BLACK LEGACY PRESS™

WWW.BLACKLEGACYPRESS.ORG

Slave Narratives

Volume XIII
Oklahoma Narratives

By
United States.
Work Projects Administration

Copyright © 2024 by BLACKLEGACYPRESS.ORG

All rights reserved. No part of this publication may be reproduced or transmitted in any form or by any means electronic or mechanical, including information storage and retrieval systems without permission in writing from the publisher, except for student research using the appropriate citations.

ISBN: 978-1-63652-201-2

SLAVE NARRATIVES

A Folk History of Slavery in the United States. From Interviews with Former Slaves

**UNITED STATES.
WORK PROJECTS ADMINISTRATION**

TYPEWRITTEN RECORDS PREPARED BY
THE FEDERAL WRITERS' PROJECT
1936-1938
ASSEMBLED BY
THE LIBRARY OF CONGRESS PROJECT
WORK PROJECTS ADMINISTRATION
FOR THE DISTRICT OF COLUMBIA
SPONSORED BY THE LIBRARY OF
CONGRESS

WASHINGTON 1941

VOLUME XIII
OKLAHOMA NARRATIVES

Prepared by
The Federal Writers' Project of
The Works Progress Administration
For the State of Oklahoma

CONTENTS

Isaac Adams	1
Alice Alexander	7
Phoebe Banks	11
Nancy Rogers Bean	17
Prince Bee	21
Lewis Bonner	25
Francis Bridges	29
John Brown	33
Sallie Carder	37
Betty Foreman Chessier	41
Polly Colbert	45
George Conrad, Jr.	53
Martha Cunningham	61
William Curtis	65
Lucinda Davis	71
Anthony Dawson	87
Alice Douglass	99
Doc Daniel Dowdy	103
Joanna Draper	109
Mrs. Esther Easter	119
Eliza Evans	123
Lizzie Farmer	129
Della Fountain	137
Nancy Gardner	145

Octavia George 149

Mary Grayson 155

Robert R. Grinstead 167

Mattie Hardman 173

Annie Hawkins 177

Ida Henry 181

Morris Hillyer 187

Hal Hutson 195

William Hutson 199

Mrs. Isabella Jackson 205

Nellie Johnson 209

Ms. Josie Jordan 215

"Uncle" George G. King 221

Martha King 227

George Kye 231

Ben Lawson 237

Mary Lindsay 241

Mrs. Mattie Logan 253

Kiziah Love 261

Daniel William Lucas 271

Bert Luster 275

Stephen Mccray 281

Hannah Mcfarland 285

Marshall Mack 289

Allen V. Manning 293

Bob Maynard 305

Jane Montgomery ... 311

Amanda Oliver ... 315

Salomon Oliver ... 319

Phyllis Petite ... 323

Matilda Poe ... 331

Henry F. Pyles ... 335

Chaney Richardson ... 351

Red Richardson ... 359

Betty Robertson ... 363

Harriet Robinson ... 369

Katie Rowe ... 377

Morris Sheppard ... 389

Andrew Simms ... 401

Liza Smith ... 405

Lou Smith ... 409

James Southall ... 417

Beauregard Tenneyson ... 423

William Walters ... 427

Mary Frances Webb ... 429

Easter Wells ... 433

John White ... 441

Charley Williams ... 451

Sarah Wilson ... 469

Tom W. Woods ... 481

Annie Young ... 487

Oklahoma Writers' Project
Ex-Slaves

ISAAC ADAMS
Age 87 yrs. Tulsa, Okla.

I was born in Louisiana, way before the War. I think it was about ten years before, because I can remember everything so well about the start of the War, and I believe I was about ten years old.

My Mammy belonged to Mr. Sack P. Gee. I don't know what his real given name was, but it maybe was Saxon. Anyways we all called him Master Sack.

He was a kind of youngish man, and was mighty rich. I think he was born in England. Anyway his pappy was from England, and I think he went back before I was born.

Master Sack had a big plantation ten miles north of Arcadia, Louisiana, and his land run ten miles along both sides. He would leave in a buggy and be gone all day and still not get all over it.

There was all kinds of land on it, and he raised cane and oats and wheat and lots of corn and cotton. His cotton fields was the biggest anywheres in that part, and when chopping and picking times come he would get negroes from other people to help out. I never was no good at picking, but I was a terror with a hoe!

I was the only child my Mammy had. She was just a

young girl, and my Master did not own her very long. He got her from Mr. Addison Hilliard, where my pappy belonged. I think she was going to have me when he got her; anyways I come along pretty soon, and my mammy never was very well afterwards. Maybe Master Sack sent her back over to my pappy. I don't know.

Mammy was the house girl at Mr. Sack's because she wasn't very strong, and when I was four or five years old she died. I was big enough to do little things for Mr. Sack and his daughter, so they kept me at the mansion, and I helped the house boys. Time I was nine or ten Mr. Sack's daughter was getting to be a young woman—fifteen or sixteen years old—and that was old enough to get married off in them days. They had a lot of company just before the War, and they had whole bunch of house negroes around all the time.

Old Mistress died when I was a baby, so I don't remember anything about her, but Young Mistress was a winder! She would ride horseback nearly all the time, and I had to go along with her when I got big enough. She never did go around the quarters, so I don't know nothing much about the negroes Mr. Sack had for the fields. They all looked pretty clean and healthy, though, when they would come up to the Big House. He fed them all good and they all liked him.

He had so much different kinds of land that they could raise anything they wanted, and he had more mules and horses and cattle than anybody around there. Some of the boys worked with his fillies all the time, and he went off to New Orleans ever once in a while with his race horses. He took his daughter but they never took me.

Some of his land was in pasture but most of it was all open fields, with just miles and miles of cotton rows. There was a pretty good strip along one side he called the "old" fields. That's what they called the land that was wore out and turned back. It was all growed up in young trees, and that's where he kept his horses most of the time.

The first I knowed about the War coming on was when Mr. Sack had a whole bunch of whitefolks at the Big House at a function. They didn't talk about anything else all evening and then the next time they come nearly all their menfolks wasn't there—just the womenfolks. It wasn't very long till Mr. Sack went off to Houma with some other men, and pretty soon we knew he was in the War. I don't remember ever seeing him come home. I don't think he did until it was nearly all over.

Next thing we knowed they was Confederate soldiers riding by pretty nearly every day in big droves. Sometimes they would come and buy corn and wheat and hogs, but they never did take any anyhow, like the Yankees done later on. They would pay with billets, Young Missy called them, and she didn't send them to git them cashed but saved them a long time, and then she got them cashed, but you couldn't buy anything with the money she got for them.

That Confederate money she got wasn't no good. I was in Arcadia with her at a store, and she had to pay seventy-five cents for a can of sardines for me to eat with some bread I had, and before the War you could get a can like that for two cents. Things was even higher then than later on, but that's the only time I saw her buy anything.

When the Yankees got down in that country the most of the big men paid for all the corn and meat and things they got, but some of the little bunches of them would ride up and take hogs and things like that and just ride off. They wasn't anybody at our place but the womenfolks and the negroes. Some of Mr. Sack's women kinfolks stayed there with Young Mistress.

Along at the last the negroes on our place didn't put in much stuff—jest what they would need, and could hide from the Yankees, because they would get it all took away from them if the Yankees found out they had plenty of corn and oats.

The Yankees was mighty nice about their manners, though. They camped all around our place for a while. There was three camps of them close by at one time, but they never did come and use any of our houses or cabins. There was lots of poor whites and Cajuns that lived down below us, between us and the Gulf, and the Yankees just moved into their houses and cabins and used them to camp in.

The negroes at our place and all of them around there didn't try to get away or leave when the Yankees come in. They wasn't no place to go, anyway, so they all stayed on. But they didn't do very much work. Just enough to take care of themselves and their whitefolks.

Master Sack come home before the War was quite over. I think he had been sick, because he looked thin and old and worried. All the negroes picked up and worked mighty hard after he come home, too.

One day he went into Arcadia and come home and

told us the War was over and we was all free. The negroes didn't know what to make of it, and didn't know where to go, so he told all that wanted to stay on that they could just go on like they had been and pay him shares.

About half of his negroes stayed on, and he marked off land for them to farm and made arrangements with them to let them use their cabins, and let them have mules and tools. They paid him out of their shares, and some of them finally bought the mules and some of the land. But about half went on off and tried to do better somewheres else.

I didn't stay with him because I was jest a boy and he didn't need me at the house anyway.

Late in the War my Pappy belonged to a man named Sander or Zander. Might been Alexander, but the negroes called him Mr. Sander. When pappy got free he come and asked me to go with him, and I went along and lived with him. He had a share-cropper deal with Mr. Sander and I helped him work his patch. That place was just a little east of Houma, a few miles.

When my Pappy was born his parents belonged to a Mr. Adams, so he took Adams for his last name, and I did too, because I was his son. I don't know where Mr. Adams lived, but I don't think my Pappy was born in Louisiana. Alabama, maybe. I think his parents come off the boat, because he was very black—even blacker than I am.

I lived there with my Pappy until I was about eighteen and then I married and moved around all over Louisiana from time to time. My wife give me twelve boys and five girls, but all my children are dead now but five. My wife died in 1920 and I come up here to Tulsa to live. One of my daughters takes care and looks out for me now.

I seen the old Sack P. Gee place about twenty years ago, and it was all cut up in little places and all run down. Never would have known it was one time a big plantation ten miles long.

I seen places going to rack and ruin all around—all the places I lived at in Louisiana—but I'm glad I wasn't there to see Master Sack's place go down. He was a good man and done right by all his negroes.

Yes, Lord, my old feets have been in mighty nigh every parish in Louisiana, and I seen some mighty pretty places, but I'll never forget how that old Gee plantation looked when I was a boy.

Oklahoma Writers' Project
Ex-Slaves

ALICE ALEXANDER
Age 88 yrs.
Oklahoma City, Okla.

I was 88 years old the 15th of March. I was born in 1849, at Jackson Parish, Louisiana. My mother's name was Mary Marlow, and father's Henry Marlow.

I can't remember very much 'bout slavery 'cause I was awful small, but I can remember that my mother's master, Colonel Threff died, and my mother, her husband, and us three chillun was handed down to Colonel Threff's poor kin folks. Colonel Threff owned about two or three hundred head of niggers, and all of 'em was tributed to his poor kin. Ooh wee! he sho' had jest a lot of them too! Master Joe Threff, one of his poor kin, took my mother, her husband, and three of us chillun from Louisiana to the Mississippi Line.

Down there we lived in a one-room log hut, and slept on homemade rail bed steads with cotton, and sometimes straw, mostly straw summers and cotton winners. I worked round the house and looked after de smaller chillun—I mean my mother's chillun. Mostly we ate yeller meal corn bread and sorghum malasses. I ate possums when we could get 'em, but jest couldn't stand rabbit meat. Didn't know there was any Christmas or holidays in dem days.

I can't 'membuh nothing 'bout no churches in slavery. I was a sinner and loved to dance. I remembuh I was on the floor one night dancing and I had four daughters on the floor with me and my son was playing de music—that got me! I jest stopped and said I wouldn't cut another step and I haven't. I'm a member of the Baptist Church and been for 25 or 30 years. I jined 'cause I wanted to be good 'cause I was an awful sinner.

We had a overseer back on Colonel Threff's plantation and my mother said he was the meanest man on earth. He'd jest go out in de fields and beat dem niggers, and my mother told me one day he come out in de field beating her sister and she jumped on him and nearly beat him half to death and old Master come up jest in time to see it all and fired dat overseer. Said he didn't want no man working fer him dat a woman could whip.

After de war set us free my pappy moved us away and I stayed round down there till I got to be a grown woman and married. You know I had a pretty fine wedding 'cause my pappy had worked hard and commenced to be prosperous. He had cattle, hogs, chickens and all those things like that.

A college of dem niggers got together and packed up to leave Louisiana. Me and my husband went with them. We had covered wagons, and let me tell you I walked nearly all the way from Louisiana to Oklahoma. We left in March but didn't git here till May. We came in search of education. I got a pretty fair education down there but didn't take care of it. We come to Oklahoma looking for de same thing then that darkies go North looking fer now. But we got dissapointed. What little I learned I quit taking care of it and seeing after it and lost it all.

I love to fish. I've worked hard in my days. Washed and ironed for 30 years, and paid for dis home that way. Yes sir, dis is my home. My mother died right here in dis house. She was 111 yeahs old. She is been dead 'bout 20 yeahs.

I have three daughters here married, Sussie Pruitt, Bertie Shannon, and Irene Freeman. Irene lost her husband, and he's dead now.

United States. Work Projects Administration

Oklahoma Writers' Project
Ex-Slaves
10-19-1938
1,428 words

PHOEBE BANKS
Age 78
Muskogee, Oklahoma.

In 1860, there was a little Creek Indian town of Sodom on the north bank of the Arkansas River, in a section the Indians called Chocka Bottoms, where Mose Perryman had a big farm or ranch for a long time before the Civil War. That same year, on October 17, I was born on the Perryman place, which was northwest of where I live now in Muskogee; only in them days Fort Gibson and Okmulgee was the biggest towns around and Muskogee hadn't shaped up yet.

My mother belonged to Mose Perryman when I was born; he was one of the best known Creeks in the whole nation, and one of his younger brothers, Legus Perryman, was made the big chief of the Creeks (1887) a long time after the slaves was freed. Mother's name was Eldee; my father's name was William McIntosh, because he belonged to a Creek Indian family by that name. Everybody say the McIntoshes was leaders in the Creek doings away back there in Alabama long before they come out here.

With me, there was twelve children in our family; Daniel, Stroy, Scott, Segal, Neil, Joe, Phillip, Mollie, Harriett, Sally and Queenie.

The Perryman slave cabins was all alike—just two-room log cabins, with a fireplace where mother do the cooking for us children at night after she get through working in the Master's house.

Mother was the house girl—cooking, waiting on the table, cleaning the house, spinning the yarn, knitting some of the winter clothes, taking care of the mistress girl, washing the clothes—yes, she was always busy and worked mighty hard all the time, while them Indians wouldn't hardly do nothing for themselves.

On the McIntosh plantation, my daddy said there was a big number of slaves and lots of slave children. The slave men work in the fields, chopping cotton, raising corn, cutting rails for the fences, building log cabins and fireplaces. One time when father was cutting down a tree it fell on him and after that he was only strong enough to rub down the horses and do light work around the yard. He got to be a good horse trainer and long time after slavery he helped to train horses for the Free Fairs around the country, and I suppose the first money he ever earned was made that way.

Lots of the slave owners didn't want their slaves to learn reading and writing, but the Perrymans didn't care; they even helped the younger slaves with that stuff. Mother said her master didn't care much what the slaves do; he was so lazy he didn't care for nothing.

They tell me about the war times, and that's all I remember of it. Before the War is over some of the Perryman slaves and some from the McIntosh place fix up to run away from their masters.

My father and my uncle, Jacob Perryman, was some of the fixers. Some of the Creek Indians had already lost a few slaves who slip off to the North, and they take what was left down into Texas so's they couldn't get away. Some of the other Creeks was friendly to the North and was fixing to get away up there; that's the ones my daddy and uncle was fixing to join, for they was afraid their masters would take up and move to Texas before they could get away.

They call the old Creek, who was leaving for the North, "Old Gouge" (Opoethleyohola). All our family join up with him, and there was lots of Creek Indians and slaves in the outfit when they made a break for the North. The runaways was riding ponies stolen from their masters.

When they get into the hilly country farther north in the country that belong to the Cherokee Indians, they make camp on a big creek and there the Rebel Indian soldiers catch up, but they was fought back.

Then long before morning lighten the sky, the men hurry and sling the camp kettles across the pack horses, tie the littlest children to the horses backs and get on the move farther into the mountains. They kept moving fast as they could, but the wagons made it mighty slow in the brush and the lowland swamps, so just about the time they ready to ford another creek the Indian soldiers catch up and the fighting begin all over again.

The Creek Indians and the slaves with them try to fight off them soldiers like they did before, but they get scattered around and separated so's they lose the battle. Lost their horses and wagons, and the soldiers killed lots of the Creeks and Negroes, and some of the slaves was captured and took back to their masters.

Dead all over the hills when we get away; some of the Negroes shot and wounded so bad the blood run down the saddle skirts, and some fall off their horses miles from the battle ground, and lay still on the ground. Daddy and Uncle Jacob keep our family together somehow and head across the line into Kansas. We all get to Fort Scott where there was a big army camp; daddy work in the blacksmith shop and Uncle Jacob join with the Northern soldiers to fight against the South. He come through the war and live to tell me about the fighting he been in.

He went with the soldiers down around Fort Gibson where they fight the Indians who stayed with the South. Uncle Jacob say he killed many a man during the war, and showed me the musket and sword he used to fight with; said he didn't shoot the women and children—just whack their heads off with the sword, and almost could I see the blood dripping from the point! It made me scared at his stories.

The captain of this company want his men to be brave and not get scared, so before the fighting start he put out a tub of white liquor (corn whiskey) and steam them up so's they'd be mean enough to whip their grannie! The soldiers do lots of riding and the saddle-sores get so bad they grease their body every night with snake oil so's they could keep going on.

Uncle Jacob said the biggest battle was at Honey Springs (1863). That was down near Elk Creek, close by

Checotah, below Rentiersville. He said it was the most terrible fighting he seen, but the Union soldiers whipped and went back into Fort Gibson. The Rebels was chased all over the country and couldn't find each other for a long time, the way he tell it.

After the war our family come back here and settle at Fort Gibson, but it ain't like the place my mother told me about. There was big houses and buildings of brick setting on the high land above the river when I first see it, not like she know it when the Perrymans come here years ago.

She heard the Indians talk about the old fort (1824), the one that rot down long before the Civil War. And she seen it herself when she go with the Master for trading with the stores. She said it was made by Matthew Arbuckle and his soldiers, and she talk about Companys B, C, D, K, and the Seventh Infantry who was there and made the Osage Indians stop fighting the Creeks and Cherokees. She talk of it, but that old place all gone when I first see the Fort.

Then I hear about how after the Arbuckle soldiers leave the old log fort, the Cherokee Indians take over the land and start up the town of Keetoowah. The folks who move in there make the place so wild and rascally the Cherokees give up trying to make a good town and it kinder blow away.

My husband was Tom Banks, but the boy I got ain't my own son, but I found him on my doorstep when he's about three weeks old and raise him like he is my own blood. He went to school at the manual training school at

Tullahassee and the education he got get him a teacher job at Taft (Okla), where he is now.

Oklahoma Writers' Project
Ex-Slaves
10-19-38
520 Words

NANCY ROGERS BEAN
Age about 82
Hulbert, Okla.

I'm getting old and it's easy to forget most of the happenings of slave days; anyway I was too little to know much about them, for my mammy told me I was born about six years before the War. My folks was on their way to Fort Gibson, and on the trip I was born at Boggy Depot, down in southern Oklahoma.

There was a lot of us children; I got their names somewheres here. Yes, there was George, Sarah, Emma, Stella, Sylvia, Lucinda, Rose, Dan, Pamp, Jeff, Austin, Jessie, Isaac and Andrew; we all lived in a one-room log cabin on Master Rogers' place not far from the old military road near Choteau. Mammy was raised around the Cherokee town of Tahlequah.

I got my name from the Rogers', but I was loaned around to their relatives most of the time. I helped around the house for Bill McCracken, then I was with Cornelius and Carline Wright, and when I was freed my Mistress was a Mrs. O'Neal, wife of a officer at Fort Gibson. She treated me the best of all and gave me the first doll I ever had. It was a rag doll with charcoal eyes and red thread worked in for the mouth. She allowed me one hour every day to play with it. When the War ended Mistress O'Neal wanted to take me with her to Richmond, Virginia, but my people wouldn't let me go. I wanted to stay with her, she was so good, and she promised to come back for me when I get older, but she never did.

All the time I was at the fort I hear the bugles and see the soldiers marching around, but never did I see any battles. The fighting must have been too far away.

Master Rogers kept all our family together, but my folks have told me about how the slaves was sold. One of my aunts was a mean, fighting woman. She was to be sold and when the bidding started she grabbed a hatchet, laid her hand on a log and chopped it off. Then she throwed the bleeding hand right in her master's face. Not long ago I hear she is still living in the country around Nowata, Oklahoma.

Sometimes I would try to get mean, but always I got me a whipping for it. When I was a little girl, moving around from one family to another, I done housework, ironing, peeling potatoes and helping the main cook. I went barefoot most of my life, but the master would get his shoes from the Government at Fort Gibson.

I wore cotton dresses, and the Mistress wore long dresses, with different colors for Sunday clothes, but us slaves didn't know much about Sunday in a religious way. The Master had a brother who used to preach to the Negroes on the sly. One time he was caught and the Master whipped him something awful.

Years ago I married Joe Bean. Our children died as babies. Twenty year ago Joe Bean and I separated for good and all.

The good Lord knows I'm glad slavery is over. Now I can stay peaceful in one place—that's all I aim to do.

United States. Work Projects Administration

Oklahoma Writers' Project
Ex-Slaves
[Date stamp: AUG 16 1937]

PRINCE BEE
Age 85 yrs.
Red Bird, Okla.

I don't know how old I was when I found myself standing on the toppen part of a high stump with a lot of white folks walking around looking at the little scared boy that was me. Pretty soon the old master, (that's my first master) Saul Nudville, he say to me that I'm now belonging to Major Bee and for me to get down off the auction block.

I do that. Major Bee he comes over and right away I know I'm going to like him. Then when I get to the Major's plantation and see his oldest daughter Mary and all her brothers and sisters, and see how kind she is to all them and to all the colored children, why, I just keeps right on liking 'em more all the time.

They was about nine white children on the place and Mary had to watch out for them 'cause the mother was dead.

That Mary gal seen to it that we children got the best food on the place, the fattest possum and the hottest fish. When the possum was all browned, and the sweet 'taters swimming in the good mellow gravy, then she call us for to eat. Um-um-h! That was tasty eating!

And from the garden come the vegetables like okra and corn and onions that Mary would mix all up in the soup pot with lean meats. That would rest kinder easy on the stomach too, 'specially if they was a bit of red squirrel meats in with the stew!

Major Bee say it wasn't good for me to learn reading and writing. Reckoned it would ruin me. But they sent me to Sunday School. Sometimes. Wasn't many of the slaves knew how to read the Bible either, but they all got the religion anyhow. I believed in it then and I still do.

That religion I got in them way back days is still with me. And it ain't this pie crust religion such as the folks are getting these days. The old time religion had some filling between the crusts, wasn't so many empty words like they is today.

They was haunts in them way back days, too. How's I know? 'Cause I stayed right with the haunts one whole night when I get caught in a norther when the Major sends me to another plantation for to bring back some cows he's bargained for. That was a cold night and a frightful one.

The blizzard overtook me and it was dark on the way. I come to an old gin house that everybody said was the hauntinest place in all the county. But I went in account of the cold and then when the noises started I was just too scared to move, so there I stood in the corner, all the time 'til morning come.

There was nobody I could see, but I could hear peoples

feet a-tromping and stomping around the room and they go up and down the stairway like they was running a race.

Sometimes the noises would be right by my side and I would feel like a hot wind passing around me, and lights would flash all over the room. Nobody could I see. When daylight come I went through that door without looking back and headed for the plantation, forgetting all about the cows that Major Bee sent me for to get.

When I tells them about the thing, Mary she won't let the old Major scold, and she fixes me up with some warm foods and I is all right again. But I stays me away from that gin place, even in the daylight, account of the haunts.

When the War come along the Major got kinder mean with some of the slaves, but not with me. I never did try to run off, but some of 'em did. One of my brothers tried and got caught.

The old Master whipped him 'til the blood spurted all over his body, the bull whip cutting in deeper all the time. He finish up the whipping with a wet coarse towel and the end got my brother in the eye. He was blinded in the one eye but the other eye is good enough he can see they ain't no use trying to run away no more.

After the War they was more whippings. This time it was the night riders—them Klan folks didn't fool with mean Negroes. The mean Negroes was whipped and some of them shot when they do something the Klan folks didn't like, and when they come a-riding up in the night, all covered with white spreads, they was something bound to happen.

Them way back days is gone and I is mighty glad. The Negroes of today needs another leader like Booker Washington. Get the young folks to working, that's what they need, and get some filling in their pie crust religion so's when they meet the Lord their soul won't be empty like is their pocketbooks today!

Oklahoma Writers' Project
Ex-Slaves

LEWIS BONNER
Age 87 yrs.
507 N. Durland
Oklahoma City, Oklahoma

I was born 7 miles north of Palestine, Texas, on Matt Swanson's place in 1850, but I kin not remember the date. My mistress was name Celia Swanson. My mistress was so good to me till I jest loved her.

My family and all slaves on our place was treated good. Mighty few floggings went on 'round and about. Master was the overseer over his darkies and didn't use no other'n. I waited table and churned in the Big House.

I ate at the table with my mistress and her family and nothing was evah said. We ate bacon, greens, Irish potatoes and such as we git now. Aunt Chaddy was the cook and nurse for all the chillun on the place.

We used to hear slaves on de other places hollering from whippings, but master never whipped his niggers 'less they lied. Sometimes slaves from other places would run off and come to our place. Master would take them back and tell the slave-holders how to treat them so dey wouldn't run off again.

Mistress had a little stool for me in the big house, and

if I got sleepy, she put me on the foot of her bed and I stayed there til morning, got up washed my face and hands and got ready to wait on the table.

There was four or five hundred slaves on our place. One morning during slavery, my father killed 18 white men and ran away. They said he was lazy and whipped him, and he just killed all of 'em he could, which was 18 of 'em. He stayed away 3 years without being found. He come back and killed 7 before they could kill him. When he was on the place he jest made bluing.

My mother worked in the field and weaved cloth. Shirts dat she made lasted 12 months, even if wore and washed and ironed every day. Pants could not be ripped with two men pulling on dem with all their might. You talking 'bout clothes, them was some clothes then. Clothes made now jest don't come up to them near abouts.

Doing of slavery, we had the best church, lots better than today. I am a Baptist from head to foot, yes sir, yes sir. Jest couldn't be nothing else. In the first place, I wouldn't even try.

I knows when the war started and ceaseted. I tell you it was some war. When it was all over, the Yankees come thoo' singing, "You may die poor but you won't die a slave."

When the War was over, master told us that we could go out and take care of the crops already planted and plant the ones that need planting 'cause we knowed all 'bout the place and we would go halvers. We stayed on 3 years after slavery. We got a little money, but we got room and board and didn't have to work too hard. It was enough difference to tell you was no slaves any more.

After slavery and when I was old enough I got married. I married a gal that was a daughter of her master. He wanted to own her, but she sho' didn't return it. He kept up with her till he died and sent her money jest all the time. Before he died, he put her name in his will and told his oldest son to be sure and keep up with her. The son was sure true to his promise, for till she died, she was forever hearing from him or he would visit us, even after we moved to Oklahoma from Texas.

Our chillun and grandchillun will git her part since she is gone. She was sure a good wife and for no reason did I take the second look at no woman. That was love, which don't live no more in our hearts.

I make a few pennies selling fish worms and doing a little yard work and raising vegetables. Not much money in circulation. When I gets my old age pension, it will make things a little mite better. I guess the time will be soon.

Tain't nothing but bad treatment that makes people die young and I ain't had none.

United States. Work Projects Administration

Oklahoma Writers' Project
Ex-Slaves
[Date stamp: AUG 19 1937]

FRANCIS BRIDGES
Age 73 yrs.
Oklahoma City, Okla.

I was born in Red River County, Texas in 1864, and that makes me 73 years old. I had myself 75, and I went to my white folks and they counted it up and told me I was 73, but I always felt like I was older than that.

My husband's name is Henry Bridges. We was raised up children together and married. I had five sisters. My brother died here in Oklahoma about two years ago. He was a Fisher. Mary Russell, my sister, she lives in Parish, Texas; Willie Ann Poke, she lives in Greenville, Texas; Winnie Jackson, lives in Adonia, Texas, and Mattie White, my other sister, lives in Long Oak, Texas, White Hunt County.

Our Master was named Master Travis Wright, and we all ate nearly the same thing. Such things as barbecued rabbits, coon, possums baked with sweet potatoes and all such as that. I used to hang round the kitchen. The cook, Mama Winnie Long, used to feed all us little niggers on the flo', jest like little pigs, in tin cups and wooden spoons. We ate fish too, and I like to go fishing right this very day.

We lived right in old Master Wright's yard. His house sat way up on a high hill. It was jest a little old log hut we lived in a little old shack around the yard. They was a lot of little shacks in the yard, I can't tell jest how many, but it was quite a number of 'em. We slept in old-fashion beds that we called "corded beds", 'cause they had ropes crossed to hold the mattresses for slats. Some of 'em had beds nailed to the wall.

Master Travis Wright had one son named Sam Wright, and after old Master Travis Wright died, young Master Sam Wright come to be my mother's master. He jest died a few years ago.

My mother say dey had a nigger driver and he'd whip 'em all but his daughter. I never seen no slaves whipped, but my mother say dey had to whip her Uncle Charley Mills once for telling a story. She say he bored a hole in de wall of de store 'til he bored de hole in old Master's whiskey barrel, and he caught two jugs of whiskey and buried it in de banks of de river. When old Master found out de whiskey was gone, he tried to make Uncle Charley 'fess up, and Uncle Charley wouldn't so he brung him in and hung him and barely let his toes touch. After Uncle Charley thought he was going to kill him, he told where de whiskey was.

We didn't go to church before freedom, land no! 'cause the closest church was so far—it was 30 miles off. But I'm a member of the Baptist Church and I've been a member for some 40-odd years. I was past 40 when I heerd of a Methodist Church. My favorite song is "Companion." I didn't get to go to school 'til after slavery.

I 'member more after de War. I 'member my mother

said dey had patrollers, and if de slaves would get passes from de Master to go to de dances and didn't git back before ten o'clock dey'd beat 'em half to death.

I used to hear 'em talking 'bout Ku Klux Klan coming to the well to get water. They'd draw up a bucket of water and pour the water in they false stomachs. They false stomachs was tied on 'em with a big leather buckle. They'd jest pour de water in there to scare 'em and say, "This is the first drink of water I've had since I left Hell." They'd say all sech things to scare the cullud folks.

I heerd my mother say they sold slaves on what they called an auction block. Jest like if a slave had any portly fine looking children they'd sell them chillun jest like selling cattle. I didn't see this, jest heerd it.

After freedom, when I was old enough then to work in the field, we lived on Mr. Martin's plantation. We worked awful hard in the fields. Lawd yes'm! I've heard 'bout shucking up de corn, but give me dem cotton pickings. Fry'd pick out all de crop of cotton in one day. The women would cook and de men'd pick the cotton, I mean on dem big cotton pickings. Some would work for they meals. Then after dey'd gather all de crops, dey'd give big dances, drink whiskey, and jest cut up sumpin terrible. We didn't know anything 'bout holidays.

I've heard my husband talk 'bout "Raw head an' bloody bones." Said whenever dey mothers wanted to scare 'em to make 'em be good dey'd tell 'em dat a man was outside de door and asked her if she'd hold his head while he fixed his back bone. I don't believe in voodooing, and I don't believe in hants. I used to believe in both of 'em when I was young.

I married Jake Bridges. We had a ordinary wedding. The preacher married us and we had a license. We have two sons grown living here. My husband told me that in slavery if your Master told you to live with your brother, you had to live with him. My father's mother and dad was first cousins.

I can 'member my husband telling me he was hauling lumber from Jefferson where the saw mill was and it was cold that night, and when they got halfway back it snowed, and he stopped with an old cullud family, and he said way in the night, a knock come at de door—woke 'em up, and it was an old cullud man, and he said dis old man commence inquiring, trying to find out who dey people was and dey told him best dey could remember, and bless de Lawd, 'fore dey finished talking de found out dis old cullud man and de other cullud woman an' man dat was married was all brothers and sisters, and he told his brother it was a shame he had married his sister and dey had nine chillun. My husband sho' told me dis.

I've heerd 'em say dey old master raised chillun by those cullud women. Why, there was one white man in Texas had a cullud woman, but didn't have no chillun by her, and he had this cullud woman and her old mistress there on the same place. So, when old Mistress died he wouldn't let this cullud woman leave, and he gave her a swell home right there on the place, and she is still there I guess. They say she say sometime, she didn't want no Negro man smutting her sheets up.

I think Abraham Lincoln was a good man, and I have read a whole lots 'bout him, but I don't know much 'bout Jeff Davis. I think Booker T. Washington is a fine man, but I aint heerd so much about him.

Oklahoma Writers' Project
Ex-Slaves
[Date stamp: AUG 16 1937]

JOHN BROWN
Age (about) 87 yrs.
West Tulsa, Okla.

Most of the folks have themselves a regular birthday but this old colored man just pick out any of the days during the year—one day just about as good as another.

I been around a long time but I don't know when I got here. That's the truth. Nearest I figures it the year was 1850—the month don't make no difference nohow.

But I know the borning was down in Taloga County, Alabama, near the county seat town. Miss Abby was with my Mammy that day. She was the wife of Master John Brown. She was with all the slave women every time a baby was born, or when a plague of misery hit the folks she knew what to do and what kind of medicine to chase off the aches and pains. God bless her! She sure loved us Negroes.

Most of the time there was more'n three hundred slaves on the plantation. The oldest ones come right from Africa. My Grandmother was one of them. A savage in Africa—a slave in America. Mammy told it to me. Over there all the natives dressed naked and lived on fruits and nuts. Never see many white mens.

One day a big ship stopped off the shore and the natives hid in the brush along the beach. Grandmother was there. The ship men sent a little boat to the shore and scattered bright things and trinkets on the beach. The natives were curious. Grandmother said everybody made a rush for them things soon as the boat left. The trinkets was fewer than the peoples. Next day the white folks scatter some more. There was another scramble. The natives was feeling less scared, and the next day some of them walked up the gangplank to get things off the plank and off the deck.

The deck was covered with things like they'd found on the beach. Two-three hundred natives on the ship when they feel it move. They rush to the side but the plank was gone. Just dropped in the water when the ship moved away.

Folks on the beach started to crying and shouting. The ones on the boat was wild with fear. Grandmother was one of them who got fooled, and she say the last thing seen of that place was the natives running up and down the beach waving their arms and shouting like they was mad. The boat men come up from below where they had been hiding and drive the slaves down in the bottom and keep them quiet with the whips and clubs.

The slaves was landed at Charleston. The town folks was mighty mad 'cause the blacks was driven through the streets without any clothes, and drove off the boat men after the slaves was sold on the market. Most of that load was sold to the Brown plantation in Alabama. Grandmother was one of the bunch.

The Browns taught them to work. Made clothes for them. For a long time the natives didn't like the clothes and try to shake them off. There was three Brown boys—John, Charley and Henry. Nephews of old Lady Hyatt who was the real owner of the plantation, but the boys run the place. The old lady she lived in the town. Come out in the spring and fall to see how is the plantation doing.

She was a fine woman. The Brown boys and their wives was just as good. Wouldn't let nobody mistreat the slaves. Whippings was few and nobody get the whip 'less he need it bad. They teach the young ones how to read and write; say it was good for the Negroes to know about such things.

Sunday was a great day around the plantation. The fields was forgotten, the light chores was hurried through and everybody got ready for the church meeting.

It was out of the doors, in the yard fronting the big log where the Browns all lived. Master John's wife would start the meeting with a prayer and then would come the singing. The old timey songs.

The white folks on the next plantation would lick their slaves for trying to do like we did. No praying there, and no singing.

The Master gave out the week's supply on Saturday. Plenty of hams, lean bacon, flour, corn meal, coffee and more'n enough for the week. Nobody go hungry on that place! During the growing season all the slaves have a garden spot all their own. Three thousand acres on that place—plenty of room for gardens and field crops.

Even during the war foods was plentiful. One time the Yankee soldiers visit the place. The white folks gone and I talks with them. Asks me lots of questions—got any meats—got any potatoes—got any this—some of that—but I just shake my head and they don't look around.

The old cook fixes them up though. She fry all the eggs on the place, skillet the ham and pan the biscuits! Them soldiers fill up and leave the house friendly as anybody I ever see!

The Browns wasn't bothered with the Ku Klux Klan either. The Negroes minded their own business just like before they was free.

I stayed on the plantation 'til the last Brown die. Then I come to Oklahoma and works on the railroad 'til I was too old to hustle the grips and packages. Now I just sits thinking how much better off would I be on the old plantation.

Homesick! Just homesick for that Alabama farm like it was in them good old times!

Oklahoma Writers' Project
Ex-Slaves

SALLIE CARDER
Age 83 yrs.
Burwin, Okla.

I was born in Jackson, Tennessee, and I'm going on 83 years. My mother was Harriett Neel and father Jeff Bills, both of them named after their masters. I has one brother, J. B. Bills, but all de rest of my brothers and sisters is dead.

No sir, we never had no money while I was a slave. We jest didn't have nothing a-tall! We ate greens, corn bread, and ash cake. De only time I ever got a biscuit would be when a misdemeanor was did, and my Mistress would give a buttered biscuit to de one who could tell her who done it.

In hot weather and cold weather dere was no difference as to what we wore. We wore dresses my mother wove for us and no shoes a-tall. I never wore any shoes till I was grown and den dey was old brogans wid only two holes to lace, one on each side. During my wedding I wore a blue calico dress, a man's shirt tail as a head rag, and a pair of brogan shoes.

My Master lived in a three-story frame house painted white. My Mistress was very mean. Sometimes she would make de overseer whip negroes for looking too hard at her when she was talking to dem. Dey had four children, three girls and one boy.

I was a servant to my Master, and as he had de palsy I had to care for him, feed him and push him around. I don't know how many slaves, but he had a good deal of 'em.

About four o' clock mornings de overseer or negro carriage driver who stayed at the Big House would ring de bell to git up and git to work. De slaves would pick a heap of cotton and work till late on moonshining nights.

Dere was a white post in front of my door with ropes to tie the slaves to whip dem. Dey used a plain strap, another one with holes in it, and one dey call de cat wid nine tails which was a number of straps plated and de ends unplated. Dey would whip de slaves wid a wide strap wid holes in it and de holes would make blisters. Den dey would take de cat wid nine tails and burst de blisters and den rub de sores wid turpentine and red pepper.

I never saw any slaves auctioned off but I seen dem pass our house chained together on de way to be sold, including both men and women wid babies all chained to each other. Dere was no churches for slaves, but at nights dey would slip off and git in ditches and sing and pray, and when dey would sometimes be caught at it dey would be whipped. Some of de slaves would turn down big pots and put dere heads in dem and pray. My Mistress would tell me to be a good obedient slave and I would go to heaven. When slaves would attempt to run off dey would catch dem and chain dem and fetch 'em back and whip dem before dey was turned loose again.

De patrollers would go about in de quarters at nights to see if any of de slaves was out or slipped off. As we sleep on de dirt floors on pallets, de patrollers would walk all over and on us and if we even grunt dey would whip us. De only trouble between de whites and blacks on our plantation was when de overseer tied my mother to whip her and my father untied her and de overseer shot and killed him.

Negroes never was allowed to git sick, and when dey would look somewhat sick, de overseer would give dem some blue-mass pills and oil of some sort and make dem continue to work.

During de War de Yankees would pass through and kill up de chickens, and hogs, and cattle, and eat up all dey could find. De day of freedom de overseer went into de field and told de slaves dat dey was free, and de slaves replied, "free how?" and he told dem: "free to work and live for demselves." And dey said dey didn't know what to do, and so some of dem stayed on. I married Josh Forch. I am mother of four children and 35 grand children.

I like Abraham Lincoln. I think he was a good man and president. I didn't know much who Jeff Davis was. What I heard 'bout Booker T. Washington, he was a good man.

Now dat slavery is over, I don't want to be in nary 'nother slavery, and if ever nary 'nothern come up I wouldn't stay here.

United States. Work Projects Administration

Oklahoma Writers' Project
Ex-Slaves

BETTY FOREMAN CHESSIER
Age 94 years
Oklahoma City, Okla.

I was born July 11, 1843 in Raleigh, N. C. My mother was named Melinda Manley, the slave of Governor Manley of North Carolina, and my father was named Arnold Foreman, slave of Bob and John Foreman, two young masters. They come over from Arkansas to visit my master and my pappy and mammy met and got married, 'though my pappy only seen my mammy in the summer when his masters come to visit our master and dey took him right back. I had three sisters and two brothers and none of dem was my whole brothers and sisters. I stayed in the Big House all the time, but my sisters and brothers was gived to the master's sons and daughters whey dey got married and dey was told to send back for some more when dem died. I didn't never stay with my mammy doing of slavery. I stayed in the Big House. I slept under the dining room table with three other darkies. The flo' was well carpeted. Don't remembah my grandmammy and grandpappy, but my master was they master.

I waited on the table, kept flies off'n my mistress and went for the mail. Never made no money, but dey did give the slaves money at Christmas time. I never had over two dresses. One was calico and one gingham. I had such underclothes as dey wore then.

Master Manley and Mistress had six sons an' six darters. Dey raised dem all till dey was grown too. Dey lived in a great big house 'cross from the mansion, right in town before Master was 'lected Governor, den dey all moved in dat mansion.

Plantation folks had barbecues and "lay crop feasts" and invited the city darkies out. When I first come here I couldn't understand the folks here, 'cause dey didn't quit work on Easter Monday. That is some day in North Carolina even today. I doesn't remember any play songs, 'cause I was almost in prison. I couldn't play with any of the darkies and I doesn't remember playing in my life when I was a little girl and when I got grown I didn't want to. I wasn't hongry, I wasn't naked and I got only five licks from the white folks in my life. Dey was for being such a big forgitful girl. I saw 'em sell niggers once. The only pusson I ever seen whipped at dat whipping post was a white man.

I never got no learning; dey kept us from dat, but you know some of dem darkies learnt anyhow. We had church in the heart of town or in the basement of some old building. I went to the 'piscopal church most all the time, till I got to be a Baptist.

The slaves run away to the North 'cause dey wanted to be free. Some of my family run away sometime and dey didn't catch 'em neither. The patrollers sho' watched the streets. But when dey caught any of master's niggers without passes, dey jest locked him up in the guard house and master come down in the mawnin' and git 'em out, but dem patrollers better not whip one.

I know when the War commenced and ended. Master Manley sent me from the Big House to the office about a mile away. Jest as I got to the office door, three men rid up in blue uniforms and said, "Dinah, do you have any milk in there?" I was sent down to the office for some beans for to cook dinner, but dem men most nigh scared me to death. They never did go in dat office, but jest rid off on horseback about a quarter a mile and seem lak right now, Yankees fell out of the very sky, 'cause hundeds and hundeds was everywhere you could look to save your life. Old Mistress sent one of her grandchillun to tell me to come on, and one of the Yankees told dat child, "You tell your grandmother she ain't coming now and never will come back there as a slave." Master was setting on the mansion porch. Dem Yankees come up on de porch, go down in cellar and didn't tech one blessed thing. Old Mistress took heart trouble, 'cause dem Yankees whipped white folks going and coming.

I laid in my bed a many night scared to death of Klu Klux Klan. Dey would come to your house and ask for a drink and no more want a drink than nothing.

After the War, I went to mammy and my step-pappy. She done married again, so I left and went to Warrington and Halifax, North Carolina, jest for a little while nursing some white chillun. I stayed in Raleigh, where I was born till 7 years ago, when I come to Oklahoma to live with my only living child. I am the mother of 4 chillun and 11 grandchillun.

When I got married I jumped a broomstick. To git unmarried, all you had to do was to jump backwards over the same broomstick.

Lincoln and Booker T. Washington was two of the finest men ever lived. Don't think nothing of Jeff Davis, 'cause he was a traitor. Freedom for us was the best thing ever happened. Prayer is best thing in the world. Everybody ought to pray, 'cause prayer got us out of slavery.

Oklahoma Writer's Project
Ex-Slaves

POLLY COLBERT
Age 83 yrs.
Colbert, Oklahoma

I am now living on de forty-acre farm dat de Government give me and it is just about three miles from my old home on Master Holmes Colbert's plantation where I lived when I was a slave.

Lawsy me, times sure has changed since slavery times! Maybe I notice it more since I been living here all de time, but dere's farms 'round here dat I've seen grown timber cleared off of twice during my lifetime. Dis land was first cleared up and worked by niggers when dey was slaves. After de War nobody worked it and it just naturally growed up again wid all sorts of trees. Later, white folks cleared it up again and took grown trees off'n it and now dey are still cultivating it but it is most wore out now. Some of it won't even sprout peas. Dis same land used to grow corn without hardly any work but it sure won't do it now.

I reckon it was on account of de rich land dat us niggers dat was owned by Indians didn't have to work so hard as dey did in de old states, but I think dat Indian masters was just naturally kinder any way, leastways mine was.

My mother, Liza, was owned by de Colbert family and

my father, Tony, was owned by de Love family. When Master Holmes and Miss Betty Love was married dey fathers give my father and mother to dem for a wedding gift. I was born at Tishomingo and we moved to de farm on Red River soon after dat and I been here ever since. I had a sister and a brother, but I ain't seen dem since den.

My mother died when I was real small, and about a year after dat my father died. Master Holmes told us children not to cry, dat he and Miss Betsy would take good care of us. Dey did, too. Dey took us in de house wid dem and look after us jest as good as dey could colored children. We slept in a little room close to them and she allus seen dat we was covered up good before she went to bed. I guess she got a sight of satisfaction from taking care of us 'cause she didn't have no babies to care for.

Master Holmes and Miss Betsy was real young folks but dey was purty well fixed. He owned about 100 acres of land dat was cleared and ready for de plow and a lot dat was not in cultivation. He had de woods full of hogs and cows and he owned seven or eight grown slaves and several children. I remember Uncle Shed, Uncle Lige, Aunt Chaney, Aunt Lizzie, and Aunt Susy just as well as if it was yesterday. Master Holmes and Miss Betsy was both half-breed Choctaw Indians. Dey had both been away to school somewhere in de states and was well educated. Dey had two children but dey died when dey was little. Another little girl was born to dem after de War and she lived to be a grown woman.

Dey sure was fine young folks and provided well for us. He allus had a smokehouse full of meat, lard, sausage, dried beans, peas, corn, potatoes, turnips and collards banked up for winter. He had plenty of milk and butter for all of us, too.

Master Holmes allus say, "A hungry man caint work." And he allus saw to it that we had lots to eat.

We cooked all sorts of Indian dishes: Tom-fuller, pashofa, hickory-nut grot, Tom-budha, ash-cakes, and pound cakes besides vegetables and meat dishes. Corn or corn meal was used in all de Indian dishes. We made hominy out'n de whole grains. Tom-fuller was made from beaten corn and tasted sort of like hominy.

We would take corn and beat it like in a wooden mortar wid a wooden pestle. We would husk it by fanning it and we would den put it on to cook in a big pot. While it was cooking we'd pick out a lot of hickory-nuts, tie 'em up in a cloth and beat 'em a little and drop 'em in and cook for a long time. We called dis dish hickory-nut grot. When we made pashofa we beat de corn and cook for a little while and den we add fresh pork and cook until de meat was done. Tom-budha was green corn and fresh meat cooked together and seasoned wid tongue or pepper-grass.

We cooked on de fire place wid de pots hanging over de fire on racks and den we baked bread and cakes in a oven-skillet. We didn't use soda and baking powder. We'd put salt in de meal and scald it wid boiling water and make it into pones and bake it. We'd roll de ash cakes in wet cabbage leaves and put 'em in de hot ashes and bake 'em. We cooked potatoes, and roasting ears dat way also. We sweetened our cakes wid molasses, and dey was plenty sweet too.

Dey was lots of possums and coons and squirrels and

we nearly always had some one of these to eat. We'd parboil de possum or coon and put it in a pan and bake him wid potatoes 'round him. We used de broth to baste him and for gravy. Hit sure was fine eating dem days.

I never had much work to do. I helped 'round de house when I wanted to and I run errands for Miss Betsy. I liked to do things for her. When I got a little bigger my brother and I toted cool water to de field for de hands.

Didn't none of Master Holmes' niggers work when dey was sick. He allus saw dat dey had medicine and a doctor iffen dey needed one. 'Bout de only sickness we had was chills and fever. In de old days we made lots of our own medicine and I still does it yet. We used polecat grease for croup and rheumatism. Dog-fennel, butterfly-root, and life-everlasting boiled and mixed and made into a syrup will cure pneumonia and pleurisy. Pursley-weed, called squirrel physic, boiled into a syrup will cure chills and fever. Snake-root steeped for a long time and mixed with whiskey will cure chills and fever also.

Our clothes was all made of homespun. De women done all de spinning and de weaving but Miss Betsy cut out all de clothes and helped wid de sewing. She learned to sew when she was away to school and she learnt all her women to sew. She done all the sewing for de children. Master Holmes bought our shoes and we all had 'em to wear in de winter. We all went barefoot in de summer.

He kept mighty good teams and he had two fine saddle horses. He and Miss Betsy rode 'em all de time. She would ride wid him all over de farm and dey would go hunting a lot, too. She could shoot a gun as good as any man.

Master Holmes sure did love his wife and children and he was so proud of her. It nearly killed 'em both to give up de little boy and girl. I never did hear of him taking a drink and he was kind to everybody, both black and white, and everybody liked him. Dey had lots of company and dey never turned anybody away. We lived about four miles from de ferry on Red River on de Texas Road and lots of travelers stopped at our house.

We was 'lowed to visit de colored folks on de Eastman and Carter plantations dat joined our farm. Eastman and Carter was both white men dat married Indian wives. Dey was good to dey slaves, too, and let 'em visit us.

Old Uncle Kellup (Caleb) Colbert, Uncle Billy Hogan, Rev. John Carr, Rev. Baker, Rev. Hogue, and old Father Murrow preached for de white folks all de time and us colored folks went to church wid dem. Dey had church under brush arbors and we set off to ourselves but we could take part in de singing and sometimes a colored person would get happy and pray and shout but nobody didn't think nothing 'bout dat.

De Patrollers was de law, kind of like de policeman now. Dey sure never did whip one of Master Holmes' niggers for he didn't allow it. He didn't whip 'em hisself and he sure didn't allow anybody else to either. I was afraid of de Ku Kluxers too, and I 'spects dat Master Holmes was one of de leaders iffen de truth was known. Dey sure was scary looking.

I was scared of de Yankee soldiers. Dey come by and killed some of our cattle for beef and took our meat and lard out'n de smokehouse and dey took some corn, too. Us niggers was awful mad. We didn't know anything 'bout dem fighting to free us. We didn't specially want to be free dat I knows of.

Right after de War I went over to Bloomfield Academy to take care of a little girl, but I went back to Master Holmes and Miss Betsy at de end of two years to take care of de little girl dat was born to dem and I stayed with her until I was about fifteen. Master Holmes went to Washington as a delegate, for something for de Indians, and he took sick and died and dey buried him dere. Poor Miss Betsy nearly grieved herself to death. She stayed on at de farm till her little girl was grown and married. Her nigger men stayed on with her and rented land from her and dey sure raised a sight of truck. Didn't none of her old slaves ever move very far from her and most of them worked for her till dey was too old to work.

I left Miss Betsy purty soon after Master Holmes died and went back to de Academy and stayed three years. I married a man dat belonged to Master Holmes' cousin. His name was Colbert, too. I had a big wedding. Miss Betsy and a lot of white folks come and stayed for dinner. We danced all evening and after supper we started again and danced all night and de next day and de next night. We'd eat awhile and den we'd dance awhile.

My husband and I had nine children and now I've got seven grandchildren. My husband has been dead a long time.

My sister, Chaney, lives here close to me but her mind has got feeble and she can't recollect as much as I can. I live with my son and he is mighty good to me. I know I ain't long for dis world but I don't mind for I has lived a long time and I'll have a lot of friends in de other world and I won't be lonesome.

United States. Work Projects Administration

Oklahoma Writers' Project
Ex-Slaves
[Date stamp: NOV 5 1937]

GEORGE CONRAD, JR.
Age 77 yrs.
Oklahoma City, Okla.

I was born February 23, 1860 at Connersville, Harrison County, Kentucky. I was born and lived just 13 miles from Parish. My mother's name is Rachel Conrad, born at Bourbon County, Kentucky. My father, George Conrad, was born at Bourbon County Kentucky. My grandmother's name is Sallie Amos, and grandfather's name is Peter Amos. My grandfather, his old Master freed him and he bought my grandmother, Aunt Liza and Uncle Cy. He made the money by freighting groceries from Ohio to Maysville, Kentucky.

Our Master was named Master Joe Conrad. We sometimes called him "Mos" Joe Conrad. Master Joe Conrad stayed in a big log house with weather boarding on the outside.

I was born in a log cabin. We slept in wooden beds with rope cords for slats, and the beds had curtains around them. You see my mother was the cook for the Master, and she cooked everything—chicken, roasting ears. She cooked mostly everything we have now. They didn't have stoves; they cooked in big ovens. The skillets had three legs. I can remember the first stove that we had. I guess I was about six years old.

My old Master had 900 acres of land. My father was a stiller. He made three barrels of whisky a day. Before the War whisky sold for 12-1/2¢ and 13¢ a gallon. After the War it went up to $3 and $4 per gallon. When War broke out he had 300 barrels hid under old Master's barn.

There was 14 colored men working for old Master Joe and 7 women. I think it was on the 13th of May, all 14 of these colored men, and my father, went to the Army. When old Master Joe come to wake 'em up the next morning—I remember he called real loud, Miles, Esau, George, Frank, Arch, on down the line, and my mother told him they'd all gone to the army. Old Master went to Cynthia, Kentucky, where they had gone to enlist and begged the officer in charge to let him see all of his boys, but the officer said "No." Some way or 'nother he got a chance to see Arch, and Arch came back with him to help raise the crops.

My mother cooked and took care of the house. Aunt Sarah took care of the children. I had two little baby brothers, Charlie and John. The old Mistress would let my mother put them in her cradle and Aunt Sarah got jealous, and killed both of the babies. When they cut one of the babies open they took out two frogs. Some say she conjured the babies. Them niggers could conjure each other but they couldn't do nothing to the whitefolks, but I don't believe in it. There's an old woman living back there now (pointing around the corner of the house where he was sitting) they said her husband put a spell on her. They call 'em two-headed Negroes.

Old Master never whipped any of his slaves, except two of my uncles—Pete Conrad and Richard Sherman, now living at Falsmouth, Kentucky.

We raised corn, wheat, oats, rye and barley, in the spring. In January, February and March we'd go up to the Sugar Camp where he had a grove of maple trees. We'd make maple syrup and put up sugar in cakes. Sugar sold for $2.50 and $3 a cake. He had a regular sugar house. My old Master was rich I tell you.

Whenever a member of the white family die all the slaves would turn out, and whenever a slave would die, whitefolks and all the slaves would go. My Master had a big vault. My Mistress was buried in an iron coffin that they called a potanic coffin. I went back to see her after I was 21 years old and she look jest like she did when they buried her. All of the family was buried in them vaults, and I expect if you'd go there today they'd look the same. The slaves was buried in good handmade coffins.

I heard a lot of talk 'bout the patrollers. In them days if you went away from home and didn't have a pass they'd whip you. Sometimes they'd whip you with a long black cow whip, and then sometime they'd roast elm switches in the fire. This was called "cat-o-nine-tails", and they'd whip you with dat. We never had no jails; only punishment was just to whip you.

Now, the way the slaves travel. If a slave had been good sometimes old Master would let him ride his hoss; then, sometime they'd steal a hoss out and ride 'em and slip him back before old Master ever found it out. There was a man in them days by the name of John Brown. We called him an underground railroad man, 'cause he'd steal the slaves and carry 'em across the river in a boat. When you got on the other side you was free, 'cause you was in a free State, Ohio.

We used to sing, and I guess young folks today does too:

> "John Brown's Body Lies A 'moulding In the Clay."

and

> "They Hung John Brown On a Sour Apple Tree."

Our slaves all got very good attention when they got sick. They'd send and get a doctor for 'em. You see old Mistress Mary bought my mother, father and two children throwed in for $1,100 and she told Master Joe to always keep her slaves, not to sell 'em and always take good care of 'em.

When my father went to the army old Master told us he was gone to fight for us niggers freedom. My daddy was the only one that come back out of the 13 men that enlisted, and when my daddy come back old Master give him a buggy and hoss.

When the Yanks come, I never will forget one of 'em was named John Morgan. We carried old Master down to the barn and hid him in the hay. I felt so sorry for old Master they took all his hams, some of his whiskey, and all dey could find, hogs, chickens, and jest treated him something terrible.

The whitefolks learned my father how to read and write, but I didn't learn how to read and write 'til I enlisted in the U. S. Army in 1883.

They sent us here (Oklahoma Territory) to keep the immigrants from settling up Oklahoma. I went to Fort Riley the 1st day of October 1883, and stayed there three weeks. Left Fort Riley and went to Ft. Worth, Texas, and landed in Henryetta, Texas, on the 14th day of October 1883. Then, we had 65 miles to walk to Ft. Sill. We walked there in three days. I was assigned to my Company, Troop G. 9th Calvary, and we stayed and drilled in Ft. Sill six months, when we was assigned to duty. We got orders to come to Ft. Reno, Okla., on the 6th day of January 1885 where we was ordered to Stillwater, Okla., to move five hundred immigrants under Capt. Couch. We landed there on the 23rd day of January, Saturday evening, and Sunday was the 24th. We had general inspection Monday, January 25, 1885. We fell in line of battle, sixteen companies of soldiers, to move 500 immigrants to the Arkansas City, Kansas line.

We formed a line at 9:00 o'clock Monday morning and Captain Couch run up his white flag, and Colonel Hatch he sent the orderly up to see what he meant by putting up the flag, so Captain Couch sent word back, "If you don't fire on me, I'll leave tomorrow." Colonel Hatch turned around to the Major and told him to turn his troops back to the camp, and detailed three camps of soldiers of the 8th Cavalry to carry Captain Couch's troop of 500 immigrants to Arkansas City, Kansas. Troop L., Troop D., and Troop B. taken them back with 43 wagons and put them over the line of Kansas. Then we were ordered back to our supply camp at Camp Alice, 9 miles north of Guthrie in the Cimarron horseshoe bottom. We stayed there about three months, and Capt. Couch and his colony came back into the territory at Caldwell, Kansas June 1885.

I laid there 'til August 8, then we changed regiments with the 5th Calvary to go to Nebraska. There was a breakout with the Indians at Ft. Reno the 1st of July 1885. The Indian Agency tried to make the Indians wear citizens' clothes. They had to call General Sheridan from Washington, D. C., to quiet the Indians down. Now, we had to make a line in three divisions, fifteen miles a part, one non-commissioned officer to each squad, and these men was to go to Caldwell, Kansas and bring him to Ft. Reno that night. He came that night, so the next morning Colonel Brisbane and General Hatch reported to General Sheridan what the trouble was. General Sheridan called all the Indian Chiefs together and asked them why they rebelled against the agency, and they told them they weren't going to wear citizen's clothes. General Sheridan called his corporals and sergeants together and told them to go behind the guard house and dig a grave for this Indian agent in order to fool the Indian Chiefs. Then, he sent a detachment of soldiers to order the Indian Chiefs away from the guard house and to put this Indian agent in the ambulance that brought him to Ft. Reno and take him back to Washington, D. C., to remain there 'til he returned. The next morning he called all the Indian Chiefs to the guard house and pointed down to the grave and said that, "I have killed the agent and buried him there." The Indians tore the feathers out of their hats rejoicing that they killed the agent.

On the 12th of the same July, we had general inspection with General Foresides from Washington, then we was ordered back to our supply camp to stay there 'til we got orders of our change. On August 8, we got orders to change to go to Nebraska, to Ft. Robinson, Ft. Nibrary, and Ft. McKinney, and we left on the 8th of August.

This is my Oklahoma history. I gave this story to the Daily Oklahoman and Times at one time and they are supposed to publish it but they haven't.

Now you see that tree up there in front of my house? That tree is 50 years old. It is called the potopic tree. That was the only tree around here in 1882. This was a bald prairie. I enlisted over there where the City Market sets now. That was our starting camp under Capt. Payne, but he died.

I joined the A. M. E. Methodist Church in 1874. I love this song better than all the rest:

"Am I a Soldier of the Cross?"

Abraham Lincoln was a smart man, but he would have done more if he was not killed. I don't think his work was finished. I'll tell you the truth about Booker T. Washington. He argued our people to stay out of town and stay in the country. He was a Democrat. He was a smart man, but I think a man should live wherever he choose regardless. I never stopped work whenever I'd hear he was coming to town to speak. You know they wasn't fighting for freeing the slaves; they was fighting to keep Kansas from being a slave State; so when they had the North whipped, I mean the South had 'em whipped, they called for the Negroes to go out and fight for his freedom. Don't know nothing 'bout Jeff Davis. I've handled a lots of his money. It was counterfeited after the War.

I've been married four times. I had one wife and three women. I mean the three wasn't no good. My first wife's name: Amanda Nelson. 2nd: Pocahuntas Jackson. 3rd: Nannie Shumpard. We lived together 9 years. She tried to beat me out of my home.

United States. Work Projects Administration

Oklahoma Writers' Project
Ex-Slaves

MARTHA CUNNINGHAM
Age 81 yrs.
Oklahoma City, Oklahoma

My father's name was A. J. Brown, and my mother's name was Hattie Brown. I was born in the East, in Saveer County, Tennessee. I had twelve sisters and brothers, all are dead but two. W. S. Brown lives at 327 W. California, and Maudie Reynolds, my sister lives at Minrovie, California.

We lived in different kinds of houses just like we do now. Some was of log, some frame and some rock. I remember when we didn't have stoves to cook on, no lamps, and not even any candles until I was about six years old. We would take a rag and sop it in lard to make lights.

All of our furniture was home made, but it was nice. We had just plenty of every thing. It wasn't like it is in these days where you have to pick and scrape for something to eat.

My grandfather and grandmother gave my mother and father two slaves, an old woman and man, when they married. My grandfather owned a large plantation, and had a large number of slaves, and my father and mother owned several farms at different places. Our mother and father treated our slaves good. They ate what we ate, and they stayed with us a long time after the War. I remember though all of the slave owners weren't good to their slaves. I have seen 'em take those young fine looking negroes, put them in a pen when they got ready to whip them, strip them and lay them face down, and beat them until white whelps arose on their bodies. Yes, some of them was treated awful mean.

I saw mothers sold from their babies, and babies sold from their mothers. They would strip them, put them on the auction block and sell them—bid them off just like you would cattle. Some would sell for lots of money.

They wouldn't take the slaves to church. I don't remember when the negroes had their first schools, but it was a long time after the War.

Why, I remember when they'd have those big corn shuckings, flax pullings, and quilting parties. They would sow acres after acres of flax, then they would meet at some house or plantation and pull flax until they had finished, then give a big party. There'd be the same thing at the next plantation and so on until they'd all in that neighborhood get their crops gathered. I remember they'd have all kinds of good eats—pies, cakes, chicken, fish, fresh pork, beef,—just plenty of good eats.

I went over the battlefield at Knoxville, Tennessee, two or three hours after the Yankees and the Rebels had a battle. It was about a mile from our house, and I walked over hundreds of dead men lying on the ground. Some were fatally wounded, and we carried about six or seven to our house. I saw the doctor pick the bullets out of their flesh.

When the Yankees came they treated the slave owners awful mean. They drew a gun on my mother, made her walk for several miles one real cold night and take them up on the top of a mountain and show them where a still was. They would make her cook for 'em. They took every thing we had. I was about twelve years old at that time.

I stayed there with my mother until after my father died, then we moved to Alabama. I was about 22 years old. I married a man named Kelley. He and my brothers were railroad graders. We traveled all over Texas.

I made the Run. Came here in '89 with my mother, husband and eight children. My husband and brothers graded the streets for the townsite of Oklahoma City and platted it off.

When we made the Run, we just stood on the property until it was surveyed, then we'd pay $1.00, and the lot was ours. I camped on the corner of Robinson and Pottawatomie Streets and Robinson and Chickasaw. I owned the Northwest corner. I later sold both lots.

I am a Christian, Baptist mostly, I guess, and I believe in the Great Beyond. I don't think you have to go to church all the time to be saved, but you have to be right with the Man up yonder before you can be saved.

I am a Republican, and it makes my blood boil whenever I hear a negro say he is a democrat. They should all be Republicans.

I have been married twice. I married William Cunningham here in 1922. He is dead; in fact, both my husbands are dead, so I don't see much need of talking about them.

United States. Work Projects Administration

Oklahoma Writers' Project
Ex-Slaves
[Date stamp: AUG 19 1937]

WILLIAM CURTIS
Age 93 yrs.
McAlester, Oklahoma

"Run Nigger, run,

De Patteroll git ye!

Run Nigger, run,

He's almost here!"

"Please Mr. Patteroll,

Don't ketch me!

Jest take dat nigger

What's behind dat tree."

Lawsy, I done heard dat song all my life and it warn't no joke neither. De Patrol would git ye too if he caught ye off the plantation without a pass from your Master, and he'd whup ye too. None of us dassn't leave without a pass.

We chillun sung lots of songs and we played marbles, mumble peg, and town ball. In de winter we would set around de fire and listen to our Mammy and Pappy tell ghost tales and witch tales. I don't guess dey was sho' nuff so, but we all thought dey was.

My Mammy was bought in Virginia by our Master, Hugh McKeown. He owned a big plantation in Georgia. Soon after she come to Georgia she married my pa. Old Master was good to us. We lived for a while in the quarters behind the Big House, and my mammy was de house woman.

Somehow, in a trade, or maybe my pa was mortgaged, but anyway old Master let a man in Virginia have him and we never see him no more 'till after the War. It nigh broke our hearts when he had to leave and old Master sho' done everything he could to make it up to us.

There was four of us chillun. I didn't do no work 'till I was about fifteen years old. Old Master bought a tavern and mammy worked as house woman and I went to work at the stables. I drove the carriage and took keer of the team and carriage. I kept 'em shining too. I'd curry the horses 'till they was slick and shiny. I'd polish the harness and the carriage. Old Master and Mistress was quality and I wanted everybody to know it. They had three girls and three boys and we boys played together and went swimming together. We loved each other, I tell ye.

Old Master built us a little house jest back of de tavern and mammy raised us jest like Old Mistress did her chillun. When I didn't have to work de boys and me would go hunting. We'd kill possum, coon, squirrels and wild hogs. Old Master killed a wild hog and he give mammy her ten tiny pigs. She raised 'em and my, at the meat we had when they was butchered.

They had lots of company at de Big House, and it was de only tavern too, so they was lots of cooking to do. They would go to church on Sunday and they would spread their dinners on the ground. My, but they was feasts. We'd allus git to go as I drive the carriage and mammy looked after the food. We had our own church too, with our own preacher.

We had a spinning house where all the old women would card and spin wool in de winter and cotton in de summer. Dey made all our clothes, what few we wore. Us boys just wore long tailed shirts 'till we was 12 or 13 years old, sometimes older. I was 15 when I started driving the fambly carriage and I got to put on pants then.

Our suits was made out of jeans. That cloth wore like buckskin. We'd wear 'em for a year before they had to be patched.

We made our own brogan shoes too. We'd kill a beef and skin it and spread the skin out and let it dry a while. We'd put the hide in lime water to get the hair off, then we'd oil it and work it 'till it was soft. Next we'd take it to the bench and scrape or 'plesh' it with knives. It was then put in a tight cabinet and smoked with oak wood for about 24 hours. Smoking loosened the skin. We'd then take it out and rub it to soften it. It was blacked and oiled and it was ready to be made into shoes. It took nearly a year to get a green hide made into shoes. Twan't no wonder we had to go barefooted.

Sometimes I'd work in the wood shop, dressing wagon spokes. We made spokes with a plane, by hand on a bench.

I didn't have much work to do before I was 15 except to run errands. One of my jobs was to take corn to the mill to be ground into meal. Some one would put my sack of corn on the mule's back and help me up and I'd ride to the mill and have it ground and they'd load me back on and I'd go back home.

I remember once my meal fell off and I waited and waited for somebody to come by and help me. I got tired waiting so I toted the sack to a big log and laid it acrost it. I led my mule up to the log and after working hard for a long time I managed to get it on his back. I climbed up and jest as we started off the mule jumped and I fell off and pulled the sack off with me. I couldn't do nothing but wait and finally old Master came after me. He knowed something was wrong.

Old Master was good to all of his slaves but his overseers had orders to make 'em work. He fed 'em good and took good keer of 'em and never made 'em work iffen they was sick or even felt bad. They was two things old Master jest wouldn't 'bide and dat was for a slave to be sassy or lazy. Sometimes if dey wouldn't work or slipped off de farm dey would whip 'em. He didn't whip often. Colored overseers was worse to whip than white ones, but Master allus said, "Hadn't you all rather have a nigger overseer than a white one? I don't want to white man over my niggers." I've seen the overseer whip some but I never did get no whipping. He would strip 'em to the waist and whip 'em with a long leather strop, about as wide as two fingers and fastened to a handle.

When de war broke out everthing was changed. My young Masters had to go. T. H. McKeown, the oldest was a Lieutenant and was one of the first to go. It nigh broke all of our hearts. Pretty soon he sent for me to come and keep him company. Old Master let me go and I stayed in his quarters. He was stationed at Atlanta and Griffin, Georgia. I'd stay with him a week or two and I'd go home for a few days and I'd take back food and fruit. I stayed with him and waited on him 'till he got used to being in the army and they moved him out to fighting. I wanted to go on with him but he wouldn't let me, he told me to go back and take care of Old Master and Old Mistress. They was getting old by then. Purty soon Young Master got wounded purty bad and they sent me home. I never went back. I got a "pass" to go home. Course, after the war nothing was right no more. Yes, we was free but we didn't know what to do. We didn't want to leave our old Master and our old home. We stayed on and after a while my pappy come home to us. Dat was de best thing about de war setting us free, he could come back to us.

We all lived on at the old plantation. Old Master and old Mistress died and young Master took charge of de farm. He couldn't a'done nothing without us niggers. He didn't know how to work. He was good to us and divided the crops with us.

I never went to school much but my white folks learned me to read and write. I could always have any of their books to read, and they had lots of 'em.

Times has changed a lot since that time. I don't know where the world is much better now, that it has everthing or then when we didn't have hardly nothing, but I believe there was more religion then. We always went to church and I've seen 'em baptize from in the early morning 'till afternoon in the Chatahooche river. Folks don't hardly know nowadays jest what to believe they's so many religions, but they's only one God.

I was eighteen when I married. I had eight chillun. My wife is 86, and she lives in St. Louis, Missouri.

Oklahoma Writers' Project
Ex-Slaves
[HW: (photo)]
[Date stamp: AUG 16 1937]

LUCINDA DAVIS
Age (about) 89 yrs.
Tulsa, Okla.

"What yo' gwine do when de meat give out?
What yo' gwine do when de meat give out?
  Set in de corner wid my lips pooched out!
Lawsy!
What yo' gwine do when de meat come in?
What yo' gwine do when de meat come in?
  Set in de corner wid a greasy chin!
Lawsy!"

Dat's about de only little nigger song I know, less'n it be de one about:

"Great big nigger, laying 'hind de log—
Finger on de trigger and eye on the hawg!
Click go de trigger and bang go de gun!
Here come de owner and de buck nigger run!"

And I think I learn both of dem long after I been grown, 'cause I belong to a full-blood Creek Indian and

I didn't know nothing but Creek talk long after de Civil War. My mistress was part white and knowed English talk, but she never did talk it because none of de people talked it. I heard it sometime, but it sound like whole lot of wild shoat in de cedar brake scared at something when I do hear it. Dat was when I was little girl in time of de War.

I don't know where I been born. Nobody never did tell me. But my mammy and pappy git me after de War and I know den whose child I is. De men at de Creek Agency help 'em git me, I reckon, maybe.

First thing I remember is when I was a little girl, and I belong to old Tuskaya-hiniha. He was big man in de Upper Creek, and we have a purty good size farm, jest a little bit to de north of de wagon depot houses on de old road at Honey Springs. Dat place was about twenty-five mile south of Fort Gibson, but I don't know nothing about whar de fort is when I was a little girl at dat time. I know de Elk River 'bout two mile north of whar we live, 'cause I been there many de time.

I don't know if old Master have a white name. Lots de Upper Creek didn't have no white name. Maybe he have another Indian name, too, because Tuskaya-hiniha mean "head man warrior" in Creek, but dat what everybody call him and dat what de family call him too.

My Mistress' name was Nancy, and she was a Lott before she marry old man Tuskaya-hiniha. Her pappy name was Lott and he was purty near white. Maybe so all white. Dey have two chillun, I think, but only one stayed on de place. She was name Luwina, and her husband was dead. His name was Walker, and Luwina bring Mr. Walker's little sister, Nancy, to live at de place too.

Luwina had a little baby boy and dat de reason old Master buy me, to look after de little baby boy. He didn't have no name cause he wasn't big enough when I was with dem, but he git a name later on, I reckon. We all call him "Istidji." Dat mean "little man."

When I first remember, before de War, old Master had 'bout as many slave as I got fingers, I reckon. I can think dem off on my fingers like dis, but I can't recollect de names.

Dey call all de slaves "Istilusti." Dat mean "Black man."

Old man Tuskaya-hiniha was near 'bout blind before de War, and 'bout time of de War he go plumb blind and have to set on de long seat under de bresh shelter of de house all de time. Sometime I lead him around de yard a little, but not very much. Dat about de time all de slave begin to slip out and run off.

My own pappy was name Stephany. I think he take dat name 'cause when he little his mammy call him "Istifani." Dat mean a skeleton, and he was a skinny man. He belong to de Grayson family and I think his master name George, but I don't know. Dey big people in de Creek, and with de white folks too. My mammy name was Serena and she belong to some of de Gouge family. Dey was big people in de Upper Creek, and one de biggest men of the Gouge was name Hopoethleyoholo for his Creek name. He was a big man and went to de North in de War and died up in Kansas, I think. Dey say when he was a little boy he was called Hopoethli, which mean "good little boy", and when he git grown he make big speeches and dey stick on de "yoholo." Dat mean "loud whooper."

Dat de way de Creek made de name for young boys when I was a little girl. When de boy git old enough de big men in de town give him a name, and sometime later on when he git to going round wid de grown men dey stick on some more name. If he a good talker dey sometime stick on "yoholo", and iffen he make lots of jokes dey call him "Hadjo." If he is a good leader dey call him "Imala" and if he kind of mean dey sometime call him "fixigo."

My mammy and pappy belong to two masters, but dey live together on a place. Dat de way de Creek slaves do lots of times. Dey work patches and give de masters most all dey make, but dey have some for demselves. Dey didn't have to stay on de master's place and work like I hear de slaves of de white people and de Cherokee and Choctaw people say dey had to do.

Maybe my pappy and mammy run off and git free, or maybeso dey buy demselves out, but anyway dey move away some time and my mammy's master sell me to old man Tuskaya-hiniha when I was jest a little gal. All I have to do is stay at de house and mind de baby.

Master had a good log house and a bresh shelter out in front like all de houses had. Like a gallery, only it had de dirt for de flo' and bresh for de roof. Dey cook everything out in de yard in big pots, and dey eat out in de yard too.

Dat was sho' good stuff to eat, and it make you fat too! Roast de green corn on de ears in de ashes, and scrape off some and fry it! Grind de dry corn or pound it up and make ash cake. Den bile de greens—all kinds of greens from out in de woods—and chop up de pork and de deer meat, or de wild turkey meat; maybe all of dem, in de big pot at de same time! Fish too, and de big turtle dat lay out on de bank!

Dey always have a pot full of sofki settin right inside de house, and anybody eat when dey feel hungry. Anybody come on a visit, always give 'em some of de sofki. Ef dey don't take none de old man git mad, too!

When you make de sofki you pound up de corn real fine, den pour in de water an dreen it off to git all de little skin from off'n de grain. Den you let de grits soak and den bile it and let it stand. Sometime you put in some pounded hickory nut meats. Dat make it real good.

I don't know whar old Master git de cloth for de clothes, less'n he buy it. Befo' I can remember I think he had some slaves dat weave de cloth, but when I was dar he git it at de wagon depot at Honey Springs, I think. He go dar all de time to sell his corn, and he raise lots of corn, too.

Dat place was on de big road, what we called de road to Texas, but it go all de way up to de North, too. De traders stop at Honey Springs and old Master trade corn for what he want. He git some purty checkedy cloth one time, and everybody git a dress or a shirt made off'n it. I have dat dress 'till I git too big for it.

Everybody dress up fine when dey is a funeral. Dey take me along to mind de baby at two-three funerals, but I don't know who it is dat die. De Creek sho' take on when somebody die!

Long in de night you wake up and hear a gun go off, way off yonder somewhar. Den it go again, and den again, jest as fast as dey can ram de load in. Dat mean somebody dead. When somebody die de men go out in de yard and let de people know dat way. Den dey jest go back in de house and let de fire go out, and don't even tech de dead person till somebody git dar what has de right to tech de dead.

When somebody bad sick dey build a fire in de house, even in de summer, and don't let it die down till dat person git well or die. When dey die dey let de fire go out.

In de morning everybody dress up fine and go to de house whar de dead is and stand around in de yard outside de house and don't go in. Pretty soon along come somebody what got a right to tech and handle de dead and dey go in. I don't know what give dem de right, but I think dey has to go through some kind of medicine to git de right, and I know dey has to drink de red root and purge good before dey tech de body. When dey git de body ready dey come out and all go to de graveyard, mostly de family graveyard, right on de place or at some of the kinfolkses.

When dey git to de grave somebody shoots a gun at de north, den de west, den de south, and den de east. Iffen dey had four guns dey used 'em.

Den dey put de body down in de grave and put some extra clothes in with it and some food and a cup of coffee, maybe. Den dey takes strips of elm bark and lays over de body till it all covered up, and den throw in de dirt.

When de last dirt throwed on, everybody must clap

dey hands and smile, but you sho hadn't better step on any of de new dirt around de grave, because it bring sickness right along wid you back to your own house. Dat what dey said, anyways.

Jest soon as de grave filled up dey built a little shelter over it wid poles like a pig pen and kiver it over wid elm bark to keep de rain from soaking down in de new dirt.

Den everybody go back to de house and de family go in and scatter some kind of medicine 'round de place and build a new fire. Sometime dey feed everybody befo' dey all leave for home.

Every time dey have a funeral dey always a lot of de people say, "Didn't you hear de stikini squalling in de night?" "I hear dat stikini all de night!" De "stikini" is de screech owl, and he suppose to tell when anybody going to die right soon. I hear lots of Creek people say dey hear de screech owl close to de house, and sho' nuff somebody in de family die soon.

When de big battle come at our place at Honey Springs dey jest git through having de green corn "busk." De green corn was just ripened enough to eat. It must of been along in July.

Dat busk was jest a little busk. Dey wasn't enough men around to have a good one. But I seen lots of big ones. Ones whar dey had all de different kinds of "banga." Dey call all de dances some kind of banga. De chicken dance is de "Tolosabanga", and de "Istifanibanga" is de one whar dey make lak dey is skeletons and raw heads coming to git you.

De "Hadjobanga" is de crazy dance, and dat is a funny one. Dey all dance crazy and make up funny songs to go wid de dance. Everybody think up funny songs to sing and everybody whoop and laugh all de time.

But de worse one was de drunk dance. Dey jest dance ever whichaway, de men and de women together, and dey wrassle and hug and carry on awful! De good people don't dance dat one. Everybody sing about going to somebody elses house and sleeping wid dem, and shout, "We is all drunk and we don't know what we doing and we ain't doing wrong 'cause we is all drunk" and things like dat. Sometime de bad ones leave and go to de woods, too!

Dat kind of doing make de good people mad, and sometime dey have killings about it. When a man catch one his women—maybeso his wife or one of his daughters—been to de woods he catch her and beat her and cut off de rim of her ears!

People think maybeso dat ain't so, but I know it is!

I was combing somebody's hair one time—I ain't going tell who—and when I lift it up off'n her ears I nearly drap dead! Dar de rims cut right off'n 'em! But she was a married woman, and I think maybeso it happen when she was a young gal and got into it at one of dem drunk dances.

Dem Upper Creek took de marrying kind of light anyways. Iffen de younguns wanted to be man and wife and de old ones didn't care dey jest went ahead and dat was about all, 'cepting some presents maybe. But de Baptists changed dat a lot amongst de young ones.

I never forgit de day dat battle of de Civil War happen at Honey Springs! Old Master jest had de green corn all in, and us had been having a time gitting it in, too. Jest de women was all dat was left, 'cause de men slaves had all slipped off and left out. My uncle Abe done got up a bunch and gone to de North wid dem to fight, but I didn't know den whar he went. He was in dat same battle, and after de War dey called him Abe Colonel. Most all de slaves 'round dat place done gone off a long time before dat wid dey masters when dey go wid old man Gouge and a man named McDaniel.

We had a big tree in de yard, and a grape vine swing in it for de little baby "Istidji", and I was swinging him real early in de morning befo' de sun up. De house set in a little patch of woods wid de field in de back, but all out on de north side was a little open space, like a kind of prairie. I was swinging de baby, and all at once I seen somebody riding dis way 'cross dat prairie—jest coming a-kiting and a-laying flat out on his hoss. When he see de house he begin to give de war whoop, "Eya-a-a-a-he-ah!" When he git close to de house he holler to git out de way 'cause dey gwine be a big fight, and old Master start rapping wid his cane and yelling to git some grub and blankets in de wagon right now!

We jest leave everything setting right whar it is, 'cepting putting out de fire and grabbing all de pots and kettles. Some de nigger women run to git de mules and de wagon and some start gitting meat and corn out of de place whar we done hid it to keep de scouters from finding it befo' now. All de time we gitting ready to travel we hear dat boy on dat horse going on down de big Texas road hollering. "Eya-a-a-he-he-hah!"

Den jest as we starting to leave here come something

across dat little prairie sho' nuff! We know dey is Indians de way dey is riding, and de way dey is all strung out. Dey had a flag, and it was all red and had a big criss-cross on it dat look lak a saw horse. De man carry it and rear back on it when de wind whip it, but it flap all 'round de horse's head and de horse pitch and rear lak he know something going happen, sho!

'Bout dat time it turn kind of dark and begin to rain a little, and we git out to de big road and de rain come down hard. It rain so hard for a little while dat we jest have to stop de wagon and set dar, and den long come more soldiers dan I ever see befo'. Dey all white men, I think, and dey have on dat brown clothes dyed wid walnut and butternut, and old Master say dey de Confederate soldiers. Dey dragging some big guns on wheels and most de men slopping 'long in de rain on foot.

Den we hear de fighting up to de north 'long about what de river is, and de guns sound lak hosses loping 'cross a plank bridge way off somewhar. De head men start hollering and some de hosses start rearing and de soldiers start trotting faster up de road. We can't git out on de road so we jest strike off through de prairie and make for a creek dat got high banks and a place on it we call Rocky Cliff.

We git in a big cave in dat cliff, and spend de whole day and dat night in dar, and listen to de battle going on.

Dat place was about half-a-mile from de wagon depot at Honey Springs, and a little east of it. We can hear de guns going all day, and along in de evening here come de South side making for a getaway. Dey come riding and running by whar we is, and it don't make no difference how much de head men hollers at 'em dey can't make dat bunch slow up and stop.

After while here come de Yankees, right after 'em, and dey goes on into Honey Springs and pretty soon we see de blaze whar dey is burning de wagon depot and de houses.

De next morning we goes back to de house and find de soldiers ain't hurt nothing much. De hogs is whar dey is in de pen and de chickens come cackling 'round too. Dem soldiers going so fast dey didn't have no time to stop and take nothing, I reckon.

Den long come lots of de Yankee soldiers going back to de North, and dey looks purty wore out, but dey is laughing and joshing and going on.

Old Master pack up de wagon wid everything he can carry den, and we strike out down de big road to git out de way of any more war, is dey going be any.

Dat old Texas road jest crowded wid wagons! Everybody doing de same thing we is, and de rains done made de road so muddy and de soldiers done tromp up de mud so bad dat de wagons git stuck all de time.

De people all moving along in bunches, and every little while one bunch of wagons come up wid another bunch all stuck in de mud, and dey put all de hosses and mules on together and pull em out, and den dey go on together awhile.

At night dey camp, and de women and what few niggers dey is have to git de supper in de big pots, and de men so tired dey eat everything up from de women and de niggers, purty nigh.

After while we come to de Canadian town. Dat whar old man Gouge been and took a whole lot de folks up north wid him, and de South soldiers got in dar ahead of us and took up all de houses to sleep in.

Dey was some of de white soldiers camped dar, and dey was singing at de camp. I couldn't understand what dey sing, and I asked a Creek man what dey say and he tell me dey sing, "I wish I was in Dixie, look away—look away."

I ask him whar dat is, and he laugh and talk to de soldiers and dey all laugh, and make me mad.

De next morning we leave dat town and git to de big river. De rain make de river rise, and I never see so much water! Jest look out dar and dar all dat water!

Dey got some boats we put de stuff on, and float de wagons and swim de mules and finally git across, but it look lak we gwine all drown.

Most de folks say dey going to Boggy Depot and around Fort Washita, but old Master strike off by hisself and go way down in de bottom somewhar to live.

I don't know whar it was, but dey been some kind of fighting all around dar, 'cause we camp in houses and cabins all de time and nobody live in any of 'em.

Look like de people all git away quick, 'cause all de stuff was in de houses, but you better scout up around de house before you go up to it. Liable to be some scouters already in it!

Dem Indian soldiers jest quit de army and lots went

scouting in little bunches and took everything dey find. Iffen somebody try to stop dem dey git killed.

Sometime we find graves in de yard whar somebody jest been buried fresh, and one house had some dead people in it when old Mistress poke her head in it. We git away from dar, and no mistake!

By and by we find a little cabin and stop and stay all de time. I was de only slave by dat time. All de others done slip out and run off. We stay dar two year I reckon, 'cause we make two little crop of corn. For meat a man name Mr. Walker wid us jest went out in de woods and shoot de wild hogs. De woods was full of dem wild hogs, and lots of fish in de holes whar he could sicken 'em wid buck root and catch 'em wid his hands, all we wanted.

I don't know when de War quit off, and when I git free, but I stayed wid old man Tuskaya-hiniha long time after I was free, I reckon. I was jest a little girl, and he didn't know whar to send me to, anyways.

One day three men rid up and talk to de old man awhile in English talk. Den he called me and tell me to go wid dem to find my own family. He jest laugh and slap my behind and set me up on de hoss in front of one de men and dey take me off and leave my good checkedy dress at de house!

Before long we git to dat Canadian river again, and de men tie me on de hoss so I can't fall off. Dar was all dat water, and dey ain't no boat, and dey ain't no bridge, and we jest swim de hosses. I knowed sho' I was going to be gone dat time, but we git across.

When we come to de Creek Agency dar is my pappy

and my mammy to claim me, and I live wid dem in de Verdigris bottom above Fort Gibson till I was grown and dey is both dead. Den I marries Anderson Davis at Gibson Station, and we git our allotments on de Verdigris east of Tulsa—kind of south too, close to de Broken Arrow town.

I knowed old man Jim McHenry at dat Broken Arrow town. He done some preaching and was a good old man, I think.

I knowed when dey started dat Wealaka school across de river from de Broken Arrow town. Dey name it for de Wilaki town, but dat town was way down in de Upper Creek country close to whar I lived when I was a girl.

I had lots of children, but only two is alive now. My boy Anderson got in a mess and went to dat McAlester prison, but he got to be a trusty and dey let him marry a good woman dat got lots of property dar, and dey living all right now.

When my old man die I come to live here wid Josephine, but I'se blind and can't see nothing and all de noises pesters me a lot in de town. And de children is all so ill mannered, too. Dey jest holler at you all de time! Dey don't mind you neither!

When I could see and had my own younguns I could jest set in de corner and tell 'em what to do, and iffen dey didn't do it right I could whack 'em on de head, 'cause dey was raised de old Creek way, and dey know de old folks know de best!

United States. Work Projects Administration

Oklahoma Writers' Project
Ex-Slaves
[HR: (photo)]
[Date stamp: AUG 16 1937]

ANTHONY DAWSON
Age 105 yrs.
1008 E. Owen St.,
Tulsa, Okla.

"Run nigger, run,

De Patteroll git you!

Run nigger, run,

De Patteroll come!

"Watch nigger, watch—

De Patteroll trick you!

Watch nigger, watch,

He got a big gun!"

Dat one of the songs de slaves all knowed, and de children down on de "twenty acres" used to sing it when dey playing in de moonlight 'round de cabins in de quarters. Sometime I wonder iffen de white folks didn't make dat song up so us niggers would keep in line.

None of my old Master's boys tried to git away 'cepting two, and dey met up wid evil, both of 'em.

One of dem niggers was fotching a bull-tongue from a piece of new ground way at de back of de plantation, and bringing it to my pappy to git it sharped. My pappy was de blacksmith.

Dis boy got out in de big road to walk in de soft sand, and long come a wagon wid a white overseer and five, six, niggers going somewhar. Dey stopped and told dat boy to git in and ride. Dat was de last anybody seen him.

Dat overseer and another one was cotched after awhile, and showed up to be underground railroaders. Dey would take a bunch of niggers into town for some excuse, and on de way jest pick up a extra nigger and show him whar to go to git on de "railroad system." When de runaway niggers got to de North dey had to go in de army, and dat boy from our place got killed. He was a good boy, but dey jest talked him into it. Dem railroaders was honest, and dey didn't take no presents, but de patrollers was low white trash!

We all knowed dat if a patroller jest rode right by and didn't say nothing dat he was doing his honest job, but iffen he stopped his hoss and talked to a nigger he was after some kind of trade.

Dat other black boy was hoeing cotton way in de back of de field and de patroller rid up and down de big road, saying nothing to nobody.

De next day another white man was on de job, and long in de evening a man come by and axed de niggers about de fishing and hunting! Dat black boy seen he was de same man what was riding de day befo' and he knowed it was a underground trick. But he didn't see all de trick, bless God!

We found out afterwards dat he told his mammy about it. She worked at de big house and she stole something for him to give dat low white trash I reckon, 'cause de next day he played sick along in de evening and de black overlooker—he was my uncle—sent him back to de quarters.

He never did git there, but when dey started de hunt dey found him about a mile away in de woods wid his head shot off, and old Master sold his mammy to a trader right away. He never whipped his grown niggers.

Dat was de way it worked. Dey was all kinds of white folks jest like dey is now. One man in Sesesh clothes would shoot you if you tried to run away. Maybe another Sesesh would help slip you out to the underground and say "God bless you poor black devil", and some of dem dat was poor would help you if you could bring 'em sumpin you stole, lak a silver dish or spoons or a couple big hams. I couldn't blame them poor white folks, wid the men in the War and the women and children hongry. The niggers didn't belong to them nohow, and they had to live somehow. But now and then they was a devil on earth, walking in the sight of God and spreading iniquity before him. He was de low-down Sesesh dat would take what a poor runaway nigger had to give for his chance to git away, and den give him 'structions dat would lead him right into de hands of de patrollers and git him caught or shot!

Yes, dat's de way it was. Devils and good people walking in de road at de same time, and nobody could tell one from t'other.

I remember about de trickery so good 'cause I was "grown and out" at that time. When I was a little boy I was a house boy, 'cause my mammy was the house woman, but when the war broke I already been sent to the fields and mammy was still at de house.

I was born on July 25, 1832. I know, 'cause old Master keep de book on his slaves jest like on his own family. He was a good man, and old Mistress was de best woman in de world!

De plantation had more than 500 acres and most was in cotton and tobacco. But we raised corn and oats, and lots of cattle and horses, and plenty of sheep for wool.

I was born on the plantation, soon after my pappy and mammy was brought to it. I don't remember whether they was bought or come from my Mistress's father. He was mighty rich and had several hundred niggers. When she was married he give her 40 niggers. One of them was my pappy's brother. His name was John, and he was my master's overlooker.

We called a white man boss the "overseer", but a nigger was a overlooker. John could read and write and figger, and old Master didn't have no white overseer.

Master's name was Levi Dawson, and his plantation was 18 miles east of Greenville, North Carolina. It was a beautiful place, with all the fences around the Big House and along the front made out of barked poles, rider style, and all whitewashed.

The Big House set back from the big road about a quarter of a mile. It was only one story, but it had lots of rooms.

There was four rooms in a bunch on one side and four in a bunch on the other, with a wide hall in between. They was made of square adzed logs, all weatherboarded on the outside and planked up and plastered on the inside. Then they was a long gallery clean across the front with big pillars made out of bricks and plastered over. They called it the passage 'cause it din't have no floor excepting bricks, and a buggy could drive right under it. Mostly it was used to set under and talk and play cards and drink the best whiskey old Master could buy.

Back in behind the big house was the kitchen, and the smokehouse in another place made of plank, and all was whitewashed and painted white all the time.

Old Mistress was named Miss Susie and she was born an Isley. She brought 40 niggers from her pappy as a present, and Master Levi jest had 4 or 5, but he had got all his land from his pappy. She had the niggers and he had the land. That's the way it was, and that's the way it stayed! She never let him punish one of her niggers and he never asked her about buying or selling land. Her pappy was richer than his pappy, and she was sure quality!

My pappy's name was Anthony, and mammy's name was Chanie. He was the blacksmith and fixed the wagons, but he couldn't read and figger like uncle John. Mammy was the head house woman but didn't know any letters either.

They was both black like me. Old man Isley, where they come from, had lots of niggers, but I don't think they was off the boat.

You can set the letters up and I can't tell them, but

you can't fool me with the figgers, 'less they are mighty big numbers.

Master Levi had three sons and no daughters. The oldest son was Simeon. He was in the Sesesh army. The other two boys was too young. I can't remember their names. They was a lot younger and I was grown and out befo' they got big.

Old Master was a fine Christian but he like his juleps anyways. He let us niggers have preachings and prayers, and would give us a parole to go 10 or 15 miles to a camp meeting and stay two or three days with nobody but Uncle John to stand for us. Mostly we had white preachers, but when we had a black preacher that was Heaven.

We didn't have no voodoo women nor conjure folks at our 20 acres. We all knowed about the Word and the unseen Son of God and we didn't put no stock in conjure.

Course we had luck charms and good and bad signs, but everybody got dem things even nowadays. My boy had a white officer in the Big War and he tells me that man had a li'l old doll tied around his wrist on a gold chain.

We used herbs and roots for common ailments, like sassafras and boneset and peach tree poultices and coon root tea, but when a nigger got bad sick Old Master sent for a white doctor. I remember that old doctor. He lived in Greenville and he had to come 18 miles in a buggy.

When he give some nigger medicine he would be afraid the nigger was like lots of them that believed in conjure, and he would say, "If you don't take that medicine like I tell you and I have to come back here to see you

I going to break your dam black neck next time I come out here!"

When it was bad weather sometime the black boy sent after him had to carry a lantern to show him the way back. If that nigger on his mule got too fur ahead so old doctor couldn't see de light he sho' catch de devil from that old doctor and from old Master, too, less'n he was one of old Missy's house niggers, and then old Master jest grumble to satisfy the doctor.

Down in the quarters we had the spinning house, where the old woman card the wool and run the loom. They made double weave for the winter time, and all the white folks and slaves had good clothes and good food.

Master made us all eat all we could hold. He would come to the smokehouse and look in and say, "You niggers ain't cutting down that smoke side and that souse lak you ought to! You made dat meat and you got to help eat it up!"

Never no work on Sunday 'cepting the regular chores. The overlooker made everybody clean up and wash de children up and after the praying we had games. Antny over and marbles and "I Spy" and de likes of that. Some times de boys would go down in de woods and git a possum. I love possum and sweet taters, but de coon meat more delicate and de har don't stink up de meat.

I wasn't at the quarters much as a boy. I was at the big house with my mammy, and I had to swing the fly bresh over my old Mistress when she was sewing or eating or taking her nap. Sometime I would keep the flies off'n old Master, and when I would get tired and let the bresh slap his neck he would kick at me and cuss me, but he never did reach me. He had a way of keeping us little niggers scared to death and never hurting nobody.

I was down in the field burning bresh when I first heard the guns in the War. De fighting was de battle at Kingston, North Carolina, and it lasted four days and nights. After while bunches of Sesesh come riding by hauling wounded people in wagons, and then pretty soon big bunches of Yankees come by, but dey didn't ack like dey was trying very hard to ketch up.

Dey had de country in charge quite some time, and they had forages coming round all the time. By dat time old Master done buried his money and all de silver and de big clock, but the Yankees didn't pear to search out dat kind of stuff. All dey ask about was did anybody find a bottle of brandy!

When de War ended up most all de niggers stay with old Master and work on de shares, until de land git divided up and sold off and the young niggers git scattered to town.

I never did have no truck wid de Ku Kluckers, but I had to step mighty high to keep out'n it! De sho' nuff Kluxes never did bother around us 'cause we minded our own business and never give no trouble.

We wouldn't let no niggers come 'round our place talking 'bout delegates and voting, and we jest all stayed on the place. But dey was some low white trash and some devilish niggers made out like dey was Ku Klux ranging 'round de country stealing hosses and taking things.

Old Master said dey wasn't shore enough, so I reckon he knowed who the regular ones was.

These bunches that come around robbing got into our neighborhood and old Master told me I better not have my old horse at the house, 'cause if I had him they would know nobody had been there stealing and it wouldn't do no good to hide anything 'cause they would tear up the place hunting what I had and maybe whip or kill me.

"Your old hoss aint no good, Tony, and you better kill him to make them think you already been raided on," old Master told me, so I led him out and knocked him in the head with an axe, and then we hid all our grub and waited for the Kluckers to come most any night, but they never did come. I borried a hoss to use in the day and took him back home every night for about a year.

The niggers kept talking about being free, but they wasn't free then and they ain't now.

Putting them free jest like putting goat hair on a sheep. When it rain de goat come a running and git in de shelter, 'cause his hair won't shed the rain and he git cold, but de sheep ain't got sense enough to git in the shelter but jest stand out and let it rain on him all day.

But the good Lord fix the sheep up wid a woolly jacket that turn the water off, and he don't git cold, so he don't have to have no brains.

De nigger during slavery was like de sheep. He couldn't take care of hisself but his Master looked out for him and he didn't have to use his brains. De master's protection was like de wooly coat.

But de 'mancipation come and take off de woolly coat and leave de nigger wid no protection and he cain't take care of hisself either.

When de niggers was sot free lots of them got mighty uppity, and everybody wanted to be a delegate to something or other. The Yankees told us we could go down and vote in the 'lections and our color was good enough to run for anything. Heaps of niggers believed them. You cain't fault them for that, 'cause they didn't have no better sense, but I knowed the black folks didn't have no business mixing in until they knowed more.

It was a long time after the War before I went down to vote and everything quiet by that time, but I heard people talk about the fights at the schoolhouse when they had the first election.

I jest stayed on around the old place a long time, and then I got on another piece of ground and farmed, not far from Greenville until 1900. Then I moved to Hearn, Texas, and stayed with my son Ed until 1903 when we moved to Sapulpa in the Creek Nation. We come to Tulsa several years ago, and I been living with him ever since.

I can't move off my bed now, but one time I was strong as a young bull. I raised seven boys and seven girls. My boys was named Edward, Joseph, Furney, Julius, James, and William, and my girls was Luvenia, Olivia, Chanie Mamie, Rebecca and Susie.

I always been a deep Christian and depend on God and know his unseen Son, the King of Glory. I learned about Him when I was a little boy. Old Master was a good man, but on some of the plantations the masters wasn't good men and the niggers didn't get the Word.

I never did get no reading and writing 'cause I never did go to the schools. I thought I was too big, but they had schools and the young ones went.

But I could figger, and I was a good farmer, and now I bless the Lord for all his good works. Everybody don't know it I reckon, but we all needed each other. The blacks needed the whites, and still do.

There's a difference in the color of the skin, but the souls is all white, or all black, 'pending on the man's life and not on his skin. The old fashioned meetings is busted up into a thousand different kinds of churches and only one God to look after them. All is confusion, but I ain't going to worry my old head about 'em.

United States. Work Projects Administration

Oklahoma Writers' Project
Ex-Slaves
[Date stamp AUG 19 1937]

ALICE DOUGLASS
Age 77 yrs.
Oklahoma City, Okla.

I was born December 22, 1860 in Sumner County, Tennessee. My mother—I mean mammy, 'cause what did we know 'bout mother and mamma. Master and Mistress made dey chillun call all nigger women, "Black Mammy." Jest as I was saying my mammy was named Millie Elkins and my pappy was named Isaac Garrett. My sisters and brothers was Frank, Susie and Mollie. They is all in Nashville, Tennessee right now. They lived in log houses. I 'member my grandpappy and when he died. I allus slept in the Big House in a cradle wid white babies.

We all the time wore cotton dresses and we weaved our own cloth. The boys jest wore shirts. Some wore shoes, and I sho' did. I kin see 'em now as they measured my feets to git my shoes. We had doctors to wait on us iffen we got sick and ailing. We wore asafedida to keep all diseases offen us.

When a nigger man got ready to marry, he go and tell his master that they was a woman on sech and sech a farm that he'd lak to have. Iffen master give his resent, then he go and ask her master and iffen he say yes, well, they jest jump the broomstick. Mens could jest see their wives on Sadday nite.

They laid peoples 'cross barrels and whupped 'em wid bull whups till the blood come. They'd half feed 'em and niggers'd steal food and cook all night. The things we was forced to do then the whites is doing of their own free will now. You gotta reap jest what you sow 'cause the Good Book says it.

They used to bid niggers off and then load 'em on wagons and take 'em to cotton farms to work. I never seen no cotton till I come heah. Peoples make big miration 'bout girls having babies at 11 years old. And you better have them whitefolks some babies iffen you didn't wanta be sold. Though a funny thing to me is, iffen a nigger woman had a baby on the boat on the way to the cotton farms, they throwed it in the river. Taking 'em to them cotton farms is jest the reason niggers is so plentiful in the South today.

I ain't got no education a'tall. In dem days you better not be caught with a newspaper, else you got a beating and your back almost cut off. When niggers got free, whitefolks killed 'em by the carload, 'cause they said it was a nigger uprising. I used to lay on the flo' with the whitefolks and hear 'em pass. Them patrollers roved trying to ketch niggers without passes to whup 'em. They was sometimes called bush whackers.

We went to white folks' church. I was a great big girl before we went to cullud church. We'd stay out and play while they worshipped. We jest played marbles—girls, white chillun and all.

The Yankees come thoo' and took all the meat and everything they could find. They took horses, food and all. Mammy cooked their vittles. One come in our cabin and took a sack of dried fruit with my mammy's shoes on the top. I tried to make 'em leave mammy's shoes too but he didn't.

I stayed in the house with the whitefolks till I was 19. They lak to kept me in there too long. That's why I'm selfish as I am. Within three weeks after I was out of the house, I married William Douglass. Whitefolks now don't want you to tech 'em, and I slept with white chillun till I was 19. You kin cook for 'em and put your hands in they vittles and they don't say nothing, but jest you tech one!

We stayed on, on the place, three or four years and it was right then mammy give us our pappy's name. We moved from the place to one three or four miles from our master's place, and mammy cooked there a long time.

Abraham Lincoln gits too much praise. I say, shucks, give God the praise. Lincoln come thoo' Gallitan, Tennessee and stopped at Hotel Tavern with his wife. They was dressed jest lak tramps and nobody knowed it was him and his wife till he got to the White House and writ back and told 'em to look 'twixt the leaves in the table where he had set and they sho' nuff found out it was him.

I never mentions Jeff Davis. He ain't wuff it.

Booker T. Washington was all right in his place. He come here and told these whitefolks jest what he thought. Course he wouldn't have done that way down South. I declare to God he sho' told 'em enough. They toted him 'round on their hands. No Jim Crow here then.

I jined the church 'cause I had religion round 60 years ago. People oughta be religious sho'; what for they wanta live in sin and die and go to the Bad Man. To git to Heaven, you sho' ought to work some. I want a resting place somewhar, 'cause I ain't got none here. I am a member of Tabernacle Baptist Church, and I help build the first church in Oklahoma City.

I got three boys and three girls. I don't know none's age. I give 'em the best education I could.

Slave Narratives

Oklahoma Writers' Project
Ex-Slaves
[Date stamp: AUG 13 1937]

DOC DANIEL DOWDY
Age 81 yrs.
Oklahoma City, Oklahoma

I was born June 6, 1856 in Madison County, Georgia. Father was named Joe Dowdy and mother was named Mary Dowdy. There was 9 of us boys, George, Smith, Lewis, Henry, William, myself, Newt, James and Jeff. There was one girl and she was my twin, and her name was Sarah. My mother and father come from Richmond, Va., to Georgia. Father lived on one side of the river and my mother on the other side. My father would come over ever week to visit us. Noah Meadows bought my father and Elizabeth Davis, daughter of the old master took my mother. They married in Noah Meadows' house.

My mother was the cook in the Big House. They'd give us pot likker with bread crumbs in it. Sometimes meat, jest sometimes, very seldom. I liked black-eyed peas and still do till now. We lived in weatherboard house. Our parents had corded-up beds with ropes and us chillun slept on the floor for most part or in a hole bored in a log. Our house had one window jest big enough to stick your head out of, and one door, and this one door faced the Big House which was your master's house. This was so that you couldn't git out 'less somebody seen you.

My job was picking up chips and keeping the calves and cows separate so that the calves wouldn't suck the cows dry. Mostly, we had Saturday afternoons off to wash. I was show boy doing [HW: during] the war, me and my sister, 'cause we was twins. My mother couldn't be bought 'cause she done had 9 boys for one farm and neither my father, 'cause he was the father of 'em. I was religious and didn't play much, but I sho' did like to listen to preachings. I did used to play marbles sometimes.

We jest wore shirts and nothing else both winter and summer. They was a little heavier in winter and that's all. No shoes ever. I had none till after I was set free. I guess I was almost 12 years old then.

The overseer on our place was a large tall, black man. We had plenty poor white neighbors. They was one of our biggest troubles. They'd allus look in our window and door all the time.

I saw slaves sold. I can see that old block now. My cousin Eliza was a pretty girl, really good looking. Her master was her father. When the girls in the big house had beaux coming to see 'em, they'd ask, "Who is that pretty gal?" So they decided to git rid of her right away. The day they sold her will allus be remembered. They stripped her to be bid off and looked at. I wasn't allowed to stand in the crowd. I was laying down under a fig brush. The man that bought Eliza was from New York. The Negroes had made up nuff money to buy her off theyself, but they wouldn't let that happen. There was a man bidding for her who was a Swedeland. He allus bid for the good looking cullud gals and bought 'em for his own use. He ask the man from New York, "Whut you gonna do with her when you git 'er?" The man from New York said, "None of your damn business, but you ain't got money nuff to buy 'er." When the man from New York had done bought her, he said, "Eliza, you are free from now on." She left and went to New York with him. Mama and Eliza both cried when she was being showed off, and master told 'em to shet up before he knocked they brains out.

Iffen you didn't do nothing wrong, they whipped you now and then anyhow. I called a boy Johnny once and he took me 'hind the garden and poured it on me and made me call him master. It was from then on I started to fear the white man. I come to think of him as a bear. Sometimes fellows would be a little late making it in and they got whipped with a cow-hide. The same man whut whipped me to make me call him master, well, he whipped my mamma. He tied her to a tree and beat her unmerciful and cut her tender parts. I don't know why he tied her to that tree.

The first time you was caught trying to read or write, you was whipped with a cow-hide, the next time with a cat-o-nine tails and the third time they cut the first jint offen your forefinger. They was very severe. You most allus got 30 and 9 lashes.

They carried news from one plantation by whut they call relay. Iffen you was caught, they whipped you till you said, "Oh, pray Master!" One day a man gitting whipped was saying "Oh pray master, Lord have mercy!" They'd say "Keep whipping that nigger Goddamn him." He was whipped till he said, "Oh pray Master, I gotta nuff." Then they said, "Let him up now, 'cause he's praying to the right man."

My father was the preacher and an educated man. You

know the sermon they give him to preach?—Servant, Obey Your Master. Our favorite baptizing hymn was On Jordan's Stormy Bank I Stand. My favorite song is Nobody Knows the Trouble I've Seen.

Oh, them patrollers! They had a chief and he git'em together and iffen they caught you without a pass and sometimes with a pass, they'd beat you. But iffen you had a pass, they had to answer to the law. One old master had two slaves, brothers, on his place. They was both preachers. Mitchell was a hardshell Baptist and Andrew was a Missionary Baptist. One day the patroller chief was rambling thoo' the place and found some letters writ to Mitchell and Andrew. He went to the master and said, "Did you know you had some niggers that could read and write?" Master said, "No, but I might have, who do you 'spect?" The patroller answered, "Mitchell and Andrew." The old master said, "I never knowed Andrew to tell me a lie 'bout nothing!"

Mitchell was called first and asked could he read and write. He was scared stiff. He said, "Naw-sir." Andrew was called and asked. He said, "Yes-sir." He was asked iffen Mitchell could. He said, "Sho', better'n me." The master told John Arnold, the patroller chief, not to bother 'em. He gloried in they spunk. When the old master died, he left all of his niggers a home apiece. We had Ku Klux Klans till the government sent Federal officers out and put a stop to their ravaging and sent 'em to Sing Sing.

Doing the war my father was carpenter. His young master come to him 'cause he was a preacher and asked him must he go to the front and my father told him not to go 'cause he wouldn't make it. He went on jest the same and when he come back my father had to tote him in the house 'cause he had one leg tore off. The Yankees come thoo', ramshacked houses, leave poor horses and take fat ones and turn the poor ones in the corn they left. They took everthing they could. They cussed niggers who dodged 'em for being fools and make 'em show 'em everything they knowed whar was.

Our old master was mighty old and him and the women folks cried when we was freed. He told us we was free as he was.

I come to Oklahoma in 1906. I come out of that riot in 1906. Some fellow knocked up a colored woman or something and we waded right in and believe me we made Atlanta a fit place to live in. It is one of the best cities in America.

I married Miss Emmaline Witt. I carried her to the preacher one of the coldest nights I ever rid. I have three chillun and don't know how many grandchillun. My chillun is one a nurse, one in Arizona for his health and the other doing first one thing and another.

I think Abraham Lincoln was the greatest human being ever been on earth 'cepting the Apostle Paul. Who any better'n a man who liberated 4,000,000 Negroes? Some said he wasn't a Christian, but he told some friends once, "I'm going to leave you and may never see you again (and he didn't) so I'm going to take the Divine Spirit with me and leave it with you."

Jeff Davis was as bloody as he could be. I don't lak him a'tall. But you know good things come from enemies. I don't even admire George Washington. White men from the south that will help the Negro is far and few between.

Booker T. Washington was a great man. He made some blunders and mistakes, but he was a great man. He is the father of industrial education and you know that sho' is a great thing.

The white folks was ignorant. You know the better you prepare yourself the better you act. Iffen they had put some sense in our heads 'stead of sticks on our heads, we'ud been better off and more benefit to 'em.

I had something from within that made me fear God and taught me how to pray. People say God don't hear sinners pray, but he do. Everybody ought to be Christians so not to be lost.

I work in real estate and can do a lot of work. I don't use no crutches and no cane and walk all the time, never hardly ride. I come in at 1 and 2 o'clock a. m. and get up between 8 and 9 a. m. 'cept Sundays, I get up at 7 or 8 a. m. so I can be ready to go to Sunday School. I cook for my own self all the time too. I am a Baptist and a member of Tabernacle Baptist Church. I am a trustee in my church too.

Oklahoma Writers' Project
Ex-Slaves
[Date stamp: AUG 19 1937]

JOANNA DRAPER
Age 83 yrs.
Tulsa, Okla.

Most folks can't remember many things happened to 'em when they only eight years old, but one of my biggest tribulations come about dat time and I never will forget it! That was when I was took away from my own mammy and pappy and sent off and bound out to another man, way off two-three hundred miles away from whar I live. And dat's the last time I ever see either one of them, or any my own kinfolks!

Whar I was born was at Hazelhurst, Mississippi. Jest a little piece east of Hazelhurst, close to the Pearl River, and that place was a kind of new plantation what my Master, Dr. Alexander, bought when he moved into Mississippi from up in Virginia awhile before the War.

They said my mammy brings me down to Mississippi, and I was born jest right after she got there. My mammy's name was Margaret, and she was born under the Ramson's, back in Tennessee. She belonged to Dave Ramson, and his pappy had come to Tennessee to settle on war land, and he had knowed Dr. Alexander's people back in Virginia too. My pappy's name was Addison, and he always belonged to Dr. Alexander. Old doctor bought my mammy 'cause my pappy liked her. Old doctor live in Tennessee a little while before he go on down in Mississippi.

Old doctor's wife named Dinah, and she sho' was a good woman, but I don't remember about old doctor much. He was away all the time, it seem like.

When I is about six year old they take me into the Big House to learn to be a house woman, and they show me how to cook and clean up and take care of babies. That Big House wasn't very fine, but it was mighty big and cool, and made out of logs with a big hall, but it didn't have no long gallery like most the houses around there had.

They was lots of big trees in the yard, and most the ground was new ground 'round that place, 'cause the old Doctor jest started to done farming on it when I was took away, but he had some more places not so far away, over towards the river that was old ground and made big crops for him. I went to one of the places one time, but they wasn't nobody on 'em but niggers and a white overseer. I don't know how many niggers old Doctor had, but Master John Deeson say he had about a hundred.

At old Doctor's house I didn't have to work very hard. Jest had to help the cooks and peel the potatoes and pick the guineas and chickens and do things like that. Sometime I had to watch the baby. He was a little boy, and they would bring him into the kitchen for me to watch. I had to git up way before daylight and make the fire in the kitchen fireplace and bring in some fresh water, and go get the milk what been down in the spring all night, and do things like that until breakfast ready. Old Master and old Mistress come in the big hall to eat in the summer, and I stand behind them and shoo off the flies.

Old doctor didn't have no spinning and weaving niggers 'cause he say they don't do enough work and he buy all the cloth he use for everybody's clothes. He can do that 'cause he had lots of money. He was big rich, and he keep a whole lot of hard money in the house all the time, but none of the slaves know it but me. Sometimes I would have the baby in the Mistress' room and she would go git three or four big wood boxes full of hard money for us to play with. I would make fences out of the money all across the floor, to keep the baby satisfied, and when he go to sleep I would put the money back in the boxes. I never did know how much they is, but a whole lot.

Even after the War start old Doctor have that money, and he would exchange money for people. Sometimes he would go out and be gone a long time, and come back with a lot more money he got from somewhar.

Right at the first they made him a high officer in the War and he done doctoring somewhar at a hospital most of the time. But he could go on both sides of the War, and sometime he would come in at night and bring old Mistress pretty little things, and I heard him tell her he got them in the North.

One day I was fanning him and I asked him is he been to the North and he kick out at me and tell to shut up my black mouth, and it nearly scared me to death the way he look at me! Nearly every time he been gone and come in and tell Mistress he been in the North he have a lot more hard money to put away in them boxes, too!

One evening long come a man and eat supper at the house and stay all night. He was a nice mannered man, and I like to wait on him. The next morning I hear him ask old Doctor what is my name, and old Doctor start in to try to sell me to that man. The man say he can't buy me 'cause old Doctor say he want a thousand dollars, and then old Doctor say he will bind me out to him.

I run away from the house and went out to the cabin whar my mammy and pappy was, but they tell me to go on back to the Big House 'cause maybe I am just scared. But about that time old Doctor and the man come and old Doctor make me go with the man. We go in his buggy a long ways off to the South, and after he stop two or three night at peoples houses and put me out to stay with the niggers he come to his own house. I ask him how far it is back home and he say about a hundred miles or more, and laugh, and ask me if I know how far that is.

I wants to know if I can go back to my mammy some time, and he say "Sho', of course you can, some of these times. You don't belong to me, Jo, I'se jest your boss and not your master."

He live in a big old rottendy house, but he aint farming none of the land. Jest as soon as he git home he go off again, and sometimes he only come in at night for a little while.

His wife's name was Kate and his name was Mr. John. I was there about a week before I found out they name was Deeson. They had two children, a girl about my size name Joanna like me, and a little baby boy name Johnny. One day Mistress Kate tell me I the only nigger they got. I been thinking maybe they had some somewhar on a plantation, but she say they aint got no plantation and they aint been at that place very long either.

That little girl Joanna and me kind of take up together, and she was a mighty nice mannered little girl, too. Her mammy raised her good. Her mammy was mighty sickly all the time, and that's the reason they bind me to do the work.

Mr. John was in some kind of business in the War too, but I never see him with no soldier clothes on but one time. One night he come in with them on, but the next morning he come to breakfast in jest his plain clothes again. Then he go off again.

I sho' had a hard row at that house. It was old and rackady, and I had to scrub off the staircase and the floors all the time, and git the breakfast for Mistress Kate and the two children. Then I could have my own breakfast in the kitchen. Mistress Kate always get the supper, though.

Some days she go off with the two children and leave me at the house all day by myself, and I think maybe I run off, but I didn't know whar to go.

After I been at that place two years Mr. John come home and stay. He done some kind of trading in Jackson, Mississippi, and he would be gone three or four days at a time, but I never did know what kind of trading it was.

About the time he come home to stay I seen the first Ku Klux I ever seen one night. I was going down the road in the moonlight and I heard a hog grunting out in the bushes at the side of the road. I jest walk right on and in a little ways I hear another hog in some more bushes. This time I stop and listen, and they's another hog grunts across the road, and about that time two mens dressed up in long white skirts steps out into the road in front of me! I was so scared the goose bumps jump up all over me 'cause I didn't know what they is! They didn't say a word to me, but jest walked on past me and went on back the way I had come. Then I see two more mens step out of the woods and I run from that as fast as I can go!

I ast Miss Kate what they is and she say they Ku Klux, and I better not go walking off down the road any more. I seen them two, three times after that, though, but they was riding hosses them times.

I stayed at Mr. John's place two more years, and he got so grumpy and his wife got so mean I make up my mind to run off. I bundle up my clothes in a little bundle and hide them, and then I wait until Miss Kate take the children and go off somewhere, and I light out on foot. I had me a piece of that hard money what Master Dr. Alexander had give me one time at Christmas. I had kept it all that time and nobody knowed I had it, not even Joanna. Old Doctor told me it was fifty dollars, and I thought I could live on it for a while.

I never had been away from that place, not even to another plantation in all the four years I was with the Deesons, and I didn't know which-a-way to go, so I jest started west.

I been walking about all evening it seem like, and I come to a little town with jest a few houses. I see a nigger man and ask him whar I can git something to eat, and I say I got fifty dollars.

"What you doing wid fifty dollars, child? Where you

belong at, anyhow?" He ask me, and I tell him I belong to Master John Deeson, but I is running away. I explain that I jest bound out to Mr. John, but Dr. Alexander my real master, and then that man tell me the first time I knowed it that I aint a slave no more!

That man Deeson never did tell me, and his wife never did!

Well, dat man asked me about the fifty dollars, and then I found out that it was jest fifty cents!

I can't begin to tell about all the hard times I had working for something to eat and roaming around after that. I don't know why I never did try to git back up around Hazelhurst and hunt up my pappy and mammy, but I reckon I was jest ignorant and didn't know how to go about it. Anyways I never did see them no more.

In about three years or a little over I met Bryce Draper on a farm in Mississippi and we was married. His mammy had had a harder time than I had. She had five children by a man that belong to her master, Mr. Bryce and already named one of the boys—that my husband—Bryce after him, and then he take her in and sell her off away from all her children!

One was jest a little baby, and the master give it laudanum, but it didn't die, and he sold her off and lied and said she was a young girl and didn't have no husband, 'cause the man what bought her said he didn't want to buy no woman and take her away from a family. That new master name was Draper.

The last year of the War Mr. Draper die, and his wife already dead, and he give all his farm to his two slaves and set them free. One of them slaves was my husband's mammy.

Then right away the whites come and robbed the place of every thing they could haul off, and run his mammy and the other niggers off! Then she went and found her boy, that was my husband, and he live with her until she died, jest before we is married.

We lived in Mississippi a long time, and then we hear about how they better to the Negroes up in the North, and we go up to Kansas, but they ain't no better there, and we come down to Indian Territory in the Creek Nation in 1898, jest as they getting in that Spanish War.

We leased a little farm from the Creek Nation for $15 an acre, but when they give out the allotments we had to give it up. Then we rent 100 acres from some Indians close to Wagoner, and we farm it all with my family. We had enough to do it too!

For children we had John and Joe, and Henry, and Jim and Robert and Will that was big enough to work, and then the girls big enough was Mary, Nellie, Izora, Dora, and the baby. Dora married Max Colbert. His people belonged to the Colberts that had Colbert's Crossin' on the Red River way before the War, and he was a freedman and got allotment.

I lives with Dora now, and we is all happy, and I don't like to talk about the days of the slavery times, 'cause they never did mean nothing to me but misery, from the time I was eight years old.

I never will forgive that white man for not telling me

I was free, and not helping me to git back to my mammy and pappy! Lots of white people done that.

United States. Work Projects Administration

Oklahoma Writers' Project
Ex-Slaves

MRS. ESTHER EASTER
Age 85 yrs.
Tulsa, Okla.

I was born near Memphis, Tenn., on the old Ben Moore plantation, but I don't know anything about the Old South because Master Ben moves us all up into Missouri (about 14-miles east of Westport, now Kansas City), long before they started fighting about slavery.

Mary Collier was my mother's name before she was a Moore. About my father, I dunno. Mammy was sickly most of the time when I was a baby, and she was so thin and poorly when they move to Missouri the white folks afraid she going die on the way.

But she fool 'em, and she live two-three year after that. That's what good Old Master Ben tells me when I gets older.

I stay with Master Ben's married daughter, Mary, till the coming of the War. Times was good before the War, and I wasn't suffering none from slavery, except once in a while the Mistress would fan me with the stick—bet I needed it, too.

When the War come along Master he say to leave Mistress Mary and get ready to go to Texas. Jim Moore, one of the meanest men I ever see, was the son of Master Ben; he's going take us there.

Demon Jim, that's what I call him when he ain't round the place, but when he's home it was always Master Jim 'cause he was reckless with the whip. He was a Rebel officer fighting round the country and didn't take us slaves to Texas right away. So I stayed on at his place not far from Master Ben's plantation.

Master Jim's wife was a demon, just like her husband. Used the whip all the time, and every time Master Jim come home he whip me 'cause the Mistress say I been mean.

One time I tell him, you better put me in your pocket (sell me), Master Jim, else I'se going run away'. He don't pay no mind, and I don't try to run away 'cause of the whips.

I done see one whipping and that enough. They wasn't no fooling about it. A runaway slave from the Jenkin's plantation was brought back, and there was a public whipping, so's the slaves could see what happens when they tries to get away.

The runaway was chained to the whipping post, and I was full of misery when I see the lash cutting deep into that boy's skin. He swell up like a dead horse, but he gets over it, only he was never no count for work no more.

While Master Jim is out fighting the Yanks, the Mistress is fiddling round with a neighbor man, Mister Headsmith. I is young then, but I knows enough that Master Jim's going be mighty mad when he hears about it.

The Mistress didn't know I knows her secret, and I'm fixing to even up for some of them whippings she put off on me. That's why I tell Master Jim next time he come home.

See that crack in the wall? Master Jim say yes, and I say, it's just like the open door when the eyes are close to the wall. He peek and see into the bedroom.

That's how I find out about the Mistress and Mister Headsmith, I tells him, and I see he's getting mad.

What you mean? And Master Jim grabs me hard by the arm like I was trying to get away.

I see them in the bed.

That's all I say. The Demon's got him and Master Jim tears out of the room looking for the Mistress.

Then I hears loud talking and pretty soon the Mistress is screaming and calling for help, and if old Master Ben hadn't drop in just then and stop the fight, why, I guess she be beat almost to death, that how mad the Master was.

Then Master Ben gets mad 'cause his boy Jim ain't got us down in Texas yet. Then we stay up all the night packing for the trip. Master Jim takes us, but the Mistress stay at home, and I wonder if Master Jim beat her again when he gets back.

We rides the wagons all the way, how many days, I dunno. The country was wild most of the way, and I know now that we come through the same country where I lives now, only it was to the east. (The trip was evidently made over the "Texas Road.") And we keeps on riding and comes to the big river that's all brown and red looking, (Red River) and the next thing I was sold to Mrs. Vaughn at Bonham, Texas, and there I stays till after the slaves is free.

The new Mistress was a widow, no children round the place, and she treat me mighty good. She was good white folks—like old Master Ben, powerful good.

When the word get to us that the slaves is free, the Mistress says I is free to go anywheres I want. And I tell her this talk about being free sounds like foolishment to me—anyway, where can I go? She just pat me on the shoulder and say I better stay right there with her, and that's what I do for a long time. Then I hears about how the white folks down at Dallas pays big money for house girls and there I goes.

That's all I ever do after that—work at the houses till I gets too old to hobble on these tired old feets and legs, then I just sits down.

Just sits down and wishes for old Master Ben to come and get me, and take care of this old woman like he use to do when she is just a little black child on the plantation in Missouri!

God Bless old Master Ben—he was good white folks!

Oklahoma Writers' Project
Ex-Slaves

ELIZA EVANS
Age 87
McAlester, Okla.

I sho' remember de days when I was a slave and belonged to de best old Master what ever was, Mr. John Mixon. We lived in Selma, Dallas County, Alabama.

My grandma was a refugee from Africa. You know dey was white men who went slipping 'round and would capture or entice black folks onto their boats and fetch them over here and sell 'em for slaves. Well, grandma was a little girl 'bout eight or nine years old and her parents had sent her out to get wood. Dey was going to have a feast. Dey was going to roast a baby. Wasn't that awful? Well, they captured her and put a stick in her mouth. The stick held her mouth wide open so she wouldn't cry out. When she got to de boat she was so tired out she didn't do nothing.

They was a lot of more colored folks on de boat. It took about four months to get across on de boat and Mr. John Mixon met the boat and bought her. I think he gave five hundred dollars for her. She was named Gigi, but Master John called her Gracie. She was so good and they thought so much of her dat they gave her a grand wedding when she was married. Master John told her he'd never sell none of her chillun. He kept dat promise and he never did sell any of her grandchillun either. He thought it was wrong to separate famblys. She was one hundred and three years old when she died. I guess her mind got kind of feeble 'cause she wandered off and fell into a mill race and was drowned.

Master John Mixon had two big plantations. I believe he owned about four hundred slaves, chillun and all. He allowed us to have church one time a month with de white folks and we had prayer meeting every Sunday. Sometimes when de men would do something like being sassy or lazy and dey knowed dey was gonna be whipped, dey'd slip off and hide in de woods. When dey'd slip back to get some food dey would all pray for 'em dat Master wouldn't have 'em whipped too hard, and for fear the Patroller would hear 'em they'd put their faces down in a dinner pot. I'd sit out and watch for the Patroller. He was a white man who was appointed to catch runaway niggers. We all knew him. His name was Howard Campbell. He had a big pack of dogs. The lead hound was named Venus. There was five or six in the pack, and they was vicious too.

My father was a carriage driver and he allus took the family to church. My mother went along to take care of the little chilluns. She'd take me too. They was Methodist and after they would take the sacrament we would allus go up and take it. The niggers could use the whitefolks church in the afternoon.

De Big House was a grand place. It was a two-story house made out of logs dat had been peeled and smoothed off. There was five big rooms and a big open hall wid a wide front porch clean across de front. De porch had big posts and pretty banisters. It was painted white and had green shutters on de windows. De kitchen was back of de Big House.

De slaves quarters was about a quarter of a mile from de Big House. Their houses was made of logs and the cracks was daubed with mud. They would have two rooms. Our bedsteads was made of poplar wood and we kept them scrubbed white with sand. We used roped woven together for slats. Our mattresses were made of cotton, grass, or even shucks. My mother had a feather bed. The chairs was made from cedar with split white oak bottoms.

Each family kept their own home and cooked and served their own meals. We used wooden trays and wooden spoons. Once a week all the cullud chillun went to the Big House to eat dinner. The table was out in de yard. My nickname was "Speck". I didn't like to eat bread and milk when I went up there and I'd just sit there. Finally they'd let me go in de house and my mother would feed me. She was the house woman and my Auntie was cook. I don't know why they had us up there unless it was so they could laugh at us.

None of old Master's young niggers never did much work. He say he want 'em to grow up strong. He gave us lots to eat. He had a store of bacon, milk, bread, beans and molasses. In summer we had vegetables. My mother could make awful good corn pone. She would take meal and put salt in it and pour boiling water over it and make into pones. She'd wrap these pones in wet cabbage or collard leaves and roll dem into hot ashes and bake dem. They sho' was good. We'd have possum and coon and fish too.

The boys never wore no britches in de summer time. Boys fifteen years old would wear long shirts with no sleeves and they went barefooted. De girls dressed in shimmys. They was a sort of dress with two seams in it and no sleeves.

Old Master had his slaves to get up about five o'clock. Dey did an ordinary day's work. He never whipped them unless they was lazy or sassy or had a fight. Sometimes his slaves would run away but they allus come back. We didn't have no truck with railroaders 'cause we like our home.

A woman cussed my mother and it made her mad and they had a fight. Old Master had them both whipped. My mother got ten licks and de other woman got twenty-five. Old Mistress sho' was mad 'cause mother got whipped. Said he wouldn't have done it if she had known it. Old Mistress taught mother how to read and write and mother taught my father. I went to school jest one day so I can't read and write now.

Weddings was big days. We'd have big dinners and dances once in a while [HW: and] when somebody died they'd hold a wake. They'd sit up all night and sing and pray and talk. At midnight they'd serve sandwiches and coffee. Sometimes we'd all get together and play ring plays and dance.

Once the Yankee soldiers come. I was big enough to tote pails and piggins then. These soldiers made us chillun tote water to fill their canteens and water their horses. We toted the water on our heads. Another time we heard the Yankee's was coming and old Master had about fifteen hundred pounds of meat. They was hauling it off to bury it and hide it when the Yankees caught them. The soldiers ate and wasted every bit of that good meat. We didn't like them a bit.

One time some Yankee soldiers stopped and started talking to me—they asked me what my name was. "I say Liza," and they say, "Liza who?" I thought a minute and I shook my head, "Jest Liza, I ain't got no other name."

He say, "Who live up yonder in dat Big House?" I say, "Mr. John Mixon." He say, "You are Liza Mixon." He say, "Do anybody ever call you nigger?" And I say, "Yes Sir." He say, "Next time anybody call you nigger you tell 'em dat you is a Negro and your name is Miss Liza Mixon." The more I thought of that the more I liked it and I made up my mind to do jest what he told me to.

My job was minding the calves back while the cows was being milked. One evening I was minding the calves and old Master come along. He say, "What you doin' nigger?" I say real pert like, "I ain't no nigger, I'se a Negro and I'm Miss Liza Mixon." Old Master sho' was surprised and he picks up a switch and starts at me.

Law, but I was skeered! I hadn't never had no whipping so I run fast as I can to Grandma Gracie. I hid behind her and she say, "What's the matter of you child?" And I say, "Master John gwine whip me." And she say, "What you done?" And I say, "Nothing." She say she know better and 'bout that time Master John got there. He say, "Gracie, dat little nigger sassed me." She say, "Lawsie child, what does ail you?" I told them what the Yankee soldier told me to say and Grandma Gracie took my dress and lift it over my head and pins my hands inside, and Lawsie, how she whipped me and I dassent holler loud either. I jest said dat [HW: to] de wrong person. [TR: "didn't I?" at end was crossed out.]

I'se getting old now and can't work no more. I jest sits here and thinks about old times. They was good times. We didn't want to be freed. We hated the Yankee soldiers. Abe Lincoln was a good man though, wasn't he? I tries to be a good Christian 'cause I wants to go to Heaven when I die.

Oklahoma Writers' Project
Ex-Slaves

LIZZIE FARMER
Age 80 years
McAlester, Okla.

"Cousin Lizzie!"

"What."

"I'se seventy years old."

And I say, "Whut's you telling me for. I ain't got nothing to do with your age!"

I knowed I was one year older than she was and it sorta riled me for her to talk about it. I never would tell folks my age for I knowed white folks didn't want no old woman working for 'em and I just wouldn't tell 'em how old I really was. Dat was nine years ago and I guess I'm seventy five now. I can't work much now.

I was born four years before de War.—"The one what set the cullud folks free." We lived on a big plantation in Texas. Old Master's name was John Booker and he was good to us all. My mammy died just at de close of de War and de young mistress took me and kept me and I growed up with her chillun. I thought I was quality sure nuff and I never would go to school 'cause I couldn't go 'long to de same school with de white chillun. Young mistress taught me how to knit, spin, weave, crochet, sew and embroider.

I couldn't recollect my age and young Mistress told me to say, "I'se born de second year of de War dat set de cullud folks free," and the only time she ever git mad at me was when I forgot to say it jest as she told me to. She take hold of me and shook me. I recollects all it, all de time.

Young mistress' name was Elizabeth Booker McNew. I'se named after her. She finally gave me to my aunt when I was a big girl and I never lived wid white folks any more. I never saw my pappy till I was grown.

In the cullud quarters, we cooked on a fireplace in big iron pots. Our bread was baked in iron skillets with lids and we would set the skillet on de fire and put coals of fire on de lid. Bread was mighty good cooked like dat. We made our own candles. We had a candle mold and we would put a string in the center of the mold and pour melted tallow in it and let it harden. We would make eight at one time. Quality folks had brass lamps.

When we went to cook our vegetables we would put a big piece of hog jowl in de pot. We'd put in a lot of snap beans and when dey was about half done we'd put in a mess of cabbage and when it was about half done we'd put in some squash and when it was about half done we'd put in some okra. Then when it was done we would take it out a layer at a time. Go 'way! It makes me hungry to talk about it.

When we cooked possum dat was a feast. We would skin him and dress him and put him on top de house and let him freeze for two days or nights. Then we'd boil him with red pepper, and take him out and put him in a pan and slice sweet 'taters and put round him and roast him. My, dat was good eating.

It was a long time after de War 'fore all de niggers knowed dey was really free. My grandpappy was Master Booker's overseer. He wouldn't have a white man over his niggers. I saw grandpappy whip one man with a long whip. Master Booker was good and wouldn't whip 'em less'n he had to. De niggers dassent leave de farm without a pass for fear of de Ku Kluxers and patrolers.

We would have dances and play parties and have sho' nuff good times. We had "ring plays." We'd all catch hands and march round, den we'd drop all hands 'cept our pardners and we'd swing round and sing:

> "You steal my pardner, and I steal yours,
>
> Miss Mary Jane.
>
> My true lover's gone away,
>
> Miss Mary Jane!

> "Steal all round and don't slight none,
>
> Miss Mary Jane.
>
> He's lost out but I'se got one,
>
> Miss Mary Jane!"

We always played at log rollin's an' cotton pickin's.

Sometimes we would have a wedding and my what a good time we'd have. Old Master's daughter, Miss Janie, got married and it took us more'n three weeks to get ready for it. De house was cleaned from top to bottom and us chillun had to run errands. Seemed like we was allers under foot, at least dat was what mammy said. I never will fergit all the good things they cooked up. Rows of pies and cakes, baked chicken and ham, my, it makes my mouth water jest thinking of it. After de wedding and de feast de white folks danced all night and us cullud folks ate all night.

When one of de cullud folks die we would allers hold a "wake." We would set up with de corpse and sing and pray and at midnight we'd all eat and den we'd sing and pray some more.

In de evening after work was done we'd sit round and de older folks would sing songs. One of de favorites was:

"Miss Ca'line gal,

Yes Ma'am

Did you see dem buzzards?

Yes Ma'am,

Did you see dem floppin',

How did ye' like 'em?

Mighty well.

"Miss Ca'line gal,

Yes Ma'am,

Did you see dem buzzards?

Yes Ma'am,

Did you see dem sailin',

Yes Ma'am.

How did you like 'em?

Mighty well."

I've heered folks talk about conjures and hoodoo charms. I have a hoss shoe over de door dat will bring good luck. I sho' do believe certain things bring bad luck. I hate to hear a scrinch (screech) owl holler at night. Whenever a scrinch owl git in dat tree at night and start to holler I gits me a stick and I say, "Confound you, I'll make yet set up dar and say 'Umph huh'," so I goes out and time I gits dar he is gone. If you tie a knot in de corner of de bed sheet he will leave, or turn your hat wrong side out too. Dey's all good and will make a scrinch owl leave every time.

I believes in dreams and visions too. I dreamed one night dat I had tall palings all 'round my house and I went out in de yard and dere was a big black hoss and I say, "How come you is in my yard? I'll jest put you out jest lak you got in." I opened de gate but he wouldn't go out and finally he run in de door and through the house and went towards de East. Right after dat my son died. I saw dat hoss again de other night. A black hoss allus means death. Seeing it de other night might mean I'se gwineter die.

I know one time a woman named May Runnels wanted to go to church about a mile away and her old man wouldn't go with her. It made her mad and she say, "I'll be dammed if I don't go." She had to go through a grave yard and when she was about half way across it a icy hand jest slap her and her mouth was twisted way 'round fer about three months. Dat was a lesson to her fer cussing.

One time there was a nigger what belonged on a adjoining farm to Master John Bookers and dey told us dis story:

"Dis nigger went down to de spring and found a terrapin and he say, 'What brung you here?' Jest imagine how he felt when it say to him, 'Teeth and tongue brung me here, and teeth and tongue will bring you here.' He run to de house and told his Master dat he found a terrapin dat could talk. Dey went back and he asked de terrapin what bring him here and it wouldn't say a word. Old Master didn't like it 'cause he went down there jest to see a common ordinary terrapin and he told de nigger he was going to git into trouble fer telling him a lie. Next day the nigger seen de terrapin and it say de same thing again. Soon after dat dis nigger was lynched right close to de place he saw de terrapin."

Master John Booker had two niggers what had a habit of slipping across de river and killing old Master's hogs and hiding de meat in de loft of de house. Master had a big blue hog and one day he missed him and he sent Ned to look fer him. Ned knowed all de time dat he had killed it and had it hid in his loft. He hunted and called "Pig-oo-ie, Pig." Somebody done stole old Master's big blue hog. Dey couldn't find it but old Master thought Ned knowed something 'bout it. One night he found out Ned was gonna kill another hog and had asked John to go with him. He borrowed John's clothes and blacked his face and met Ned at de river. Soon dey find a nice big one and Ned say, "John, I'll drive him round and you kill him." So he drove him past old Master but he didn't want to kill his own hog so he made lak he'd like to kill him but he missed him. Finally Ned got tired and said. "I'll kill him, you drive him by me." So Master John drove him by him and Ned knock de hog on de head and cut his throat and dey load him on de canoe. When dey was nearly 'cross de river Old Master dip up some water and wash his face a little, then he look at Ned and he say, "Ned you look sick, I believe you've got lepersy." Ned row on little more and he jump in de river and Master had a hard time finding him again. He had the overseer whip Ned for that.

I think Lincoln was a wonderful man. Everybody was sorry when he died, but I never heerd of Jeff Davis.

United States. Work Projects Administration

Oklahoma Writers' Project
Ex-Slaves
10-19-38
1,876-words

DELLA FOUNTAIN
Age 69 years
McAlester, Oklahoma

I was born after de War of de Rebellion but I 'member lots o' things dat my parents told me 'bout slavery.

My grandmother was captured in Africa. Traders come dere in a big boat and dey had all sorts of purty gew-gaws—red handkerchiefs, dress goods, beads, bells, and trinkets in bright colors. Dey would pull up at de shore and entice de colored folks onto de boat to see de purty things. Befo' de darkies realized it dey would be out from shore. Dat's de way she was captured. Fifteen to twenty-five would pay dem for de trip as dey all brought good prices.

I was born and raised in Louisiana, near Winfield. My mother's Master was John Rogers and his wife was Miss Millie. Dey was awful good to deir slaves and he never whupped his grown niggers.

I 'member when I was a child dat we didn't have hardly anything to keep house wid, but we got along purty well I guess. Our furniture was home-made and we cooked on de fireplace.

We saved all our oak-wood ashes, and would put a barrel on a slanting scaffold and put sticks and shucks in de bottom of de barrel and den fill it wid de ashes. We'd pour water in it and let it drip. Dese drippings made pure lye. We used dis wid cracklings and meat scraps to make our soap.

Father took a good-sized pine long and split it open, planed it down smooth and bored holes in de bottom and drove pegs in dem for legs; dis was our battling bench. We'd spread our wet clothes on dis and rub soap on 'em and take a paddle and beat de dirt out. We got 'em clean but had to be careful not to wear 'em out wid de paddle.

We had no tubs either, so father took a hollow log and split it open and put partitions in it. He bored a hole in each section and drove a peg in it. He next cut two forked poles and drove 'em in de ground and rested de ends of de hollow log in dese forks. We'd fill de log trough wid water and rinse our clothes. We could pull out de pegs and let de water out. We had no brooms either, so we made brush brooms to sweep our floors.

Dere was lots of wild game near our home. I 'member father and two more men going out and killing six deer in jest a little while. Dey was plentiful, and so was squirrels, coon, possums and quail. Dere was lots of bears, too. We'd be in de field working and hear de dogs, and father and de boys would go to 'em and maybe dey'd have a bear. We liked bear meat. It was dark, but awful good and sweet.

De grown folks used to have big times at log-rollings, corn-shuckings and quiltings. Dey'd have a big supper and a big dance at night. Us children would play ring plays, play with home-made rag dolls, or we'd take big leaves and pin 'em together wid thorns and make hats and dresses. We'd ride saplings, too. All of us would pull a sapling down and one would climb up in it near de top and git a good hold on it, and dey would turn it loose. It took a purty good holding to stay wid it, I can tell you.

All de ladies rode horseback, and dey rode side-saddles. I had a purty side-saddle when I growed up. De saddle seat was flowered plush. I had a purty riding habit, too. De skirt was so long dat it almost touched de ground.

We spun and wove all our clothes. I had to spin three broaches ever night before bedtime. Mother would take bark and make dye to give us different colored dresses.

Red oak and sweet gum made purple. Bois d'arc made yellow or orange. Walnut made a purty brown. We knitted our socks and stockings, too.

We celebrated Christmas by having a big dance and egg-nog for ever' body.

During slavery young colored boys and girls didn't do much work but just growed up, care-free and happy. De first work boys done was to learn to hitch up de team to Master's carriage and take de young folks for a drive.

My older brothers and sisters told me lots of things dey done during slave days. My brother Joe felt mighty big after freedom and strutted about. One day he took his younger brother, Ol wid him to where father was building a house. Dey played 'bout de house and come up to where a white man and father was talking. De white man was rolling a little ball of mud in his hands and he just pitched it over on Ol's foot. It didn't hurt him a mite, but

Joe bridled up and he started to git smart, and father told him he'd break his neck if he didn't go on home and keep his mouth shet. Father finally had to whup Joe to make him know he was black. He give father and mother lots of concern, for dey was afraid the Ku Kluxers would git him. One day he was playing wid a axe and chopped off brother Ol's finger. Mother told him she was going to kill him when she caught him. He took to de woods. His three sisters and two neighbor girls run him nearly all day but couldn't catch him. Late in de evening, he come up to a white neighbor's house and she told him to go in and git under de bed and dey couldn't find him. Curtains come down to de floor and as he was tired he decided to risk it. He hadn't much more dan got hid when he heard de girls coming. He heard de woman say, "He's under de bed." He knowed he was caught, and he put up a fight, but dey took him to mother. He got a whupping, but he was shocked dat mother didn't kill him like she said she was. He didn't mind de whupping. He growed up to be a good man, and was de apple of my mother's eye.

Father knowed a man that stole his Master's horse out and rode him to a dance. For some reason de horse died. De poor man knowed he was up against it, and he let in to begging de men to help him git de horse on his back so he could put him back in his stable and his Master would think he died dere. Poor fellow, he really did think he could tote dat horse on his back. He couldn't git anybody to help him, so he went to the woods. He was shot by a patroller 'cause he wouldn't surrender. Dey captured him but he died.

Paul Castleberry was a white preacher. De colored would go to church de same as de whites. He give de colored instructions on obeying Masters. He say, "while your Master is going f'om pillar to post, looking after your intrusts, you is always doing some devilment." I 'spect dat was jest about de truth.

My sister played wid Miss Millie's little girl, Mollie. De big house was on a high hill and at de foot of de hill. Nearly a half-mile away was a big creek wid a big wooden bridge across it. Soldiers come by ever' few days, and you could hear deir horses when dey struck de bridge. Sister and Mollie would run upstairs and look down de hill, and if it was Confederate soldiers dey would run back and tell Miss Millie and dey would start putting out de best food dey had. If dey saw Yankee soldiers, dey would run down and tell 'em and dey'd start hiding things.

De Yankees come through dere and took ever' body's horses. Lots of people took deir horses and cows and hid 'em in some low place in de deep wood.

Miss Millie had a young horse and she had 'em take him to de wheat field and hide him. De wheat was as high as he was. De Yankees come by, and a man had stopped dere just before dey come. He was riding an old horse, and he was wearing a long linen-duster—a duster was a long coat dat was worn over de suit to protect it from de dust.

Dis smart-aleck hid behind de house and as de soldiers rode up he shot at 'em. Dey started shooting at him and he started running, and his coat was sticking straight out behind him. De soldiers surely wasn't trying to hit him, but dey sure did scare him plenty. Miss Millie was certain dey was going to find her horse but dey didn't.

Master John Rogers was good to all his slaves, and they all loved him and would a'died for him. One day he was sitting in his yard and Mollie come running down stairs and told him de Yankees was coming. He never say nothing, but kept sitting dere. Dat morning he had a big sack of money and he give it to my mother to hide for him. She ripped her mattress, and put it in de middle of it and sewed it up. She den made up de bed and put de covers on it. De Yankees searched de house and took de jewelry and silverware and old Master's gold mug, but dey didn't find his money.

My parents lived close to de old plantation dat they lived on when dey was slaves. De big house was still dere, but it was sure dilapidated. Ever'body was poor after de War, whites and blacks alike. I really think de colored was de best off, for they knowed all 'bout hardships and hard work and de white folks didn't.

At first some of 'em was too proud to do drudgery work, but most of 'em went right to work and build up deir homes again. Food, clothes, and in fact everything needed, was scarce.

Mother always say, "If you visit on New Years, you'll visit all de year." We always had black-eyed peas and hog jowl for New Year's dinner, for it brought good luck.

The Nineteenth of June was Emancipation Day, and we always had a big picnic and speeches.

I knowed one woman who was a conjur woman. Lots of people went to her to git her to break a evil spell dat some one had over them. She'd brew a tea from herbs and give to 'em to drink, and it always cured 'em.

I've seen people use all kinds o' roots and herbs for medicine, and I also seen 'em use all kind of things for cures. I've knowed 'em to put wood lice in a bag and tie 'em 'round a baby's neck so it'd teeth easy.

Black-haw root, sour dock, bear grass, grape root, bull nettle, sweet-gum bark and red-oak bark boiled separately and mixed, makes a good blood medicine.

United States. Work Projects Administration

Oklahoma Writers' Project
Ex-Slaves

NANCY GARDNER
Age 79 yrs.
Oklahoma City, Oklahoma

Well, to tell you de truth I don't know my age, but I was born in 1858, in Franklin, Tennessee. Now, you can figger for yourself and tell how old I is. I is de daughter of Prophet and Callie Isaiah, and dey was natives of Tennessee. Dere was three of us children, two boys and myself. I'm de only girl. My brothers names was Prophet and Billie Isaiah. I don't 'member much about dem as we was separated when I was seven years old. I'll never forget when me, my ma and my auntie had to leave my pa and brothers. It is jest as clear in my mind now as it was den, and dat's been about seventy years ago.

Oh God! I tell you it was awful dat day when old Jeff Davis had a bunch of us sent to Memphis to be sold. I can see old Major Clifton now. He was a big nigger trader you know. Well, dey took us on up dere to Memphis and we was sold jest like cattle. Dey sold me and ma together and dey sold pa and de boys together. Dey was sent to Mississippi and we was sent to Alabama. My pa, O how my ma was grieved to death about him! She didn't live long after dat. She didn't live long enough to be set free. Poor ma, she died a slave, but she is saved though. I know she is, and I'll be wid her some day.

It was thirty years before my pa knew if we was still living. Finally in some way he heard dat I was still alive, and he began writing me. Course I was grown and married den and me and my husband had moved to Missouri. Well, my pa started out to see me and on his way he was drowned in de Missouri River, and I never saw him alive after we was sold in Memphis.

I can't tell you much 'bout work during de slave days 'cause you see I was jest a baby you might say when de War broke out. I do remember our Master's name though, it was Dr. Perkins, and he was a good Master. Ma and pa sure hated to have to leave him, he was so good to dem. He was a rich man, and had a big fine house and thousands of acres of land. He was good to his niggers too. We had a good house too, better dan some of dese houses I see folks living in now. Course Dr. Perkins niggers had to work, but dey didn't mind 'cause he would let dem have little patches of dey own such as 'tatoes, corn, cotton and garden. Jest a little, you know. He couldn't let dem have much, there was so many on Dr. Perkins plantation.

I don't remember seeing anybody sick in slavery time. You see I was jest a kid and dere's a lot of things I can't remember.

I am a Christian. I jined de church nigh on seventy years ago and when I say dat, I don't mean I jest jined de church. I mean I gave myself up to de Heavenly Father, and I've been gwine straight down de line for Him ever since. You know in dem days, we didn't get religion like young folks do now. Young folks today jest find de church and den call theyselves Christians, but they aint.

I remember jest as well when I was converted. One day

I was thinking 'bout a sermon de preacher had preached and a voice spoke to me and said, "De Holy Ghost is over your head. Accept it!" Right den I got down on my knees and prayed to God dat I might understand dat voice, and God Almighty in a vision told me dat I should find de church. I could hardly wait for de next service so I could find it, and when I was in de water getting my baptisement, dat same voice spoke and said, "Now you have accepted don't turn back 'cause I will be wid you always!" O you don't know nothing 'bout dat kind of religion!

I 'member one night shortly after I jined de church I was laying in bed and dere was a vine tied 'round my waist and dat vine extended into de elements. O my God! I can see it now! I looked up dat vine and away in de elements I could see my Divine Master and he spoke to me and said, "When you get in trouble shake dis vine; I'm your Master and I will hear your cry."

I knowed old Jeff Davis good. Why I was jest as close to him as I am to dat table. I've talked wid him too. I reckon I do know dat scoundrel! Why, he didn't want de niggers to be free! He was known as a mean old rascal all over de South.

Abraham Lincoln? Now you is talking 'bout de niggers friend! Why dat was de best man God ever let tramp de earth! Everybody was mighty sad when poor old Abraham was 'sassinated, 'cause he did a mighty good deed for de colored race before he left dis world.

I wasn't here long during slavery, but I saw enough of it to know it was mighty hard going for most of de niggers den, and young folks wouldn't stand for dat kind of treatment now. I know most of the young folks would be killed, but they jest wouldn't stand for it. I would hate to have to go through wid my little share of it again.

Oklahoma Writers' Project
Ex-Slaves

OCTAVIA GEORGE
Age 85 yrs.
Oklahoma City, Okla.

I was born in Mansieur, Louisiana, 1852, Avoir Parish. I am the daughter of Alfred and Clementine Joseph. I don't know much about my grandparents other than my mother told me my grandfather's name was Fransuai, and was one time a king in Africa.

Most of the slaves lived in log cabins, and the beds were home-made. The mattresses were made out of moss gathered from trees, and we used to have lots of fun gathering that moss to make those mattresses.

My job was taking care of the white children up at the Big House (that is what they called the house where our master lived), and I also had to feed the little Negro children. I remember quite well how those poor little children used to have to eat. They were fed in boxes and troughs, under the house. They were fed corn meal mush and beans. When this was poured into their box they would gather around it the same as we see pigs, horses and cattle gather around troughs today.

We were never given any money, but were able to get a little money this way: our Master would let us have two or three acres of land each year to plant for ourselves, and we could have what we raised on it. We could not allow our work on these two or three acres to interfere with Master's work, but we had to work our little crops on Sundays. Now remind you, all the Negroes didn't get these two or three acres, only good masters allowed their slaves to have a little crop of their own. We would take the money from our little crops and buy a few clothes and something for Christmas. The men would save enough money out of the crops to buy their Christmas whiskey. It was all right for the slaves to get drunk on Christmas and New Years Day; no one was whipped for getting drunk on those days. We were allowed to have a garden and from this we gathered vegetables to eat; on Sundays we could have duck, fish, and pork.

We didn't know anything about any clothes other than cotton; everything we wore was made of cotton, except our shoes, they were made from pieces of leather cut out of a raw cowhide.

Our Master and Mistress was good, they let us go to church with them, have our little two- or three-acre crops and any other thing that the good masters would let their slaves do. They lived in a big fine house and had a fine barn. Their barn was much better than the house we lived in. Master Depriest (our master) was a Frenchman, and had eight or nine children, and they were sure mean. They would fight us, but we were not allowed to fight our little Master or Mistress as we had to call them.

The overseer on Master's plantation was a mean old fellow, he carried his gun all the time and would ride a big fine horse and go from one bunch of slaves to the other. Some poor white folks lived close to us. They could not own slaves and they had to work for the rich plantation owners. I believe that those poor white folk are to blame for the Negroes stealing because they would get the Negroes to steal their master's corn, hogs, chickens and many other things and sell it to them for practically nothing.

We had to work plenty hard, because our Master had a large plantation. Don't know just how many acres it was, but we had to be up at 5 o'clock in the morning and would work until dark than we would have to go home and do our night work, that is cook, milk, and feed the stock.

The slaves were punished for stealing, running off, not doing what their master told them and for talking back to their master. If any of these rules were disobeyed their feet and hands were chained together and they were put across a log or a barrel and whipped until the blood came from them.

There were no jails; the white man was the slaves' jail. If whipping didn't settle the crime the Negro committed—the next thing would be to hang him or burn him at stake.

I've seen them sell slaves. The whites would auction them off just as we do cattle and horses today. The big fine healthy slaves were worth more than those that were not quite so good. I have seen men sold from their wives and I thought that was such a crime. I knew that God would settle thing someday.

Slaves would run away but most of the time they were caught. The Master would put blood hounds on their trail, and sometimes the slave would kill the blood hound and make his escape. If a slave once tried to run away and was caught, he would be whipped almost to death, and from then on if he was sent any place they would chain their meanest blood hound to him.

Funerals were very simple for slaves, they could not carry the body to the church they would just take it to the grave yard and bury it. They were not even allowed to sing a song at the cemetery. Old Mistress used to tell us ghost stories after funerals and they would nearly scare me to death. She would tell of seeing men with no head, and see cattle that would suddenly turn to cats, and she made us believe if a fire was close to a cemetery it was coming from a ghost.

I used to hear quite a bit about voodoo, but that some thing I never believed in, therefore, I didn't pay any attention to it.

When a slave was sick, the master would get a good doctor for him if he was a good slave, but if he wasn't considered a good slave he would be given cheap medical care. Some of the doctors would not go to the cabin where the slaves were, and the slave would have to be carried on his bed to his master's back porch and the doctor would see him there.

When the news came that we were free, all of us were hid on the Mississippi River. We had been there for several days, and we had to catch fish with our hands and roast them for food. I remember quite well when old Master came down to there and hollered, Come on out niggers; you are free now and you can do as you please! We all went to the Big House and there we found old Miss crying and talking about how she hated to lose her good niggers.

Abraham Lincoln! Why we mourned three months for that man when he died! I wouldn't miss a morning getting my black arm band and placing it on in remembrance of Abraham, who was the best friend the Negroes ever had. Now old Jeff Davis, I didn't care a thing about him. He was a Democrat and none of them mean anything to the Negro. And if these young Negroes don't quit messing with the democratic bunch they are going to be right back where we started from. If they only knew as I know they would struggle to keep such from happening, because although I had a good master I wouldn't want to go through it again.

United States. Work Projects Administration

Oklahoma Writers' Project
Ex-Slaves

MARY GRAYSON
Age 83 yrs.
Tulsa, Oklahoma

I am what we colored people call a "native." That means that I didn't come into the Indian country from somewhere in the Old South, after the War, like so many negroes did, but I was born here in the old Creek Nation, and my master was a Creek Indian. That was eighty three years ago, so I am told.

My mammy belonged to white people back in Alabama when she was born—down in the southern part I think, for she told me that after she was a sizeable girl her white people moved into the eastern part of Alabama where there was a lot of Creeks. Some of them Creeks was mixed up with the whites, and some of the big men in the Creeks who come to talk to her master was almost white, it looked like. "My white folks moved around a lot when I was a little girl", she told me.

When mammy was about 10 or 13 years old some of the Creeks begun to come out to the Territory in little bunches. They wasn't the ones who was taken out here by the soldiers and contractor men—they come on ahead by themselves and most of them had plenty of money, too. A Creek come to my mammy's master and bought her to bring out here, but she heard she was being sold and run off into the woods. There was an old clay pit, dug way back into a high bank, where the slaves had been getting clay to mix with hog hair scrapings to make chinking for the big log houses that they built for the master and the cabins they made for themselves. Well, my mammy run and hid way back in that old clay pit, and it was way after dark before the master and the other man found her.

The Creek man that bought her was a kind sort of a man, mammy said, and wouldn't let the master punish her. He took her away and was kind to her, but he decided she was too young to breed and he sold her to another Creek who had several slaves already, and he brought her out to the Territory.

The McIntosh men was the leaders in the bunch that come out at that time, and one of the bunch, named Jim Perryman, bought my mammy and married her to one of his "boys", but after he waited a while and she didn't have a baby he decided she was no good breeder and he sold her to Mose Perryman.

Mose Perryman was my master, and he was a cousin to Legus Perryman, who was a big man in the Tribe. He was a lot younger than Mose, and laughed at Mose for buying my mammy, but he got fooled, because my mammy got married to Mose's slave boy Jacob, the way the slaves was married them days, and went ahead and had ten children for Mr. Mose.

Mose Perryman owned my pappy and his older brother, Hector, and one of the McIntosh men, Oona, I think his name was, owned my pappy's brother William. I can remember when I first heard about there was going to be a war. The older children would talk about it, but they didn't say it was a war all over the country. They would talk about a war going to be "back in Alabama", and I guess they had heard the Creeks talking about it that way.

When I was born we lived in the Choska bottoms, and Mr. Mose Perryman had a lot of land broke in all up and down the Arkansas river along there. After the War, when I had got to be a young woman, there was quite a settlement grew up at Choska (pronounced Choe-skey) right across the river east of where Haskell now is, but when I was a child before the War all the whole bottoms was marshy kind of wilderness except where farms had been cleared out. The land was very rich, and the Creeks who got to settle there were lucky. They always had big crops. All west of us was high ground, toward Gibson station and Fort Gibson, and the land was sandy. Some of the McIntoshes lived over that way, and my Uncle William belonged to one of them.

We slaves didn't have a hard time at all before the War. I have had people who were slaves of white folks back in the old states tell me that they had to work awfully hard and their masters were cruel to them sometimes, but all the Negroes I knew who belonged to Creeks always had plenty of clothes and lots to eat and we all lived in good log cabins we built. We worked the farm and tended to the horses and cattle and hogs, and some of the older women worked around the owner's house, but each Negro family looked after a part of the fields and worked the crops like they belonged to us.

When I first heard talk about the War the slaves were allowed to go and see one another sometimes and often they were sent on errands several miles with a wagon or on a horse, but pretty soon we were all kept at home, and nobody was allowed to come around and talk to us. But we heard what was going on.

The McIntosh men got nearly everybody to side with them about the War, but we Negroes got word somehow that the Cherokees over back of Ft. Gibson was not going to be in the War, and that there were some Union people over there who would help slaves to get away, but we children didn't know anything about what we heard our parents whispering about, and they would stop if they heard us listening. Most of the Creeks who lived in our part of the country, between the Arkansas and the Verdigris, and some even south of the Arkansas, belonged to the Lower Creeks and sided with the South, but down below us along the Canadian River they were Upper Creeks and there was a good deal of talk about them going with the North. Some of the Negroes tried to get away and go down to them, but I don't know of any from our neighborhood that went to them.

Some Upper Creeks came up into the Choska bottoms talking around among the folks there about siding with the North. They were talking, they said, for old man Gouge, who was a big man among the Upper Creeks. His Indian name was Opoeth-le-ya-hola, and he got away into Kansas with a big bunch of Creeks and Seminoles during the War.

Before that time, I remember one night my uncle William brought another Negro man to our cabin and talked a long time with my pappy, but pretty soon some of the Perryman Negroes told them that Mr. Mose was coming down and they went off into the woods to talk. But Mr. Mose didn't come down. When pappy came back Mammy cried quite a while, and we children could hear them arguing late at night. Then my uncle Hector slipped over to our cabin several times and talked to pappy, and mammy began to fix up grub, but she didn't give us children but a little bit of it, and told us to stay around with her at the cabin and not go playing with the other children.

Then early one morning, about daylight, old Mr. Mose came down to the cabin in his buggy, waving a shot gun and hollering at the top of his voice. I never saw a man so mad in all my life, before nor since!

He yelled in at mammy to "git them children together and git up to my house before I beat you and all of them to death!" Mammy began to cry and plead that she didn't know anything, but he acted like he was going to shoot sure enough, so we all ran to mammy and started for Mr. Mose's house as fast as we could trot.

We had to pass all the other Negro cabins on the way, and we could see that they were all empty, and it looked like everything in them had been tore up. Straw and corn shucks all over the place, where somebody had tore up the mattresses, and all the pans and kettles gone off the outside walls where they used to hang them.

At one place we saw two Negro boys loading some iron kettles on a wagon, and a little further on was some boys catching chickens in a yard, but we could see all the Negroes had left in a big hurry.

I asked mammy where everybody had gone and she said, "Up to Mr. Mose's house, where we are going. He's calling us all in."

"Will pappy be up there too?" I asked her.

"No. Your pappy and your Uncle Hector and your Uncle William and a lot of other menfolks won't be here any more. They went away. That's why Mr. Mose is so mad, so if any of you younguns say anything about any strange men coming to our place I'll break your necks!" Mammy was sure scared!

We all thought sure she was going to get a big whipping, but Mr. Mose just looked at her a minute and then told her to get back to the cabin and bring all the clothes, and bed ticks and all kinds of cloth we had and come back ready to travel.

"We're going to take all you black devils to a place where there won't no more of you run away!" he yelled after us. So we got ready to leave as quick as we could. I kept crying about my pappy, but mammy would say, "Don't you worry about your pappy, he's free now. Better be worrying about us. No telling where we all will end up!" There was four or five Creek families and their Negroes all got together to leave, with all their stuff packed in buggies and wagons, and being toted by the Negroes or carried tied on horses, jack asses, mules and milk cattle. I reckon it was a funny looking sight, or it would be to a person now; the way we was all loaded down with all manner of baggage when we met at the old ford across the Arkansas that lead to the Creek Agency. The Agency stood on a high hill a few miles across the river from where we lived, but we couldn't see it from our place down in the Choska bottoms. But as soon as we got up on the upland east of the bottoms we could look across and see the hill.

When we got to a grove at the foot of the hill near the agency Mr. Mose and the other masters went up to the

Agency for a while. I suppose they found out up there what everybody was supposed to do and where they was supposed to go, for when we started on it wasn't long until several more families and their slaves had joined the party and we made quite a big crowd.

The little Negro boys had to carry a little bundle apiece, but Mr. Mose didn't make the little girls carry anything and let us ride if we could find anything to ride on. My mammy had to help lead the cows part of the time, but a lot of the time she got to ride an old horse, and she would put me up behind her. It nearly scared me to death, because I had never been on a horse before, and she had to hold on to me all the time to keep me from falling off.

Of course I was too small to know what was going on then, but I could tell that all the masters and the Negroes seemed to be mighty worried and careful all the time. Of course I know now that the Creeks were all split up over the War, and nobody was able to tell who would be friendly to us or who would try to poison us or kill us, or at least rob us. There was a lot of bushwhacking all through that country by little groups of men who was just out to get all they could. They would appear like they was the enemy of anybody they run across, just to have an excuse to rob them or burn up their stuff. If you said you was with the South they would be with the North and if you claimed to be with the Yankees they would be with the South, so our party was kind of upset all the time we was passing through the country along the Canadian. That was where old Gouge had been talking against the South. I've heard my folks say that he was a wonderful speaker, too.

We all had to move along mighty slow, on account of the ones on foot, and we wouldn't get very far in one day, then we Negroes had to fix up a place to camp and get wood and cook supper for everybody. Sometimes we would come to a place to camp that somebody knew about and we would find it all tromped down by horses and the spring all filled in and ruined. I reckon old Gouge's people would tear up things when they left, or maybe some Southern bushwhackers would do it. I don't know which.

When we got down to where the North Fork runs into the Canadian we went around the place where the Creek town was. There was lots of Creeks down there who was on the other side, so we passed around that place and forded across west of there. The ford was a bad one, and it took us a long time to get across. Everybody got wet and a lot of the stuff on the wagons got wet. Pretty soon we got down into the Chickasaw country, and everybody was friendly to us, but the Chickasaw people didn't treat their slaves like the Creeks did. They was more strict, like the people in Texas and other places. The Chickasaws seemed lighter color than the Creeks but they talked more in Indian among themselves and to their slaves. Our masters talked English nearly all the time except when they were talking to Creeks who didn't talk good English, and we Negroes never did learn very good Creek. I could always understand it, and can yet, a little, but I never did try to talk it much. Mammy and pappy used English to us all the time.

Mr. Mose found a place for us to stop close to Fort Washita, and got us places to stay and work. I don't know which direction we were from Fort Washita, but I know we were not very far. I don't know how many years we were down in there, but I know it was over two for we worked on crops at two different places, I remember.

Then one day Mr. Mose came and told us that the War was over and that we would have to root for ourselves after that. Then he just rode away and I never saw him after that until after we had got back up into the Choska country. Mammy heard that the Negroes were going to get equal rights with the Creeks, and that she should go to the Creek Agency to draw for us, so we set out to try to get back.

We started out on foot, and would go a little ways each day, and mammy would try to get a little something to do to get us some food. Two or three times she got paid in money, so she had some money when we got back. After three or four days of walking we came across some more Negroes who had a horse, and mammy paid them to let us children ride and tie with their children for a day or two. They had their children on the horse, so two or three little ones would get on with a larger one to guide the horse and we would ride a while and get off and tie the horse and start walking on down the road. Then when the others caught up with the horse they would ride until they caught up with us. Pretty soon the old people got afraid to have us do that, so we just led the horse and some of the little ones rode it.

We had our hardest times when we would get to a river or big creek. If the water was swift the horse didn't do any good, for it would shy at the water and the little ones couldn't stay on, so we would have to just wait until someone came along in a wagon and maybe have to pay them with some of our money or some of our goods we were bringing back to haul us across. Sometimes we had to wait all day before anyone would come along in a wagon.

We were coming north all this time, up through the Seminole Nation, but when we got to Weeleetka we met a Creek family of freedmen who were going to the Agency too, and mammy paid them to take us along in their wagon. When we got to the Agency mammy met a Negro who had seen pappy and knew where he was, so we sent word to him and he came and found us. He had been through most of the War in the Union army.

When we got away into the Cherokee country some of them called the "Pins" helped to smuggle him on up into Missouri and over into Kansas, but he soon found that he couldn't get along and stay safe unless he went with the Army. He went with them until the War was over, and was around Gibson quite a lot. When he was there he tried to find out where we had gone but said he never could find out. He was in the battle of Honey Springs, he said, but never was hurt or sick. When we got back together we cleared a selection of land a little east of the Choska bottoms, near where Clarksville now is, and farmed until I was a great big girl.

I went to school at a little school called Blackjack school. I think it was a kind of mission school and not one of the Creek nation schools, because my first teacher was Miss Betty Weaver and she was not a Creek but a Cherokee. Then we had two white teachers, Miss King and John Kernan, and another Cherokee was in charge. His name was Ross, and he was killed one day when his horse fell off a bridge across the Verdigris, on the way from Tullahassee to Gibson Station.

When I got to be a young woman I went to Okmulgee and worked for some people near there for several years, then I married Tate Grayson. We got our freedmen's allotments on Mingo Creek, east of Tulsa, and lived there until our children were grown and Tate died, then I came to live with my daughter in Tulsa.

United States. Work Projects Administration

Oklahoma Writers' Project
Ex-Slaves

ROBERT R. GRINSTEAD
Age 80 yrs.
Oklahoma City, Okla.

I was born in Lawrence County, Mississippi, February 17, 1857. My father's name is Elias Grinstead, a German, and my mother's name is Ann Greenstead after that of her master. I am a son by my mother and her Master. I have four other half brothers William (Bill) oldest, Albert, Silas, and John.

I was only eight years of age at freedom and for that reason I was too young to work and on account of being the son of my Master's I received no hard treatment and did little or no work. Yet, I wore the same clothing as did the rest of the slaves: a shirt of lowell for summer and shirt and trousers for winter and no shoes. I could walk through a briar patch in my bare feet without sticking one in the bottom of my feet as they were so hard and resistant.

I was the only child of my Master as he had no wife. When the War broke out he went to the War and left the plantation in charge of his overseer and his two sisters. As the overseers were hard for them to get along with they were oftener without an overseer as with one, and therefore they used one of the Negroes as overseer for the most of the time.

Across the river was another large plantation and slave owner by the name of Master Wilson. We called him Master too, for he was a close friend and neighbor to our Mistresses. There was one Negro man slave who decided to not work after Master went to the War and the white overseer was fired and the Negro overseer was acting as overseer, so my Mistress gave him a note to take across the river to Master Wilson. The note was an order to whip this Negro and as he couldn't read he didn't know what the note contained until after Master Wilson read it and gave orders to his men to tie him for his whipping. After this, the whipping was so severe that they never had any more trouble in making this Negro slave work and they never had to send him back again to Master Wilson to be whipped. The fun part of this above incidence was the Negro carried his own note and went alone to be whipped and didn't know it 'til the lashes was being put on him.

My Master's plantation was about 2 miles long and 1-1/2 mile wide and he owned between 30 or 40 slaves. The Negro overseer would wake up the slaves and have them in the field before they could see how to work each morning and as they would go to work so soon their breakfast was carried to the field to them. One morning the breakfast was taken to the field and the slaves were hoeing cotton and among them was a lad about 15 years of age who could not hoe as fast as the older slaves and the breakfast was sat at the end of the rows and as they would hoe out to the end they would eat, and if you would be late hoeing to the end the first to go to the end would began eating and eat everything. So, this 15 year old lad in order to get out to eat before everything was gone did not hoe his row good and the overseer, who was white at this time, whipped him so severely that he could not eat nor work, that day.

The Negroes went to church with the white people and joined their church. The church was Baptist in denomination, and they built a pen in the church in which the Negroes sat, and when they would take sacrament the Negroes would be served after the whites were through and one of the Negro group would pass it around to the others within the pen.

As there were no dances held on the plantation the Negroes would oftimes slip off and go at nights to a nearby dance or peanut parching or rice suppers at nights after work. Some of the slaves would be allowed to make for themselves rice patches which they would gather and save for the dances. To prepare this rice for cooking after harvested they would burn a trough into a log, they called mortar and with a large wooden mallet they called pessel, and which they would pound upon the rice until hulled and ready for cooking. This rice would be boiled with just salt and water and eaten as a great feast with delight.

During slavery some of the Negro slaves would kill snakes and skin them and wear these snake skins to prevent being voodooed they said. When some of the slaves would take sick and the home remedies would fail to cure them our Mistress would allow one of the Negro men slaves to go to the white doctor and get some medicine for the patient. The doctor would ask questions as to the actions of the patient and from said description would send medicine without ever going to see the patient and his medicine would always cure the patient of his disease if consulted in time.

After the news came that brought our freedom a white union officer with 20 trained Negro soldiers visited the plantations and saw that the Negroes received their freedom. He would put on a demonstration with his Negro soldiers by having them line up and then at a command they would all rush forward and stand their guns up together on the stock end without a one falling and get back into line and upon another command they would rush forward and each get his gun again without allowing one to fall and again reline up.

When I was large enough to pay attention to my color and to that of the other slaves I wondered to myself why I was not black like the rest of the slaves and concluded to myself that I would when I got grown like they were as I knew not then that I was the son of my Master.

During the War and as the men and our Master all went to the War the Negroes or a Negro would have to go to the Mistress' homes each morning and start fires and never, did I ever hear of a rape case under such close conditions as Negroes going into the bed rooms each morning of the white mistress to start fires.

My first wife was name Tracy Smith. As I had been free for over 12 years. We had ordinary marriage ceremony. I have 11 grown children, 15 or 20 grandchildren and 3 great grandchildren.

I think Abraham Lincoln was a fine old gentlemen and as to Jeff Davis I don't think he was what he should have been, and as to Booker T. Washington I think his idea of educating or training Negroes as servants to serve the white race appealed more to the white race than the Negroes.

My viewpoint as to slavery is that it was as much detrimental to the white race as it was to the Negroes, as one elevated ones minds too highly, and the other degraded ones mind too lowly.

United States. Work Projects Administration

Oklahoma Writers' Project
Ex-Slaves
[Date stamp: NOV 5 1937]

MATTIE HARDMAN
Age 78 yrs.
Oklahoma City, Okla.

I was born January 2, 1859, at Gunalis, Texas. My father's name was William Tensley and my mother's name Mildred Howard. They was brought from Virginia. I did have 8 brothers and sisters but all of them are dead.

My Master was name William Henry Howard. Since I was too young to work I nursed my sisters' children while they worked. The cooking was done all up to the general kitchen at Masters house and when slaves come from work they would send their children up to the kitchen to bring their meals to their homes in the quarters. Our Mistress would have one of the cooks to dish up vegetables and she herself would slice or serve the meat to see that it wasn't wasted, as seemingly it was thought so precious.

As my mother worked 'round the Big House quite a deal I would go up to the Big House with her and play with the white children who seemed to like for me to come to play with them. One day in anger while playing I called one of the white girls, "old black dog" and they pretended they would tell their mother (my Mistress) about it.

I was scared, as they saw, and they promised me they would not tell if I'd promise to not do it again, and which I was so glad to do and be let off so lightly.

For summer I wore a cotton slip and for winter my mother knitted at nights after her days work was done so I wore red flannels for underwear and thick linsey for an over-dress, and had knitted stockings and bought shoes. As my Master was a doctor he made his slaves wear suitable clothes in accordance to the weather. We also wore gloves my mother knitted in winter.

My Mistress was good to all of the slaves. On Sunday morning she would make all the Negro children come to the Big House and she would stand on the front steps and read the Catechism to us who sat or stood in front on the ground.

My Master was also good. On Wednesdays and Friday nights he would make the slaves come up to the Big House and he would read the Bible to them and he would pray. He was a doctor and very fractious and exact. He didn't allow the slaves to claim they forgot to do thus and so nor did he allow them to make the expression, "I thought so and so." He would say to them if they did: "Who told you, you could think!"

They had 10 children, 7 boys and 3 girls. Their house was a large 2-story log house painted white. My father was overseer on the plantation.

The plantation consisted of 400 acres and about 40 slaves including children. The slaves were so seldom punished until they never'd worry about being punished. They treated their slaves as though they loved them.

The poor white neighbors were also good and treated the slaves good, for my Master would warn them to not bother his Negroes. My Mistress always told the slaves she wanted all of them to visit her and come to her funeral and burial when she died and named the men slaves she wanted to be her pallbearers, all of which was carried out as she planned even though it was after freedom.

The slaves even who lived adjoining our plantation would have church at our Big House. They would hold church on Sundays and Sunday nights.

As my mother worked a deal for her Mistress she had an inkling or overheard that they was going to be set free long before the day they were. She called all the slaves on the plantation together and broke to them this news after they had promised her they would not spread the news so that it would get back to our Master. So, everybody kept the news until Saturday night June 19th, when Master called all the slaves to the big gate and told them they were all free, but could stay right on in their homes if they had no places to go and which all of them did. They went right out and gathered the crop just like they'd always done, and some of them remained there several years.

My first husband was name, S. W. Warnley. We had 4 children, 1 girl and three boys and 3 grandchildren. I now have two grandchildren.

Now that slavery is over I sometime wish 'twas still existing for some of our lazy folks, so that so many of them wouldn't or couldn't loaf around so much lowering our race, walking the streets day by day and running from house to house living corruptible lives which is keeping the race down as though there be no good ones among us.

Oklahoma Writers' Project
Ex-Slaves
[Date stamp: AUG 16 1937]

ANNIE HAWKINS
Age 90
Colbert, Okla

I calls myself 90, but I don't know jest how old I really am but I was a good sized gal when we moved from Georgia to Texas. We come on a big boat and one night the stars fell. Talk about being scared! We all run and hid and hollered and prayed. We thought the end of the world had come.

I never had no whitefolks that was good to me. We all worked jest like dogs and had about half enough to eat and got whupped for everything. Our days was a constant misery to us. I know lots of niggers that was slaves had a good time but we never did. Seems hard that I can't say anything good for any of 'em but I sho' can't. When I was small my job was to tote cool water to the field to the hands. It kept me busy going back and forth and I had to be sho' my old Mistress had a cool drink when she wanted it, too. Mother and my sister and me worked in the field all day and come in time to clear away the things and cook supper. When we was through in the kitchen we would spin fer a long time. Mother would spin and we would card.

My old Master was Dave Giles, the meanest man that

ever lived. He didn't have many slaves, my mammy, and me, and my sister, Uncle Bill, and Truman. He had owned my grandma but he give her a bad whupping and she never did git over it and died. We all done as much work as a dozen niggers—we knowed we had to.

I seen old Master git mad at Truman and he buckled him down across a barrel and whupped him till he cut the blood out of him and then he rubbed salt and pepper in the raw places. It looked like Truman would die it hurt so bad. I know that don't sound reasonable that a white man in a Christian community would do such a thing but you can't realize how heartless he was. People didn't know about it and we dassent tell for we knowed he'd kill us if we did. You must remember he owned us body and soul and they wasn't anything we could do about it. Old Mistress and her three girls was mean to us too.

One time me and my sister was spinning and old Mistress went to the well-house and she found a chicken snake and killed it. She brought it back and she throwed it around my sister's neck. She jest laughed and laughed about it. She thought it was a big joke.

Old Master stayed drunk all the time. I reckon that is the reason he was so fetched mean. My, how we hated him! He finally killed hisself drinking and I remember Old Mistress called us in to look at him in his coffin. We all marched by him slow like and I jest happened to look up and caught my sister's eye and we both jest natchelly laughed—Why shouldn't we? We was glad he was dead. It's a good thing we had our laugh fer old Mistress took us out and whupped us with a broomstick. She didn't make us sorry though.

Old Master and Mistress lived in a nice big house on top of a hill and us darkies lived in log cabins with log floors. Our dresses was made out of coarse cloth like cotton sacking and and [TR: sic] it sho' lasted a long time. It ort to been called mule-hide for it was about that tough.

We went to church sometimes. They had to let us do that or folks would have found out how mean they was to us. Old Master'd give us a pass to show the patroller. We was glad to git the chance to git away and we always went to church.

During the War we seen lots of soldiers. Some of them was Yankees and some were Sesesh soldiers. My job every day was to take a big tray of food and set it on a stump about a quarter of a mile from our house. I done this twice a day and ever time I went back the dishes would be empty. I never did see nobody and didn't nobody tell me why I was to take the food up there but of course it was either for soliders [TR: sic] that was scouting 'round or it may been for some lowdown dirty bushwhacker, and again it might a been for some of old Master's folks scouting 'round to keep out of the army.

We was the happiest folks in the world when we knowed we was free. We couldn't realize it at first but how we did shout and cry for joy when we did realize it. We was afraid to leave the place at first for fear old Mistress would bring us back or the pateroller would git us. Old Mistress died soon after the War and we didn't care either. She didn't never do nothing to make us love her. We was jest as glad as when old Master died. I don't know what become of the three gals. They was about grown.

We moved away jest as far away as we could and I

married soon after. My husband died and I married again. I been married four times and all my husbands died. The last time I married it was to a man that belonged to a Indian man, Sam Love. He was a good owner and was one of the best men that ever lived. My husband never did move far away from him and he loved him like a father. He always looked after him till he died. My husband has been dead five years.

I have had fifteen children. Four pairs of twins, and only four of them are living. The good Lawd wouldn't let me keep them. I'se lived through three wars so you see I'se no baby.

Oklahoma Writers' Project
Ex-Slaves
[Date stamp: NOV 5 1937]

IDA HENRY
Age 83
Oklahoma City, Okla.

I was born in Marshall, Texas, in 1854. Me mother was named Millie Henderson and me father Silas Hall. Me mother was sold in South Carolina to Mister Hall, who brought her to Texas. Me father was born and raised by Master John Hall. Me mother's and father's family consisted of five girls and one boy. My sisters' names were: Margrette, Chalette, Lottie, Gracy and Loyo, and me brother's name was Dock Howard. I lived with me mother and father in a log house on Master Hall's plantation. We would be sorry when dark, as de patrollers would walk through de quarters and homes of de slaves all times of night wid pine torch lights to whip de niggers found away from deir home.

At nights when me mother would slip away for a visit to some of de neighbors homes, she would raise up the old plank floor to de log cabin and make pallets on de ground and put us to bed and put the floor back down so dat we couldn't be seen or found by the patrollers on their stroll around at nights.

My grandmother Lottie would always tell us to not let Master catch you in a lie, and to always tell him de truth.

I was a house girl to me Mistress and nursed, cooked, and carried de children to and from school. In summer we girls wore cotton slips and yarn dresses for winter. When I got married I was dress in blue serge and was de third person to marry in it. Wedding dresses was not worn after de wedding in dem days by niggers as we was taught by our Mistress dat it was bad luck to wear de wedding dress after marriage. Therefore, 'twas handed down from one generation to the other one.

Me Mistress was sometimes good and sometimes mean. One day de cook was waiting de table and when passing around de potatoes, old Mistress felt of one and as hit wasn't soft done, she exclaimed to de cook, "What you bring these raw potatoes out here for?" and grab a fork and stuck it in her eye and put hit out. She, de cook, lived about 10 years and died.

Me Mistress was de mother of five children, Crock, Jim, Boss and two girls name, Lea and Annie.

Dere home was a large two-story white house wid de large white posts.

As me Master went to de War de old overseer tried himself in meanness over de slaves as seemingly he tried to be important. One day de slaves caught him and one held him whilst another knocked him in de head and killed him.

Master's plantation was about 300 acres and he had 'bout 160 slaves. Before de slaves killed our overseer, he would work 'em night and day. De slaves was punished when dey didn't do as much work as de overseer wanted 'em to do.

He would lock 'em in jail some nights without food and kept 'em dere all night, and after whipping 'em de next morning would only give 'em bread and water to work on till noon.

When a slave was hard to catch for punishment dey would make 'em wear ball and chains. De ball was 'bout de size of de head and made of lead.

On Sunday mornings before breakfast our Mistress would call us together, read de Bible and show us pictures of de Devil in de Bible and tell us dat if we was not good and if we would steal and tell lies dat old Satan would git us.

Close to our Master's plantation lived several families of old "poor white trash" who would steal me Master's hogs and chickens and come and tell me Mistress dat dey seen some of de slaves knock one of dere hogs in de head. Dis continued up till Master returned from de War and caught de old white trash stealing his hogs. De niggers did at times steal Master's hogs and chickens, and I would put biscuits and pieces of chicken in a sack under me dress dat hung from me waist, as I waited de table for me Mistress, and later would slip off and eat it as dey never gave de slaves none of dis sort of food.

We had church Sundays and our preacher Rev. Pat Williams would preach and our Master and family and other nearby white neighbors would ofttime attend our services. De patrollers wouldn't allow de slaves to hold night services, and one night dey caught me mother out praying. Dey stripped her naked and tied her hands together and wid a rope tied to de hand cuffs and threw one end of de rope over a limb and tied de other end to de pommel of a saddle on a horse. As me mother weighed 'bout 200, dey pulled her up so dat her toes could barely touch de ground and whipped her. Dat same night she ran away and stayed over a day and returned.

During de fall months dey would have corn shucking and cotton pickings and would give a prize to de one who would pick de highest amount of cotton or shuck de largest pile of corn. De prize would usually be a suit of clothes or something to wear and which would be given at some later date.

We could only have dances during holidays, but dances was held on other plantations. One night a traveler visiting me Master and wanted his boots shined. So Master gave de boots to one of de slaves to shine and de slave put de boots on and went to a dance and danced so much dat his feet swelled so dat when he returned he could not pull 'em off.

De next morning as de slave did not show up with de boots dey went to look for him and found him lying down trying to pull de boots off. He told his Master dat he had put de boots on to shine 'em and could not pull 'em off. So Master had to go to town and buy de traveler another pair of boots. Before he could run away de slave was beaten wid 500 lashes.

De War dat brought our freedom lasted about two years. Me Master went and carried one of de slaves for a servant. He was kind and good and from dat day on he never whipped another slave nor did he allow any of his slaves whipped. Dis time lasted from January to June de 19th when we was set free in de State of Texas.

Lincoln and Davis both died short of promise. I means dat dey both died before dey carried out dere plans and promises for freeing de slaves.

United States. Work Projects Administration

Oklahoma Writers' Project
Ex-Slaves

MORRIS HILLYER
Age 84 yrs.
Alderson, Okla.

My father was Gabe Hillyer and my mother was Clarisay Hillyer, and our home was in Rome, Georgia. Our owner was Judge Hillyer. He was de last United States senator to Washington, D. C., before de War.

My mother died when I was only a few days old and the only mother I ever knew was Judge Hillyer's wife, Miss Jane. Her nine children were all older than I was and when mother died Miss Jane said mother had raised her children and she would raise hers. So she took us into her house and we never lived at de quarters any more. I had two sisters, Sally and Sylvia, and we had a room in de Big House and sister Sally didn't do nothing else but look after me. I used to stand with my thumb in my mouth and hold to Miss Jane's apron while she knitted.

When Judge Hillyer was elected he sold out his farm and gave his slaves to his children. He owned about twelve or fourteen slaves at this time. He gave me and my sister Sylvia to his son, Dr. Hillyer, and my father to another one of his sons who was studying law. Father stayed with him and took care of him until he graduated.

Father learned to be a good carpenter while he lived with George Hillyer. George never married until after de War.

Dr. Hillyer lived on a big plantation but he practiced medicine all de time. He didn't have much time to look after de farm but he had good overseers and they sure didn't beat his slaves or mistreat 'em in any way. Dr. Hillyer married a rich girl, Miss Mary Cooley, and her father gave her fifteen slaves when she married and Judge Hillyer gave him five so he had a purty good start from de first and he knowed how to make money so he was a wealthy man when de Rebellion started.

My sister and I didn't know how to act when we was sent out there among strangers. We had to live in de quarters just like de other niggers, and we didn't especially like it. I guess I was a sort of bad boy.

There was several more boys about my age and we didn't have any work to do but just busy ourselves by getting into mischief. We'd ride de calves, chase de pigs, kill de chickens, break up hens nests, and in fact do most everything we hadn't ought to do. Finally they put us to toting water to de field hands, minding de gaps, taking de cows to pasture and as dat kept us purty busy we wasn't so bad after dat.

My happiest days was when I was with de old Judge and Miss Jane. I can sit here and think of them old times and it seems like it was just yesterday dat it all happened. He was a great hand to go to town every day and lounge around wid his cronies. I used to go with him, and my how they would argue. Sometimes they would get mad and shake their canes in each other's faces. I guess they was talking politics.

Our old Master liked cats better than any man I ever saw, and he always had five or six that followed him about de place like dogs. When he went to eat they was always close to him and just as soon as he finished he would always feed them. When he was gone us boys used to throw at his cats or set de dogs on 'em. We was always careful dat no one saw us for if he had known about it he would a-whipped us and no mistake. I wouldn't a-blamed him either, for I like cats now. I think they are lots of company.

He was a typical Southern gentleman, medium sized, and wore a Van Dyke beard. He never whipped his slaves, and he didn't have a one dat wouldn't a-died for him.

Judge Hillyer had one son, William, dat wouldn't go to college. He made fun of his brothers for going to school so long, and said that he would be ashamed to go and stay five or six years. After de War he settled down and studied law in Judge Akin's office and opened a office in Athens, Georgia, and he made de best lawyer of them all.

Us boys used to go hunting with Master William. He hunted rabbits, quails, squirrels, and sometimes he would kill a deer. He hunted mostly with dogs. He never used a gun but very little. Lead was so scarce and cost so much dat he couldn't afford to waste a bullet on rabbits or snakes. He made his own bullets. The dogs would chase a rabbit into a hollow tree and we'd take a stick and twist him out. Sometimes we'd have nearly all de hide twisted off him when we'd git him out.

Old Judge Hillyer smoked a pipe with a long stem. He used to give me ten cents a day to fill it for him. He told me I had to have $36 at the end of the year, but I never made it. There was a store right close to us and I'd go down there and spend my money for lemon stick candy, ginger cakes, peanuts, and firecrackers. Old Master knowed I wouldn't save it, and he didn't care if I did spent it for it was mine to do with just as I pleased.

Every time a circus come to town I'd run off and they wouldn't see me again all day. Seemed like I just couldn't help it. I wouldn't take time to git permission to go. One time to punish me for running off he tied me up by my thumbs, and I had to stay home while de rest went. I didn't dare try to git loose and run off for I knowed I'd git my jacket tanned if I did. Old Master never laid his hand on me, but I knowed he would if I didn't do as he told me. He never told us twice to do anything either.

Coins had curious names in them days. A dime was called a thrip. Fourpen was about the same value as three cents or maybe a little more. It took three of 'em to make a thrip. There was all sorts of paper money.

Every first Tuesday slaves were brought in from Virginia and sold on de block. De auctioneer was Cap'n Dorsey. E. M. Cobb was de slave bringer. They would stand de slaves up on de block and talk about what a fine looking specimen of black manhood or womanhood dey was, tell how healthy dey was, look in their mouth and examine their teeth just like they was a horse, and talk about de kind of work they would be fit for and could do. Young healthy boys and girls brought the best prices. I guess they figured dat they would grow to be valuable. I used to stand around and watch de sales take place but it never entered my mind to be afraid for I knowed old Judge wasn't going to sell me. I thought I was an important member of his family.

Old Judge bought every roguish nigger in the country. He'd take him home and give him the key to everything on de place and say to help hisself. Soon as he got all he wanted to eat he'd quit being a rogue. Old Judge said that was what made niggers steal—they was hungry.

They used to scare us kids by telling us dat a runaway nigger would git us. De timber was awful heavy in de river bottoms, and dey was one nigger dat run off from his master and lived for years in these bottoms. He was there all during de War and come out after de surrender. Every man in dat country owned him at some time or other. His owner sold him to a man who was sure he could catch him—he never did, so he sold him to another slave owner and so on till nearly everybody had him. He changed hands about six or seven times. They would come in droves with blood hounds and hunt for him but dey couldn't catch him for he knowed them woods too well. He'd feed de dogs and make friends with 'em and they wouldn't bother him. He lived on nuts, fruit, and wild game, and niggers would slip food to him. He'd slip into town and get whiskey and trade it to de niggers for food.

Judge Hillyer never 'lowanced his niggers and dey could always have anything on de place to eat. We had so much freedom dat other slave owners in our neighborhood didn't like for us to come among their slaves for they said we was free niggers and would make their slaves discontented.

After I went to live with Judge Hillyer's son, Dr. Hillyer, one of my jobs was to tote the girls books to school every morning. All the plantation owners had a colored boy dat did that. After we had toted de books to de school house we'd go back down de road a piece and line up and have the "gone-bying-est" fight you ever see. We'd have regular battles. If I got licked in de morning I'd go home and rest up and I'd give somebody a good licking dat evening. I reckon I caught up with my fighting for in all my working life I have always worked with gangs of men of from one to two-hundred and I never struck a man and no man ever struck me.

Jim Williams was a patroller, and how he did like to catch a nigger off de farm without a permit so he could whip him. Jim thought he was de best man in de country and could whip de best of 'em. One night John Hardin, a big husky feller, was out late. He met Jim and knowed he was in for it. Jim said, "John I'm gonna give you a white man's chance. I'm gonna let you fight me and if you are de best man, well and good."

John say, "Master Jim, I can't fight wid you. Come on and give me my licking, and let me go on home."

But Jim wouldn't do it, and he slapped John and called him some names and told him he is a coward to fight him. All dis made John awful mad and he flew into him and give him the terriblest licking a man ever toted. He went on home but knew he would git into trouble over it.

Jim talked around over the country about what he was going to do to John but everybody told him dat he brought it all on hisself. He never did try to git another nigger to fight with him.

Yes, I guess charms keep off bad luck. I have wore 'em but money always was my best lucky piece. I've made lots of money but I never made good use of it.

I was always afraid of ghosts but I never saw one. There was a graveyard beside de road from our house to town and I always was afraid to go by it. I'd shut my eyes and run for dear life till I was past de grave yard. I had heard dat there was a headless man dat stayed there on cold rainy days or foggy nights he'd hide by de fence and throw his head at you. Once a man got hit and he fell right down dead. I believed dat tale and you can imagine how I felt whenever I had to go past there by myself and on foot.

I saw lots of Ku Kluxers but I wasn't afraid of them. I knowed I hadn't done nothing and they wasn't after me. One time I met a bunch of 'em and one of 'em said, "Who is dis feller?" Another one said, "Oh, dat's Gabe's foolish boy, come on, don't bother him." I always did think dat voice sounded natural but I never did say anything about it. It sounded powerful like one of old Judge's boys. Dey rode on and didn't bother me and I never was a bit afraid of 'em any more.

I went to school one month after de War. I never learned much but I learned to read some where along de road dat I come over. My father come from Athens, Georgia, and took us away with him. I learned the carpenter's trade from him. He was so mean to me dat I run away when I was nineteen. I went back to Rome, Georgia, and got a job with a bridge gang and spent two years with 'em. I went then to Henderson, Kentucky, and worked for ten years. There was hundreds of colored people coming to de mines at Krebs and Alderson and I decided to come along, too. I never worked in de mines but I did all sorts of carpentering for them.

I married in Atoka, Oklahoma, thirty-three years ago. I never had no children.

I've made lots of money but somehow it always got away from me. But me and my wife have our little home here and we are both still able to work a little, so I guess we are making it all right.

Oklahoma Writers' Project
Ex-Slaves

HAL HUTSON
Age 90 yrs.
Oklahoma City, Okla.

I was born at Galveston, Tennessee, October 12, 1847. There were 11 children: 7 brothers; Andrew, George, Clent, Gilbert, Frank, Mack and Horace; and 3 girls: Rosie, Marie and Nancy. We were all Hutsons. Together with my mother and father we worked for the same man whose name was Mr. Barton Brown, but who we all call Master Brown, and sometimes Mr. Brown.

Master Brown had a good weather-board house, two story, with five or six rooms. They lived pretty well. He had eight children. We lived in one-room log huts. There were a long string of them huts. We slept on the floor like hogs. Girls and boys slept together—jest everybody slept every whar. We never knew what biscuits were! We ate "seconds and shorts" (wheat ground once) for bread. Ate rabbits, possums baked with taters, beans, and bean soup. No chicken, fish and the like. My favorite dish now is beans.

Master Brown owned about 36 or 40 slaves, I can't recall jest now, and about 200 acres of ground. There was very little cotton raised in Galveston—I mean jest some corn. Sometimes we would shuck corn all night. He would not let us raise gardens of our own, but didn't mind us raising corn and a few other truck vegetables to sell for a little spending change.

I learned to read, write and figger at an early age. Master Brown's boy and I were the same age you see (14 years old) and he would send me to school to protect his kids, and I would have to sit up there until school was out. So while sitting there I listened to what the white teacher was telling the kids, and caught on how to read, write and figger—but I never let on, 'cause if I was caught trying to read or figger dey would whip me something terrible. After I caught on how to figger the white kids would ask me to teach them. Master Brown would often say: "My God O'mighty, never do for that nigger to learn to figger."

We weren't allowed to count change. If we borrowed a fifty-cent piece, we would have to pay back a fifty-cent piece—not five dimes or fifty pennies or ten nickels.

We went barefooted the year round and wore long shirts split on each side. All of us niggers called all the whites "poor white trash." The overseer was nothing but poor white trash and the meanest man that ever walked on earth. He never did whip me much 'cause I was kind of a pet. I worked up to the Big House, but he sho' did whip them others. Why, one day he was beating my mother, and I was too small to say anything, so my big brother heard her crying and came running, picked up a chunk and that overseer stopped a'beating her. The white boy was holding her on the ground and he was whipping her with a long leather whip. They said they couldn't teach her no sense and she said "I don't wanna learn no sense." The overseer's name was Charlie Clark. One day he whipped a man until he was bloody as a pig 'cause he went to the mill and stayed too long.

The patroller rode all night and iffen we were caught out later than 10:00 o'clock they would beat us, but we would git each other word by sending a man round way late at night. Always take news by night. Of course the Ku Klux Klan didn't come 'til after the war. They was something like the patrollers. Never heard of no trouble between the black and whites 'cause them niggers were afraid to resist them.

My biggest job was keeping flies off'n the table up at the Big House. When time come to go in for the day we would cut up and dance. I can't remember any of the songs jest now, but we had some that we sung. We danced a whole lots and jest sung "made up" songs.

Old Master would stay up to hear us come in. Of course Saturday afternoon was a holiday. We didn't work no holidays. Master gave us one week off for Christmas, and never worked us on Sunday, unless the "ox was in the ditch." When the slaves got sick we had white doctors, and we would wait on each other. Drink dock root tea, mullin tea, and flaxweed tea, but we never wore charms.

I think it's a good thing that slavery's over. It ought to been over a good while ago. But its going to be slavery all over again if things don't git better. But I thank God I've been a Christian for 70 years, and now is a member of Tabernacle Baptist Church and deacon of the church, and a Christian 'cause the Bible teaches me to be.

That war was a awful thing. I used to pack them soldiers water on my head, and then I worked at Fort Sill and Fort Dawson in Tennessee. Those Yankees came by nights—got behind those rebels, and took their hams, drove horses in the houses, killed their chickens and ate up the rebels food, but the Yanks didn't bother us niggers.

When freedom come old Master called us all in from the fields and told us, "All of you niggers are free as frogs now to go wherever you choose. You are your own man now." We all continued working for him at $5.00 a month. After the crops were gathered the niggers scattered out. Some went North—and we would say when they went North that they had "crossed the water."

I never married 'till after the War. Married at my mother's house 'cause my wife's mother didn't let us marry at her house, so I sent Jack Perry after her on a hoss and we had a big dinner—and jest got married.

I am the father of nine children, but jest three is living. One is a dentist in Muskogge, Dr. Andrew Hutson. All of the children are pretty well read. We never had schools for niggers until after slavery.

I think Abraham Lincoln was a great man, but I don't know much about Jeff Davis. Booker T. Washington was a fine man.

Oklahoma Writers' Project
Ex-Slaves
[Date stamp: AUG 16 1937]

WILLIAM HUTSON
Age 98 yrs.
Tulsa, Okla.

When a feller gets as old as me it's a heap easier to forget things than it is to remember, but I ain't never forgot that old plantation where good old Doctor Allison lived back there in Georgia long before the War that brought us slaves the freedom.

I hear the slaves talking about mean masters when I was a boy. They wasn't talking about Master Allison though, 'cause he was a good man and took part for the slaves when any trouble come up with the overseer.

The Mistress' name was Louisa (the same name as the gal I was married to later after the War), and she was just about as mean as was the old Master good. I was the house boy when I gets old enough to understand what the Master wants done and I does it just like he says, so I reckon that's why we always get along together.

The Master helped to raise my mammy. When I was born he says to her (my mammy tells me when I gets older): "Cheney", the old Master say, "that boy is going be different from these other children. I aims to see that he is. He's going be in the house all the time, he ain't going work in the fields; he's going to stay right with me all the time."

They was about twenty slaves on the plantation but I was the one old Master called for when he wanted something special for himself. I was the one he took with him on the trips to town, I was the one who fetch him the cooling drink after he look about the fields and sometimes I carry the little black bag when he goes a-doctoring folks with the misery away off some other farm.

The Master hear about there going be an auction one day and he figgered maybe he needed some more slaves if they was good ones, so he took me and started out early in the morning. It wasn't very far and we got there early before the auction started. Rockon that was the first time I ever see any slaves sold.

They was a long platform made of heavy planks and all the slaves was lined up on the platform, and they was stripped to the waist, men, women, and children. One or two of the women folks was bare naked. They wasn't young women neither, just middle age ones, but they was built good. Some of them was well greased and that grease covered up many a scar they'd earned for some foolishment or other.

The Master don't buy none and pretty soon we starts home. The Master was riding horseback,—he didn't ever use no buggy 'cause he said that was the way for folks to travel who was too feeble to sit in the saddle—and I rode back of him on another horse, but that horse I rides is just horse while the Master's was a real thoroughbred like maybe you see on race tracks down in the South.

That auction kept bothering me all the way back to the plantation. I kept seeing them little children standing on the flatform (platform), their mammy and pappy crying hard 'cause their young'uns is being sold. They was a lot of heartaches even they was slaves and it gets me worried.

I asked the Master is he going to have an auction and he jest laugh. I ain't never sold no slaves yet and I ain't going to, he says. And I gets easier right then. I kind of hates to think about standing up on one of them platforms, kinder sorry to leave my old mammy and the Master, so I was easy in the heart when he talked like that.

The plantation house was a big frame and the yard was shaded with trees all around. The Master's children—four boys and two girls—would play in the yard with me just like I was one of the family. And we'd go hunting and fishing. There was a creek not far away and they was good fishing in the stream and squirrels in the trees. Mighty lot of fun to catch them fishes but more fun when they is all fried brown and ready for to eat with a piece of hot pone. Ain't no fish ever taste that good since!

One thing I sort of ponders about. The old Master don't let us have no religion meetings and reading and writing is something I learn after the War. Some of the slaves talk about meeting 'round the country and wants to have preaching on the plantation. Master says NO. No preacher around here to tell about the Bible and religion will be just a puzzlement, the Master say, and we let it go at that. I reckon that was the only thing he was set against.

That and the Yankees. The Master went to the War

and stayed 'til it was most over. He was a mighty sick man when he come back to the old place, but I was there waiting for him just like always. All the time he was away I take care around the house. That's what he say for me to do when he rides away to fight the Yankees. Lot's of talk about the War but the slaves goes right on working just the same, raising cotton and tobacco.

The slaves talk a heap about Lincoln and some trys to run away to the North. Don't hear much about Jeff Davis, mostly Lincoln. He give us slaves the freedom but we was better off as we was.

The day of freedom come around just [HW: like] any other day, except the Master say for me to bring up the horses, we is going to town. That's when he hears about the slaves being free. We gets to the town and the Master goes into the store. It's pretty early but the streets was filled with folks talking and I wonder what makes the Master in such a hurry when he comes out of the store.

He gets on his horse and tells me to follow fast. When we gets back to the plantation he sounds the horn calling the slaves. They come in from the fields and meet 'round back of the kitchen building that stood separate from the Master's house. They all keeps quiet while the Master talks: "You-all is free now, and all the rest of the slaves is free too. Nobody owns you now and nobody going to own you anymore!" That was good news, I reckon, but nobody know what to do about it.

The crops was mostly in and the Master wants the folks to stay 'til the crop is finished. They talk about it the rest of that day. They wasn't no celebration 'round the place, but they wasn't no work after the Master tells us we is free. Nobody leave the place though. Not 'til in the fall when the work is through. Then some of us go into the town and gets work 'cause everybody knows the Allison slaves was the right kind of folks to have around.

That was the first money I earn and then I have to learn how to spend it. That was the hardest part 'cause the prices was high and the wages was low.

Then I moves on and meets the gal that maybe I been looking for, Louisa Baker, and right away she takes to me and we is married. Ain't been no other woman but her and she's waiting for me wherever the dead waits for the living.

I reckon she won't have so long to wait now, even if I is feeling pretty spry and got good use of the feets and hands. Ninety-eight years brings a heap of wear and some of these days the old body'll need a long time rest and then I'll join her for all the time.

I is ready for the New Day a-coming!

United States. Work Projects Administration

Oklahoma Writers' Project
Ex-Slaves
[Date stamp: AUG 16 1937]

MRS. ISABELLA JACKSON
Age 79 yrs.
Tulsa, Okla.

"Boom ... Boom! Boom ... Boom!" That's the way the old weaver go all day long when my sister, Margaret, is making cloth for the slaves down on old Doc Joe Jackson's plantation in Louisiana.

That was near the little place of Bunker, and its my birthplace, and I guess where all Mammy's children were born because she was never sold but once and nobody but the old Doc ever did own her after she come to his place.

He always say couldn't nobody get work out of Mammy but him. I guess that's just his foolery 'cause if she ain't no good the Old Doc most likely sell her to some of them white folks in Texas.

That's what they done to them mean, no account slaves—just send them to Texas. Them folks sure knew how for to handle 'em!

But I was talking about my sister, Margaret. I can still see her weaving the cloth—Boom!... Boom!—and she hear that all the day and get mighty tired. Sometimes she drop her head and go to sleep. The Mistress get her then sure. Rap her on the head with almost anything handy, but she hit pretty easy, just trying to scare her that's all.

The old Master though, he ain't so easy as that. The whippings was done by the master and the overseer just tell the old Doc about the troubles, like the old Doc say:

"You just watch the slaves and see they works and works hard, but don't lay on with the whip, because I is the only one who knows how to do it right!"

Maybe the old Master was sickened of whippings from the stories the slaves told about the plantation that joined ours on the north.

If they ever was a living Devil that plantation was his home and the owner was It! That's what the old slaves say, and when I tell you about it see if I is right.

That man got so mean even the white folks was scared of him, 'specially if he was filled with drink. That's the way he was most of the time, just before the slaves was freed.

All the time we hear about slaves on that place getting whipped or being locked in the stock—that one of them things where your head and hands is fastened through holes in a wide board, and you stands there all the day and all the night—and sometimes we hears of them staying in the stock for three-four weeks if they trys to run away to the north.

Sometimes we hears about some slave who is shot by that man while he is wild with the drink. That's what I'm telling about now.

Don't nobody know what made the master mad at the

old slave—one of the oldest on the place. Anyway, the master didn't whip him; instead of that he kills him with the gun and scares the others so bad most of 'em runs off and hides in the woods.

The drunk master just drags the old dead slave to the graveyard which is down in the corner away from the growing crops, and hunts up two of the young boys who was hiding in the barn. He takes them to dig the grave.

The master stands watching every move they make, the dead man lays there with his face to the sky, and the boys is so scared they could hardly dig. The master keeps telling them to hurry with the digging.

After while he tells them to stop and put the body in the grave. They wasn't no coffin, no box, for him. Just the old clothes that he wears in the fields.

But the grave was too short and they start to digging some more, but the master stop them. He says to put back the body in the grave, and then he jumps into the grave hisself. Right on the dead he jumps and stomps 'til the body is mashed and twisted to fit the hole. Then the old nigger is buried.

That's the way my Mammy hears it and told it to us children. She was a Christian and I know she told the truth.

Like I said, Mammy was never sold only to Master Jackson. But she's seen them slave auctions where the men, women and children was stripped naked and lined up so's the buyers could see what kind of animals they was getting for their money.

My pappy's name was Jacob Keller and my mother was Maria. They's both dead long ago, and I'm waiting for the old ship Zion that took my Mammy away, like we use to sing of in the woods:

> "It has landed my old Mammy,
> It has landed my old Mammy,
> Get on board, Get on board,
> 'Tis the Old Ship of Zion—
> Get on board!"

Oklahoma Writers' Project
Ex-Slaves
[Date stamp: AUG 16 1937]

NELLIE JOHNSON

I don't know how old I is, but I is a great big half grown gal when the time of the War come, and I can remember how everything look at that time, and what all the people do, too.

I'm pretty nigh to blind right now, and all I can do is set on this little old front porch and maybe try to keep the things picked up behing my grandchild and his wife, because she has to work and he is out selling wood most of the time.

But I didn't have to live in any such a house during the time I was young like they is, because I belonged to old Chief Rolley McIntosh, and my pappy and mammy have a big, nice, clean log house to live in, and everything round it look better than most renters got these days.

We never did call old Master anything but the Chief or the General for that's what everybody called him in them days, and he never did act towards us like we was slaves, much anyways. He was the mikko of the Kawita town long before the War and long before I was borned, and he was the chief of the Lower Creeks even before he got to be the chief of all the Creeks.

But just at the time of the War the Lower Creeks stayed with him and the Upper Creeks, at least them that lived along to the south of where we live, all go off after that old man Gouge, and he take most of the Seminole too. I hear old Tuskenugge, the big man with the Seminoles, but I never did see him, nor mighty few of the Seminoles.

My mammy tells me old General ain't been living in that Kawita town very many years when I was borned. He come up there from down in the fork of the river where the Arkansas and the Verdigris run together a little while after all the last of the Creeks come out to the Territory. His brother old Chili McIntosh, live down in that forks of the rivers too, but I don't think he ever move up into that Kawita town. It was in the narrow stretch where the Verdigris come close to the Arkansas. They got a pretty good sized white folks town there now they call Coweta, but the old Creek town was different from that. The folks lived all around in that stretch between the rivers, and my old Master was the boss of all of them.

For a long time after the Civil War they had a court at the new town called Coweta court, and a school house too, but before I was born they had a mission school down the Kawita Creek from where the town now is.

Earliest I can remember about my master was when he come to the slave settlement where we live and get out of the buggy and show a preacher all around the place. That preacher named Mr. Loughridge, and he was the man had the mission down on Kawita Creek before I was born, but at that time he had a school off at some other place. He git down out the buggy and talk to all us children, and ask us how we getting along.

I didn't even know at that time that old Chief was my

master, until my pappy tell me after he was gone. I think all the time he was another preacher.

My pappy's name was Jackson McInotsh, and my mammy name was Hagar. I think old Chief bring them out to the Territory when he come out with his brother Chili and the rest of the Creek people. My pappy tell me that old Master's pappy was killed by the Creeks because he signed up a treaty to bring his folks out here, and old Master always hated that bunch of Creeks that done that.

I think old man Gouge was one of the big men in that bunch, and he fit in the War on the Government side, after he done holler and go on so about the Government making him come out here.

Old Master have lots of land took up all around that Kawita place, and I don't know how much, but a lot more than anybody else. He have it all fenced in with good rail fence, and all the Negroes have all the horses and mules and tools they need to work it with. They all live in good log houses they built themselves, and everything they need.

Old Master's land wasn't all in one big field, but a lot of little fields scattered all over the place. He just take up land what already was a kind of prairie, and the niggers don't have to clear up much woods.

We all live around on them little farms, and we didn't have to be under any overseer like the Cherokee Negroes had lots of times. We didn't have to work if they wasn't no work to do that day.

Everybody could have a little patch of his own, too, and work it between times, on Saturdays and Sundays if he wanted to. What he made on that patch belong to him, and the old Chief never bothered the slaves about anything.

Every slave can fix up his own cabin any way he want to, and pick out a good place with a spring if he can find one. Mostly the slave houses had just one big room with a stick-and-mud chimney, just like the poor people among the Creeks had. Then they had a brush shelter built out of four poles with a roof made out of brush, set out to one side of the house where they do the cooking and eating, and sometimes the sleeping too. They set there when they is done working, and lay around on corn shuck beds, because they never did use the log house much only in cold and rainy weather.

Old Chief just treat all the Negroes like they was just hired hands, and I was a big girl before I knowed very much about belonging to him.

I was one of the youngest children in my family; only Sammy and Millie was younger than I was. My big brothers was Adam, August and Nero, and my big sisters was Flora, Nancy and Rhoda. We could work a mighty big patch for our own selves when we was all at home together, and put in all the work we had to for the old Master too, but after the War the big children all get married off and took up land of they own.

Old Chief lived in a big log house made double with a hall in between, and a lot of white folks was always coming there to see him about something. He was gone off somewhere a lot of the time, too, and he just trusted the Negroes to look after his farms and stuff. We would just go on out in the fields and work the crops just like they was our own, and he never come around excepting when we had harvest time, or to tell us what he wanted planted.

Sometimes he would send a Negro to tell us to gather up some chickens or turkeys or shoats he wanted to sell off, and sometimes he would send after loads of corn and wheat to sell. I heard my pappy say old Chief and Mr. Chili McIntosh was the first ones to have any wheat in the Territory, but I don't know about that.

Along during the War the Negro men got pretty lazy and shiftless, but my pappy and my big brothers just go right on and work like they always did. My pappy always said we better off to stay on the place and work good and behave ourselves because old Master take care of us that way. But on lots of other places the men slipped off.

I never did see many soldiers during the War, and there wasn't any fighting close to where we live. It was kind of down in the bottoms, not far from the Verdigris and that Gar Creek, and the soldiers would have bad crossings if the come by our place.

We did see some whackers riding around sometimes, in little bunches of about a dozen, but they never did bother us and never did stop. Some of the Negro girls that I knowed of mixed up with the poor Creeks and Seminoles, and some got married to them after the War, but none of my family ever did mix up with them that I knows of.

Along towards the last of the War I never did see old Chief come around any more, and somebody say he went down into Texas. He never did come back that I knows of, and I think he died down there.

One day my pappy come home and tell us all that the Creek done sign up to quit the War, and that old Master send word that we all free now and can take up some land for our own selves or just stay where we is if we want to. Pappy stayed on that place where he was at until he died.

I got to be a big girl and went down to work for a Creek family close to where they got that Checotah town now. At that time it was just all a scattered settlement of Creeks and they call it Eufaula town. After while I marry a man name Joe Johnson, at a little settlement they call Rentesville. He have his freedmen's allotment close to that place, but mine is up on the Verdigris, and we move up there to live.

We just had one child, named Louisa, and she married Tom Armstrong. They had three-four children, but one was named Ton, and it is him I live with now. My husband's been dead a long, long time now.

Oklahoma Writers' Project
Ex-Slaves
[Date stamp: AUG 16 1937]

MS. JOSIE JORDAN
Age 75 yrs.
840 East King St.,
Tulsa, Oklahoma.

I was born right in the middle of the War on the Mark Lowery plantation at Sparta, in White County, Tennessee, so I don't know anything much about them slave days except what my mammy told me long years ago. 'Course I mean the Civil War, for to us colored folks they just wasn't no other war as meanful as that one.

My mother she come from Virginia when a little girl, but never nobody tells me where at my pappy is from. His name was David Lowery when I was born, but I guess he had plenty other names, for like my mammy he was sold lots of times.

Salina was my mammy's name, and she belonged to a Mister Clark, who sold her and pappy to Mark Lowery 'cause she was a fighting, mule-headed woman.

It wasn't her fault 'cause she was a fighter. The master who owned her before Mister Clark was one of them white mens who was always whipping and beating his slaves and mammy couldn't stand it no more.

That's the way she tells me about it. She just figgured

she would be better off dead and out of her misery as to be whipped all the time, so one day the master claimed they was something wrong with her work and started to raise his whip, but mammy fought back and when the ruckus was over the Master was laying still on the ground and folks thought he was dead, he got such a heavy beating.

Mammy says he don't die and right after that she was sold to Mister Clark I been telling you about. And mammy was full of misery for a long time after she was carried to Mark Lowery's plantation where at I was born during of the War.

She had two children while belonging to Mister Clark and he wouldn't let them go with mammy and pappy. That's what caused her misery. Pappy tried to ease her mind but she jest kept a'crying for her babies, Ann and Reuban, till Mister Lowery got Clark to leave them visit with her once a month.

Mammy always says that Mark Lowery was a good master. But he'd heard things about mammy before he got her and I reckon was curious to know if they was all true. Mammy says he found out mighty quick they was.

It was mammy's second day on the plantation and Mark Lowery acted like he was going to whip her for something she'd done or hadn't, but mammy knocked him plumb through the open cellar door. He wasn't hurt, not even mad for mammy says he climbed out the cellar a'laughing, saying he was only fooling to see if she would fight.

But mammy's troubles wasn't over then, for Mark Lowery he got himself a new young wife (his first wife was dead), and mammy was round of the house most of the time after that.

Right away they had trouble. The Mistress was trying to make mammy hurry up with the work and she hit mammy with the broom stick. Mammy's mule temper boiled up all over the kitchen and the Master had to stop the fighting.

He wouldn't whip mammy for her part in the trouble, so the Mistress she sent word to her father and brothers and they come to Mister Lowery's place.

They was going to whip mammy, they was good and mad. Master was good and mad, too, and he warned 'em home.

"Whip your own slaves." He told them. "Mine have to work and if they're beat up they can't do a days work. Get on home—I'll take care of this." And they left.

My folks didn't have no food troubles at Mark Lowery's like they did somewheres else. I remember mammy told me about one master who almost starved his slaves. Mighty stingy I reckon he was.

Some of them slaves was so poorly thin they ribs would kinder rustle against each other like corn stalks a-drying in the hot winds. But they gets even one hog-killing time, and it was funny too, mammy said.

They was seven hogs, fat and ready for fall hog-killing time. Just the day before old master told off they was to be killed something happened to all them porkers. One of the field boys found them and come a-telling the master: "The hogs is all died, now they won't be any meats for the winter."

When the master gets to where at the hogs is laying, they's a lot of Negroes standing round looking sorrow-eyed at the wasted meat. The master asks: "What's the illness with 'em?"

"Malitis." They tell him, and they acts like they don't want to touch the hogs. Master says to dress them anyway for they ain't no more meat on the place.

He says to keep all the meat for the slave families, but that's because he's afraid to eat it hisself account of the hogs' got malitis.

"Don't you-all know what is malitis?" Mammy would ask the children when she was telling of the seven fat hogs and seventy lean slaves. And she would laugh, remembering how they fooled the old master so's to get all them good meats.

"One of the strongest Negroes got up early in the morning," Mammy would explain, "long 'fore the rising horn called the slaves from their cabins. He skitted to the hog pen with a heavy mallet in his hand. When he tapped Mister Hog 'tween the eyes with that mallet 'malitis' set in mighty quick, but it was a uncommon 'disease', even with hungry Negroes around all the time."

Mammy had me three sisters and a brother while on the Lowery plantation. They was Lisa, Addie, Alice and Lincoln. It was a long time after the War and we was all freed before we left old Master Lowery.

Stayed right there where we was at home, working in

the fields, living in the same old cabins, just like before the War. Never did have no big troubles after the War, except one time the Ku Klux Klan broke up a church meeting and whipped some of the Negroes.

The preacher was telling about the Bible days when the Klan rode up. They was all masked up and everybody crawled under the benches when they shouted: "We'll make you damn niggers wish you wasn't free!"

And they just about did. The preacher got the worst whipping, blood was running from his nose and mouth and ears, and they left him laying on the floor.

They whipped the women just like the men, but Mammy and the girls wasn't touched none and we run all the way back to the cabin. Layed down with all our clothes on and tried to sleep, but we's too scairt to close our eyes.

Mammy reckoned old Master Lowery was a-riding with the Klan that night, else we'd got a flogging too.

We first moved about a mile from Master Lowery's place and ever week we'd ask mammy if we children could go see old Master and she'd say: "Yes, if you-all are good niggers."

The old Master was always glad to see us children and he would give us candy and apples and treat us mighty fine.

The old plantations gone, the old Masters gone, the old slaves is gone, and I'll be a going some of these days, too, for I been here a mighty long time and they ain't nobody needs me now 'cause I is too old for any good.

United States. Work Projects Administration

Oklahoma Writers' Project
Ex-Slaves

"UNCLE" GEORGE G. KING
Age 83 yrs
Tulsa, Oklahoma

"Prayers for sale.... Prayers for sale...." Uncle George chants in sing-song fashion as he roams around Tulsa's Greenwood Negro district—pockets filled with prayer papers that are soiled and dirty with constant handling.

But they are potent, Uncle George tells those who fear the coming of some trouble, disaster or just ordinary misery, and there's a special prayer for each and every trouble—including one to keep away the bill collector when the young folks forget to make payments on the radio, the furniture, the car, or the Spring outfit purchased months ago from the credit clothier.

Its all in the Bible and the Bible is his workshop—'cause folks don't know how to pray.

He's mighty old, is Uncle George King, and he'll tell you that he was born on two-hundred acres of Hell, but the whitefolks called it Samuel Roll's plantation (six miles N.E. of Lexington, South Carolina).

Kinder small for a plantation, Uncle George explains, but plenty room for that devil overseer to lay on the lash, and plenty room for the old she-devil Mistress to whip his mammy til' she was just a piece of living raw meat!

The old Master talked hard words, but the Mistress whipped. Lot's of difference, and Uncle George ought to know, 'cause he's felt the lash layed on pretty heavy when he was no older than kindergarten children of today.

The Mistress owned the slaves and they couldn't be sold without her say-so. That's the reason George was never sold, but the Master once tried to sell him 'cause the beatings was breaking him down. Old Mistress said "No", and used it for an excuse to whip his Mammy. Uncle George remembers that, too.

They crossed her wrists and tied them with a stout cord. They made her bend over so that her arms was sticking back between her legs and fastened the arms with a stick so's she couldn't straighten up.

He saw the Mistress pull his Mammy's clothes over her head so's the lash would reach the skin. He saw the overseer lay on the whip with hide busting blows that left her laying, all a shiver, on the ground, like a wounded animal dying from the chase.

He saw the Mistress walk away, laughing, while his Mammy screamed and groaned—the old Master standing there looking sad and wretched, like he could feel the blows on Mammy's bared back and legs as much as she.

The Mistress was a great believer in the power of punishment, and Uncle George remembers the old log cabin jail built before the War, right on the plantation, where runaway slaves were stowed away 'till they would promise to behave themselves.

The old jail was full up during most of the War. Three runaway slaves were still chained to its floor when the Master gave word the Negroes were free.

They were Prince, Sanovey (his wife), and Henry, who were caught and whipped by the patrollers, and then brought back to the plantation for another beating before being locked in jail.

The Mistress ordered them chained, and the overseer would come every morning with the same question: "Will you niggers promise not to runaway no more?"

But they wouldn't promise. One at a time the overseer would loosen the chains, and lead them from the jail to cut them with powerful blows from the lash, then drag them back to be chained until the next day when more lickings were given 'cause they wouldn't promise.

The jail was emptied on the day Master Roll called together all the men, women and children to tell them they wasn't slaves no more. Uncle George tells it this way:

"The Master he says we are all free, but it don't mean we is white. And it don't mean we is equal. Just equal for to work and earn our own living and not depend on him for no more meats and clother." [TR: clothes?]

Food was scarce before the War; it was worse after the shooting and killing was over, and Uncle George says: "There wasn't no corn bread, no bacon—just trash eating trash, like when General Sherman marched down through the country taking everything the soldiers could lug away, and burning all along the way.

"Wasn't nothing to eat after he march by. Darkies

search 'round the barns, maybe find some grains of corn in the manure, and they'd parch the grains—nothing else to eat, except sometimes at night Mammy would skit out and steal scraps from the Master's house for the children.

"She had lots of hungry mouths, too. They was seven of us then, six boys and a girl, Eliza. The boys was Wesley, Simeon, Moses, Peter, William and me, George. This pappy's name was Griffin.

"But they was other pappys (Mammy told him) when Eva was born long before any of us, and Laura come next, but from a white daddy. Mammy lost them when she was sold around on the markets.

"The Klan they done lots of riding round the country. One night the come down to the old slave quarters where the cabins is all squared round each other, and called everybody outdoors. They's looking for two women.

"They picks 'em out of the crowd right quick and say they been with white men. Says their children is by white men, and they're going to get whipped so's they'll remember to stay with their own kind. The women kick and scream, but the mens grab them and roll them over a barrel and let fly with the whip."

It was a long time after the Civil War that Uncle George got his first schooling or attended regular church meetings. Like he says:

"Getting up at four o'clock in the morning, hoeing in the fields all day, doing chores when they come in from the fields, and then piddling with the weaver 'til nine or ten every night—it just didn't leave no time for reading and such, even if we was allowed to."

And religion, that came later too, for during the old plantation days Uncle George's white folks didn't think a Negro needed religion—there wasn't a Heaven for Negroes anyhow.

Finally, though, the Master gave them right to hold meetings on the plantation, and old Peter Coon was the preacher. The overseer was there with guards to keep the Negroes from getting too much riled up when old Peter started talking about Paul or some of the things in the Old Testament. That's all he would talk about; nothing 'bout Jesus, just Paul and the Old Testament.

His Mammy went to every meeting. Like he says: "She knew them good things was good for her children and she told us about the Bible."

Like his old Mammy, Uncle George is a firm believer in the power of the word. "Prayers are saving!" Uncle George says, "But they's lots of folks' don't know how to pray."

That's why he has prayers for sale—and he knows they are never failing, "If you tack 'em up on the wall and say 'em over and over every day they's sure to be answered."

United States. Work Projects Administration

Oklahoma Writers' Project
Ex-Slaves
[Date stamp: AUG 19 1937]

MARTHA KING
Age 85 yrs.
McAlester, Oklahoma

"They hung Jeff Davis to a sour apple tree!
They hung Jeff Davis to a sour apple tree!
They hung Jeff Davis to a sour apple tree!
While we go marching on!"

Dat was de song de Yankees sang when they marched by our house. They didn't harm us in any way. I guess de War was over then 'cause a few days after dat old Master say, "Matt", and I say, "Suh?" He say, "Come here. You go tell Henry I say come out here and to bring the rest of the niggers with him." I went to the north door and I say, "Henry, Master Willis say ever one of you come out here." We all went outside and line up in front of old Master. He say, "Henry". Henry say, "Yes sah". Old Master say, "Every one of you is free—as free as I am. You all can leave or stay 'round here if you want to."

We all stayed on for a long time 'cause we didn't have no other home and didn't know how to take keer of ourselves. We was kind of scared I reckon. Finally I heard my mother was in Walker County, Alabama, and I left and went to live with her.

My mother was Harriet Davis and she was born in Virginia. I don't know who my father was. My grandmother was captured in Africa when she was a little girl. A big boat was down at the edge of a bay an' the people was all excited about it an' some of the bravest went up purty close to look at it. The men on the boat told them to come on board and they could have the pretty red handkerchiefs, red and blue beads and big rings. A lot of them went on board and the ship sailed away with them. My grandmother never saw any of her folks again.

When I was about five years old they brought my grandmother, my mother and my two aunts and two uncles to Tuskaloosa from Fayettesville, Alabama. We crossed a big river on a ferry boat. They put us on the "block" and sold us. I can remember it well. A white man "cried" me off just like I was a animal or varmint or something. He said, "Here's a little nigger, who will give me a bid on her. She will make a good house gal someday." Old man Davis give him $300.00 for me. I don't know whether I was afraid or not; I don't think I cared just so I had something to eat. I was allus hungry. Miss Davis' grandmother and one of my aunts and uncles. Old man Davis bought the rest of us. Uncle Henry looked after me when he could. I could see my mother once in awhile but not often.

I had a purty easy time. I didn't have to work very hard 'till I was about ten years old. I started working in the field and I had to work in the weaving room too. We made all our own clothes. I spun and wove cotton and wool. Old Master bought our shoes. We made fancy cloth.

We could stripe the cloth or check it or leave it plain. We also wove coverlids and jeans to make mens suits out of. I could still do that if I had to.

We all went to church with the white folks. We didn't have no colored preachers. The niggers would get happy and shout all over the place. Sometimes they'd fall out doors.

The Big House was a double log, two story house, not very fine but awful comfortable. They was four big fireplace rooms downstairs and two upstairs. Then they was two sort of shed rooms. There was a big piazza across the front. The kitchen was a way off from the house, seems like it was 200 feet at least. Our quarters were close by at the back. He didn't have many slaves and they was nearly all my kinfolks. There was Aunt Emmy and Phillis, Uncles Henry, Mitchell, Louis and Andy, and the others were Uncle Logan and Uncle Nathan. They was old Mistress' slaves when she done married.

Old Master and old Mistress had three boys, Eli, Billy and Dock. They had to go to war and old Mistress sho' did cry. She say they might get killed and she might not see 'em any more. I wonder why all dem white folks didn't think of that when they sold mothers away from they chillun. I had to be sold away from my mother. Two of her boys was badly wounded but they all come back.

Abe Lincoln done everything he could for the niggers. We lost our best friend when he got killed.

United States. Work Projects Administration

Oklahoma Writers' Project
Ex-Slaves

GEORGE KYE
Age 110 yrs.
Fort Gibson, Okla.

I was born in Arkansas under Mr. Abraham Stover, on a big farm about twenty miles north of Van Buren. I was plumb grown when the Civil War come along, but I can remember back when the Cherokee Indians was in all that part of the country.

Joe Kye was my pappy's name what he was born under back in Garrison County, Virginia, and I took that name when I was freed, but I don't know whether he took it or not because he was sold off by old Master Stover when I was a child. I never have seen him since. I think he wouldn't mind good, leastways that what my mammy say.

My mammy was named Jennie and I don't think I had any brothers or sisters, but they was a whole lot of children at the quarters that I played and lived with. I didn't live with mammy because she worked all the time, and us children all stayed in one house.

It was a little one room log cabin, chinked and daubed, and you couldn't stir us with a stick. When we went to eat we had a big pan and all ate out of it. One what ate the fastest got the most.

Us children wore homespun shirts and britches and little slips, and nobody but the big boys wore any britches. I wore just a shirt until I was about 12 years old, but it had a long tall down to my calves. Four or five of us boys slept in one bed, and it was made of hewed logs with rope laced acrost it and a shuck mattress. We had stew made out of pork and potatoes, and sometimes greens and pot liquor, and we had ash cake mostly, but biscuits about once a month.

In the winter time I had brass toed shoes made on the place, and a cloth cap with ear flaps.

The work I done was hoeing and plowing, and I rid a horse a lot for old Master because I was a good rider. He would send me to run chores for him, like going to the mill. He never beat his negroes but he talked mighty cross and glared at us until he would nearly scare us to death sometimes.

He told us the rules and we lived by them and didn't make trouble, but they was a neighbor man that had some mean negroes and he nearly beat them to death. We could hear them hollering in the field sometimes. They would sleep in the cotton rows, and run off, and then they would catch the cat-o-nine tails sure nuff. He would chain them up, too, and keep them tied out to trees, and when they went to the field they would be chained together in bunches sometimes after they had been cutting up.

We didn't have no place to go to church, but old Master didn't care if we had singing and praying, and we would tie our shoes on our backs and go down the road close to the white church and all set down and put our shoes on and go up close and listen to the service.

Old Master was baptized almost every Sunday and cussed us all out on Monday. I didn't join the church until after freedom, and I always was a scoundrel for dancing. My favorite preacher was old Pete Conway. He was the only ordained colored preacher we had after freedom, and he married me.

Old Master wouldn't let us take herb medicine, and he got all our medicine in Van Buren when we was sick. But I wore a buckeye on my neck just the same.

When the War come along I was a grown man, and I went off to serve because old Master was too old to go, but he had to send somebody anyways. I served as George Stover, but every time the sergeant would call out "Abe Stover", I would answer "Here".

They had me driving a mule team wagon that Old Master furnished, and I went with the Sesesh soldiers from Van Buren to Texarkana and back a dozen times or more. I was in the War two years, right up to the day of freedom. We had a battle close to Texarkana and another big one near Van Buren, but I never left Arkansas and never got a scratch.

One time in the Texarkana battle I was behind some pine trees and the bullets cut the limbs down all over me. I dug a big hole with my bare hands before I hardly knowed how I done it.

One time two white soldiers named Levy and Briggs come to the wagon train and said they was hunting slaves for some purpose. Some of us black boys got scared because we heard they was going to Squire Mack and get a reward for catching runaways, so me and two more lit out of there.

They took out after us and we got to a big mound in the woods and hid. Somebody shot at me and I rolled into some bushes. He rid up and got down to look for me but I was on t'other side of his horse and he never did see me. When they was gone we went back to the wagons just as the regiment was pulling out and the officer didn't say nothing.

They was eleven negro boys served in my regiment for their masters. The first year was mighty hard because we couldn't get enough to eat. Some ate poke greens without no grease and took down and died.

How I knowed I was free, we was bad licked, I reckon. Anyways, we quit fighting and a Federal soldier come up to my wagon and say: "Whose mules?" "Abe Stover's mules," I says, and he tells me then, "Let me tell you, black boy, you are as free now as old Abe Stover his own self!" When he said that I jumped on top of one of them mules' back before I knowed anything!

I married Sarah Richardson, February 10, 1870, and had only eleven children. One son is a deacon and one grandson is a preacher. I am a good Baptist. Before I was married I said to the gal's old man, "I'll go to the mourners bench if you'll let me have Sal," and sure nuff I joined up just a month after I got her. I am head of the Sunday School and deacon in the St. Paul Baptist church in Muskogee now.

I lived about five miles from Van Buren until about

twelve years ago when they found oil and then they run all the negroes out and leased up the land. They never did treat the negroes good around there anyways.

I never had a hard time as a slave, but I'm glad we was set free. Sometimes we can't figger out the best thing to do, but anyways we can lead our own life now, and I'm glad the young ones can learn and get somewhere these days.

United States. Work Projects Administration

Oklahoma Writers' Project
Ex-Slaves
[Date stamp: NOV 5 1937]

BEN LAWSON
Age 84 yrs.
Oklahoma City, Okla.

I was born in Danville, Illinois. De best I can get at my age I is 84 years old. My father dey tell me was name Dennis Lawson and died before I was born. My mother's name was Ann Lawson, who I saw once. I was given by her to my Mistress, Mrs. Jane Brazier, when a kid and she was too. My mother raised me, she and her son to manhood. I got no brothers or sisters to my knowledge. I was de only slave dey had and dey raised me to be humble and fear dem as a slave and servant. As I was de only slave I slept in de same room wid my Mistress and her son who was grown, her husband and father being dead.

I worked on the farm doing general farm work, hoeing, plowing, harvesting the crop of wheat, corn, barley, oats, rice, peas, etc. To make and harvest the crops dey would hire poor white help and as dey was grown and I was a lad, dey kept me in a strain in order to keep up wid dem for if I didn't it was just too bad for my back. So's dere would be work for me to do during the bad days of winter dey built a pen under a shed and dey would lay a cloth on de ground covering the ground in the pen and wid small mesh wire on top of de pen on which de wheat was laid and wid a wooden maul I would pounder out wheat all day long, even though dey could have thrashed it as dey did de biggest part of it.

At meal time dey would give me what was left of de scraps off dey table in a plate, which I would eat most de time on de back porch in warm weather and in de kitchen in winter.

For summer I wore a lowell shirt and for winter I wore de same old lowell shirt only wid outing slips and a pair of brogan shoes or a pair of old shoes dat was thrown away by my Mistress' son.

Their house was a 3-room log house unpainted, wid only one bed room and a dining room and kitchen.

The plantation had 'bout 160 acres and was worked by my Mistress' son and myself plus poor white hired help, my being de only slave.

I was treated most harshly 'mongst a group of just white people and who seemed to think me de old work ox for all de hardest work. De nearest other Negro slaves were 'bout 15 or 20 miles from me.

When I was grown I ran away one night and walked and rode de rods under stage coaches to Paducah, Kentucky. I got me a job and worked as a roustabout on a boat where I learned to gamble wid dice. I fought and gambled all up and down de Mississippi River, and in de course of time I had 'bout $3,000, but I lost it.

I don't know de month or de year I was born in but I can 'member de sinking of de biggest circus show in de Mississippi River at Mobile, Alabama when I was 10 to 14 years old, I ain't sure which.

There wasn't no children for me to play with and it seem like I never was a child but was just always a man. I wasn't never told dat I was free, and I didn't know nothing 'bout de War much dat brought my freedom. Dey kept all of dat away from me and I couldn't read or write so I didn't know.

I've been married only once. My wife is 54 years old, and her name is Hattie Lawson. We have no children. Since we married after freedom there wasn't nothing unusual at our wedding.

United States. Work Projects Administration

Oklahoma Writers' Project
Ex-Slaves
[Date stamp: AUG 16 1937]

MARY LINDSAY
Age 91 yrs.
Tulsa, Oklahoma.

My slavery days wasn't like most people tell you about, 'cause I was give to my young Mistress and sent away to Texas when I was jest a little girl, and I didn't live on a big plantation a very long tine.

I got an old family Bible what say I was born on September 20, in 1846, but I don't know who put de writing in it unless it was my mammy's mistress. My mammy had de book when she die.

My mammy come out to the Indian country from Mississippi two years before I was born. She was the slave of a Chickasaw part-breed name Sobe Love. He was the kinsfolks of Mr. Benjamin Love, and Mr. Henry Love what bring two big bunches of the Chickasaws out from Mississippi to the Choctaw country when the Chickasaws sign up de treaty to leave Mississippi, and the whole Love family settle 'round on the Red River below Fort Washita. There whar I was born.

My mammy say dey have a terrible hard time again the sickness when they first come out into that country, because it was low and swampy and all full of cane brakes, and everybody have the smallpox and the malaria and fever all the time. Lots of the Chickasaw families nearly died off.

Old Sobe Love marry her off to a slave named William, what belong to a full-blood Chickasaw man name Chick-a-lathe, and I was one of de children.

De children belong to the owner of the mother, and me and my brother Franklin, what we called "Bruner", was born under the name of Love and then old Master Sobe bought my pappy William, and we was all Love slaves then. My mammy had two more girls, name Hatty and Rena.

My mammy name was Mary, and I was named after her. Old Mistress name was Lottie, and they had a daughter name Mary. Old Master Sobe was powerful rich, and he had about a hundred slaves and four or five big pieces of that bottom land broke out for farms. He had niggers on all the places, but didn't have no overseers, jest hisself and he went around and seen that everybody behave and do they work right.

Old Master Sobe was a mighty big man in the tribe, and so was all his kinfolks, and they went to Fort Washita and to Boggy Depot all the time on business, and leave the Negroes to look after old Mistress and the young daughter. She was almost grown along about that time, when I can first remember about things.

'Cause my name was Mary, and so was my mammy's and my young Mistress' too. Old Master Sobe called me Mary-Ka-Chubbe to show which Mary he was talking about.

Miss Mary have a black woman name Vici what wait on her all the time, and do the carding and spinning and cooking 'round the house, and Vici belong to Miss Mary. I never did go 'round the Big House, but jest stayed in the quarters with my mammy and pappy and helped in the field a little.

Then one day Miss Mary run off with a man and married him, and old Master Sobe nearly went crazy! The man was name Bill Merrick, and he was a poor blacksmith and didn't have two pair of britches to his name, and old Master Sobe said he jest stole Miss Mary 'cause she was rich, and no other reason. 'Cause he was a white man and she was mostly Chickasaw Indian.

Anyways old Master Sobe wouldn't even speak to Mr. Bill, and wouldn't let him set foot on the place. He jest reared and pitched around, and threatened to shoot him if he set eyes on him, and Mr. Bill took Miss Mary and left out for Texas. He set up a blacksmith shop on the big road between Bonham and Honey Grove, and lived there until he died.

Miss Mary done took Vici along with her, and pretty soon she come back home and stay a while, and old Master Sobe kind of soften up a little bit and give her some money to git started on, and he give her me too.

Dat jest nearly broke my old mammy's and pappy's heart, to have me took away off from them, but they couldn't say nothing and I had to go along with Miss Mary back to Texas. When we git away from the Big House I jest cried and cried until I couldn't hardly see, my eyes was so swole up, but Miss Mary said she gwine to be good to me.

I ask her how come Master Sobe didn't give her some of the grown boys and she say she reckon it because he didn't want to help her husband out none, but jest wanted to help her. If he give her a man her husband have him working in the blacksmith shop, she reckon.

Master Bill Merrick was a hard worker, and he was more sober than most the men in them days, and he never tell me to do nothing. He jest let Miss Mary tell me what to do. They have a log house close to the shop, and a little patch of a field at first, but after awhile he git more land, and then Miss Mary tell me and Vici we got to help in the field too.

That sho' was hard living then! I have to git up at three o'clock sometimes so I have time to water the hosses and slop the hogs and feed the chickens and milk the cows, and then git back to the house and git the breakfast. That was during the times when Miss Mary was having and nursing her two children, and old Vici had to stay with her all the time. Master Bill never did do none of that kind of work, but he had to be in the shop sometimes until way late in the night, and sometimes before daylight, to shoe peoples hosses and oxen and fix wagons.

He never did tell me to do that work, but he never done it his own self and I had to do it if anybody do it.

He was the slowest one white man I ever did see. He jest move 'round like de dead lice falling off'n him all the time, and everytime he go to say anything he talk so slow that when he say one word you could walk from here to way over there before he say de next word. He don't look sick, and he was powerful strong in his arms, but he act like he don't feel good jest the same.

I remember when the War come. Mostly by the people passing 'long the big road, we heard about it. First they was a lot of wagons hauling farm stuff into town to sell, and then purty soon they was soldiers on the wagons, and they was coming out into the country to git the stuff and buying it right at the place they find it.

Then purty soon they commence to be little bunches of mens in soldier clothes riding up and down the road going somewhar. They seem like they was mostly young boys like, and they jest laughing and jollying and going on like they was on a picnic.

Then the soldiers come 'round and got a lot of the white men and took them off to the War even iffen they didn't want to go. Master Bill never did want to go, 'cause he had his wife and two little children, and anyways he was gitting all the work he could do fixing wagons and shoeing hosses, with all the traffic on de road at that time. Master Bill had jest two hosses, for him and his wife to ride and to work to the buggy, and he had one old yoke of oxen and some more cattle. He got some kind of a paper in town and he kept it with him all the time, and when the soldiers would come to git his hosses or his cattle he would jest draw that paper on 'em and they let 'em alone.

By and by the people got so thick on the big road that they was somebody in sight all the time. They jest keep a dust kicked up all day and all night 'cepting when it rain, and they git all bogged down and be strung all up and down the road camping. They kept Master Bill in the shop all the time, fixing the things they bust trying to git the wagons out'n the mud. They was whole families of them, with they children and they slaves along, and they was coming in from every place because the Yankees was gitting in their part of the country, they say.

We all git mighty scared about the Yankees coming but I don't reckon they ever git thar, 'cause I never seen none, and we was right on the big road and we would of seen them. They was a whole lot more soldiers in them brown looking jeans, round-about jackets and cotton britches a-faunching up and down the road on their hosses, though. Them hoss soldiers would come b'iling by, going east, all day and night, and the two-three days later on they would all come tearing by going west! Dey acted like dey didn't know whar dey gwine, but I reckon dey did.

Den Master Bill git sick. I reckon he more wore out and worried than anything else, but he go down with de fever one day and it raining so hard Mistress and me and Vici can't neither one go nowhar to git no help.

We puts peach tree poultices on his head and wash him off all the time, until it quit raining so Mistress can go out on de road, and then a doctor man come from one of the bunches of soldiers and see Master Bill. He say he going be all right and jest keep him quiet, and go on.

Mistress have to tend de children and Vici have to take care of Master Bill and look after the house, and dat leave me all by myself wid all the rest of everything around the place.

I got to feed all the stock and milk the cows and work in the field too. Dat the first time I ever try to plow, and I nearly git killed, too! I got me a young yoke of oxens I broke to pull the wagon, 'cause Vici have to use the old oxens to work the field. I had to take the wagon and go 'bout ten miles west to a patch of woods Master Bill owned to git fire wood, 'cause we lived right on a flat patch of prairie, and I had to chop and haul the wood by myself. I had to git postoak to burn in the kitchen fireplace and willow for Master Bill to make charcoal out of to burn in his blacksmith fire.

Well, I hitch up them young oxen to the plow and they won't follow the row, and so I go git the old oxens. One of them old oxens didn't know me and took in after me, and I couldn't hitch 'em up. And then it begins to rain again.

After the rain was quit I git the bucket and go milk the cows, and it is time to water the hosses too, so I starts to the house with the milk and leading one of the hosses. When I gits to the gate I drops the halter across my arm and hooks the bucket of milk on my arm too, and starts to open the gate. The wind blow the gate wide open, and it slap the hoss on the flank. That was when I nearly git killed!

Out the hoss go through the gate to the yard, and down the big road, and my arm all tangled up in the halter rope and me dragging on the ground!

The first jump knock the wind out of me and I can't git loose, and that hoss drag me down the road on the run until he meet up with a passel of soldiers and they stop him.

The next thing I knowed I was laying on the back kitchen gallery, and some soldiers was pouring water on me with a bucket. My arm was broke, and I was stove up so bad that I have to lay down for a whole week, and Mistress and Vici have to do all the work.

Jest as I gitting able to walk 'round here come some soldiers and say they come to git Master Bill for the War. He still in the bed sick, and so they leave a parole paper for him to stay until he git well, and then he got to go into Bonham and go with the soldiers to blacksmith for them that got the cannons, the man said.

Mistress take on and cry and hold onto the man's coat and beg, but it don't do no good. She say they don't belong in Texas but they belong in the Chickasaw Nation, but he say that don't do no good, 'cause they living in Texas now.

Master Bill jest stew and fret so, one night he fever git way up and he go off into a kind of a sleep and about morning he died.

My broke arm begin to swell up and hurt me, and I git sick with it again, and Mistress git another doctor to come look at it.

He say I got bad blood from it how come I git so sick, and he git out his knife out'n his satchel and bleed me in the other arm. The next day he come back and bleed me again two times, and the next day one more time, and then I git so sick I puke and he quit bleeding me.

While I still sick Mistress pick up and go off to the Territory to her pappy and leave the children thar for Vici and me to look after. After while she come home for a day or two and go off again somewhere else. Then the next time she come home she say they been having big battles in the Territory and her pappy moved all his stuff down on the river, and she home to stay now.

We git along the best we can for a whole winter, but we nearly starve to death, and then the next spring when we getting a little patch planted Mistress go into Bonham and come back and say we all free and the War over.

She say, "You and Vici jest as free as I am, and a lot freer, I reckon, and they say I got to pay you if you work for me, but I ain't got no money to pay you. If you stay on with me and help me I will feed and home you and I can weave you some good dresses if you card and spin the cotton and wool."

Well, I stayed on, 'cause I didn't have no place to go, and I carded and spinned the cotton and wool and she make me just one dress. Vici didn't do nothing but jest wait on the children and Mistress.

Mistress go off again about a week, and when she come back I see she got some money, but she didn't give us any of it.

After while I asked her ain't she got some money for me, and she say no, ain't she giving me a good home? Den I starts to feeling like I aint treated right.

Every evening I git done with the work and go out in the back yard and jest stand and look off to the west towards Bonham, and wish I was at that place or some other place.

Den along come a nigger boy and say he working for a family in Bonham and he git a dollar every week. He say

Mistress got some kinfolks in Bonham and some of Master Sobe Love's niggers living close to there.

So one night I jest put that new dress in a bundle and set foot right down the big road a-walking west, and don't say nothing to nobody!

Its ten miles into Bonham, and I gits in town about daylight. I keeps on being afraid, 'cause I con't git it out'n my mind I still belong to Mistress.

Purty soon some niggers tells me a nigger name Bruner Love living down west of Greenville, and I know that my brother Franklin, 'cause we all called him Bruner. I don't remember how all I gits down to Greenville, but I know I walks most the way, and I finds Bruner. Him and his wife working on a farm, and they say my sister Hetty and my sister Rena what was little is living with my mammy way back up on the Red River. My pappy done died in time of the War and I didn't know it.

Bruner taken me in a wagon and we went to my mammy, and I lived with her until she died and Hetty was married. Then I married a boy name Henry Lindsay. His people was from Georgia and he live with them way west at Cedar Mills, Texas. That was right close to Gordonville, on the Red River.

We live at Cedar Mills until three my children was born and then we come to the Creek Nation in 1887. My last one was born here.

My oldest is named Georgia on account of her pappy. He was born in Georgia and that was in 1838, so his whitefolks got a book that say. My next child was Henry. We called him William Henry, after my pappy and his pappy. Then come Donie, and after we come here we had Madison, my youngest boy.

I lives with Henry here on this little place we got in Tulsa.

When we first come here we got some land for $15 an acre from the Creek Nation, but our papers said we can only stay as long as it is the Creek Nation. Then in 1901 comes the allotments, and we found out our land belong to a Creek Indian, and we have to pay him to let us stay on it. After while he makes us move off and we lose out all around.

But my daughter Donie git a little lot, and we trade it for this place about thirty year ago, when this town was a little place.

United States. Work Projects Administration

Oklahoma Writers' Project
Ex-Slaves

MRS. MATTIE LOGAN
Age 79 yrs.
Route 5, West Tulsa, Oklahoma.

This is a mighty fitting time to be telling about the slave days, for I'm just finished up celebrating my seventy-nine years of being around and the first part of my life was spent on the old John B. Lewis plantation down in old Mississippi.

Yes, sir! my birthday is just over. September 1 it was and the year was 1858. Borned on the John B. Lewis plantation just ten mile south of Jackson in the Mississippi country. Rankin County it was.

My mother's name was Lucinda, and father's name was Levi Miles. My mother was part Indian, for her mother was a half-blood Cherokee Indian from Virginia.

There was children a-plenty besides me. There was Sally, Julia, Hubbard, Ada, Ira, Anthony, Henry, Amanda, Mary, John, Lucinda, Daniel and me, Mattie. That was my family.

The master's family was a large one, too. Six children was born to the Master and Mistress. Her name, his first wife, was Jennie, the second and last was named, Louise. The children was, Rebecca, Mollie, Jennie, Susie, Silas, and Begerlan. They kind of leaned to females.

My mother belonged to Mistress Jennie who thought a heap of her, and why shouldn't she? Mother nursed all Miss Jennie's children because all of her young ones and my mammy's was born so close together it wasn't no trouble at all for mammy to raise the whole kaboodle of them. I was born about the same time as the baby Jennie. They say I nursed on one breast while that white child, Jennie, pulled away at the other!

That was a pretty good idea for the Mistress, for it didn't keep her tied to the place and she could visit around with her friends most any time she wanted 'thout having to worry if the babies would be fed or not.

Mammy was the house girl and account of that and because her family was so large, the Mistress fixed up a two room cabin right back of the Big House and that's where we lived. The cabin had a fireplace in one of the rooms, just like the rest of the slave cabins which was set in a row away from the Big House. In one room was bunk beds, just plain old two-by-fours with holes bored through the plank so's ropes could be fastened in and across for to hold the corn-shuck mattress.

My brothers and sisters was allowed to play with the Master's children, but not with the children who belonged to the field Negroes. We just played yard games like marbles and tossing a ball. I don't rightly remember much about games, for there wasn't too much fun in them days even if we did get raised with the Master's family. We wasn't allowed to learn any reading or writing. They say if they catched a slave learning them things they'd pull his finger nails off! I never saw that done, though.

Each slave cabin had a stone fireplace in the end, just like ours, and over the flames at daybreak was prepared the morning meal. That was the only meal the field negroes had to cook.

All the other meals was fixed up by an old man and woman who was too old for field trucking. The peas, the beans, the turnips, the potatoes, all seasoned up with fat meats and sometimes a ham bone, was cooked in a big iron kettle and when meal time come they all gathered around the pot for a-plenty of helpings! Corn bread and buttermilk made up the rest of the meal.

Ten or fifteen hogs was butchered every fall and the slaves would get the skins and maybe a ham bone. That was all, except what was mixed in with the stews. Flour was given out every Sunday morning and if a family run out of that before the next week, well, they was just out that's all!

The slaves got small amounts of vegetables from the plantation garden, but they didn't have any gardens of their own. Everybody took what old Master rationed out.

Once in a while we had rabbits and fish, but the best dish of all was the 'possum and sweet potatoes—baked together over red-hot coals in the fireplace. Now, that was something to eat!

The Lewis plantation was about three hundred acres, with usually fifty slaves working on the place. Master Lewis was a trader. He couldn't sell of our family, for we belonged to Mistress Jennie. Negro girls, the fat ones who was kinder pretty, was the most sold. Folks wanted them pretty bad but the Mistress said there wasn't going to be any selling of the girls who was mammy's children.

There was no overseer on our place, just the old Master who did all the bossing. He wasn't too mean, but I've seen him whip Old John. I'd run in the house to get away from the sight, but I could still hear Old John yelling, 'Pray, Master! Oh! Pray, Master!', but I guess that there was more howling than there was hurting at that.

My uncle Ed Miles run away to the North and joined with Yankees during the War. He was lucky to get away, for lots of them who tried it was ketched up by the patrollers. I seen some of them once. They had chains fastened around their legs, fastened short, too, just long enough to take a short step. No more running away with them chains anchoring the feets!

There wasn't any negro churches close by our plantation. All the slaves who wanted religion was allowed to join the Methodist church because that was the Mistress' church.

A doctor was called in when the slaves would get sick. He'd give pills for most all the ailments, but once in a while, like when the children would get the whooping cough, some old negro would try to cure them with home made remedies.

The whooping cough cure was by using a land turtle. Cut off his head and drain the blood into a cup. Then take a lump of sugar and dip in the blood, eat the sugar and the coughing was supposed to stop. If it did or not I don't know.

And that makes me think about another cure they use

to tell about. A cure for mean overseers. And I don't mean kill, just scare him, that's all. They say the cure was tried on an overseer who worked for Silas Stien, who was a slave owner living close by the Lewis plantation.

It seems like this overseer was of the meanest kind, always whipping the slaves for no reason at all, and the slaves tried to figure out a way to even up with him by chasing him off the place.

One of the slaves told how to cure him. Get a King snake and put the snake in the overseer's cabin. Slip the snake in about, no, not about, but just exactly nine o'clock at night. Seems like the time was important, why so, I don't remember now.

That's what the slaves did. Put in the snake and out went the overseer. Never no more did he whip the slaves on that plantation because he wasn't working there no more! When he went, when he went, or how he went nobody knows, but they all say he went. That's what counted—he was gone!

The Yankees didn't come around our plantation during the war. All we heard was, 'They'll kill all the slaves,' and such hearing was a-plenty!

After the war some man come to the plantation and told the field negroes they was free. But he didn't know about the cabin we lived in and didn't tell my folks nothing about it. They learned about the freedom from the old Master.

That was some days after the man left the place. The Master called my mother and father into the Big House and told them they was free. Free like him. But he didn't want my folks to leave and they stayed, stayed there three year after they was free to go anywhere they wanted.

The master paid them $200 a month to work for him and that wasn't so much if you stop to figure there was two grown folks and thirteen children who could do plenty of work around the place.

But that money paid for an 80-acre farm my folks bought not far from the old plantation and they moved onto it three year after the freedom come.

I think Lincoln was a mighty good man, and I think Roosevelt is trying to carry some of the good ideas Lincoln had. Lincoln would have done a heap more if he had lived.

The young negroes who are living now are selfish and shiftless. They're not worth two cents and don't have the respect for other folks to get along right. That's what I think.

I been married three times, but no children did I have. The first man was Frank Morris, the next was Jim White, and the last was John Logan. All gone. Dead.

From Mississippi I come to Idabel, Oklahoma, in 1909, two year after statehood. I moved to Muskogee in 1910, staying there while the times was good and coming to Tulsa some years ago.

I'm pretty old and can't work hard anymore, but I manage to get along. I'm glad to be free and I don't believe I could stand them slavery days now at all.

I'm my own boss, get up when I want, go to bed the same way. Nobody to say this or that about what I do.

Yes, I'm glad to be free!

United States. Work Projects Administration

Oklahoma Writers' Project
Ex-Slaves
[Date stamp: AUG 16 1937]

KIZIAH LOVE
Age 93
Colbert, Okla.

Lawd help us, I sho' remembers all about slavery times for I was a grown woman, married and had one baby when de War done broke out. That was a sorry time for some poor black folks but I guess Master Frank Colbert's niggers was about as well off as the best of 'em. I can recollect things that happened way back better than I can things that happen now. Funny ain't it?

Frank Colbert, a full blood Choctaw Indian, was my owner. He owned my mother but I don't remember much about my father. He died when I was a little youngun. My Mistress' name was Julie Colbert. She and Master Frank was de best folks that ever lived. All the niggers loved Master Frank and knowed jest what he wanted done and they tried their best to do it, too.

I married Isom Love, a slave of Sam Love, another full-blood Indian that lived on a jining farm. We lived on Master Frank's farm and Isom went back and forth to work fer his master and I worked ever day fer mine. I don't 'spect we could of done that way iffen we hadn't of had Indian masters. They let us do a lot like we pleased jest so we got our work done and didn't run off.

Old Master Frank never worked us hard and we had plenty of good food to eat. He never did like to put us under white overseers and never tried it but once. A white man come through here and stopped overnight. He looked 'round the farm and told Master Frank that he wasn't gitting half what he ought to out of his rich land. He said he could take his bunch of hands and double his amount of corn and cotton.

Master Frank told him that he never used white overseers, that he had one nigger that bossed around some when he didn't do it hisself. He also told the white man that he had one nigger named Bill that was kind of bad, that he was a good worker but he didn't like to be bothered as he liked to do his own work in his own way. The white boss told him he wouldn't have any trouble and that he could handle him all right.

Old Master hired him and things went very well for a few days. He hadn't said anything to Bill and they had got along fine. I guess the new boss got to thinking it was time for him to take Bill in hand so one morning he told him to hitch up another team before he caught his own team to go to work.

Uncle Bill told him that he didn't have time, that he had a lot of plowing to git done that morning and besides it was customary for every man to catch his own team. Of course this made the overseer mad and he grabbed a stick and started cussing and run at Uncle Bill. Old Bill grabbed a single-tree and went meeting him. Dat white man all on a sudden turned 'round and run fer dear life and I tell you, he fairly bust old Red River wide open gitting away from there and nobody never did see hide nor hair of him 'round to this day.

Master Colbert run a stage stand and a ferry on Red River and he didn't have much time to look after his farm and his niggers. He had lots of land and lots of slaves. His house was a big log house, three rooms on one side and three on the other, and there was a big open hall between them. There was a big gallery clean across the front of the house. Behind the house was the kitchen and the smokehouse. The smokehouse was always filled with plenty of good meat and lard. They would kill the polecat and dress it and take a sharp stick and run it up their back jest under the flesh. They would also run one up each leg and then turn him on his back and put him on top of the house and let him freeze all night. The next morning they'd pull the sticks out and all the scent would be on them sticks and the cat wouldn't smell at all. They'd cook it like they did possum, bake it with taters or make dumplings.

We had plenty of salt. We got that from Grand Saline. Our coffee was made from parched meal or wheat bran. We made it from dried sweet potatoes that had been parched, too.

One of our choicest dishes was "Tom Pashofa", an Indian dish. We'd take corn and beat it in a mortar with a pestle. They took out the husks with a riddle and a fanner. The riddle was a kind of a sifter. When it was beat fine enough to go through the riddle we'd put it in a pot and cook it with fresh pork or beef. We cooked our bread in a Dutch oven or in the ashes.

When we got sick we would take butterfly root and life-everlasting and boil it and made a syrup and take it for colds. Balmony and queen's delight boiled and mixed would make good blood medicine.

The slaves lived in log cabins scattered back of the house. He wasn't afraid they'd run off. They didn't know as much as the slaves in the states, I reckon. But Master Frank had a half brother that was as mean as he was good. I believe he was the meanest man the sun ever shined on. His name was Buck Colbert and he claimed he was a patroller. He was sho' bad to whup niggers. He'd stop a nigger and ask him if he had a pass and even if they did he'd read it and tell them they had stayed over time and he'd beat 'em most to death. He'd say they didn't have any business off the farm and to git back there and stay there.

One time he got mad at his baby's nurse because she couldn't git the baby to stop crying and he hit her on the head with some fire-tongs and she died. His wife got sick and she sent for me to come and take care of her baby. I sho' didn't want to go and I begged so hard for them not to make me that they sent an older woman who had a baby of her own so she could nurse the baby if necessary.

In the night the baby woke up and got to crying and Master Buck called the woman and told her to git him quiet. She was sleepy and was sort of slow and this made Buck mad and he made her strip her clothes off to her waist and he began to whip her. His wife tried to git him to quit and he told her he'd beat her iffen she didn't shut up. Sick as as she was she slipped off and went to Master Frank's and woke him up and got him to go and make Buck quit whipping her. He had beat her so that she was cut up so bad she couldn't nurse her own baby any more.

Master Buck kept on being bad till one day he got mad at one of his own brothers and killed him. This made another one of his brothers mad and he went to his house and killed him. Everybody was glad that Buck was dead.

We had lots of visitors. They'd stop at the stage inn that we kept. One morning I was cleaning the rooms and I found a piece of money in the bed where two men had slept. I thought it was a dime and I showed it to my mammy and she told me it was a five dollar piece. I sho' was happy fer I had been wanting some hoops fer my skirts like Misstress had so Mammy said she would keep my money 'til I could send fer the hoops. My brother got my money from my mammy and I didn't git my hoops fer a long time. Miss Julie give me some later.

When me and my husband got married we built us a log cabin about half-way from Master Frank's house and Master Sam Love's house. I would go to work at Master Frank's and Isom would go to work at Mister Sam's. One day I was at home with jest my baby and a runner come by and said the Yankee soldiers was coming. I looked 'round and I knowed they would git my chickens. I had 'em in a pen right close to the house to keep the varmints from gitting 'em so I decided to take up the boards in the floor and put 'em in there as the wall logs come to the ground and they couldn't git out. By the time I got my chickens under the floor and the house locked tight the soldiers had got so close I could hear their bugles blowing so I jest fairly flew over to old Master's house. Them Yankees clumb down the chimbley and got every one of my chickens and they killed about fifteen of Master Frank's hogs. He went down to their camp and told the captain about it and he paid him for his hogs and sent me some money for my chickens.

We went to church all the time. We had both white and colored preachers. Master Frank wasn't a Christian but he would help build brush-arbors fer us to have church under and we sho' would have big meetings I'll tell you.

One day Master Frank was going through the woods close to where niggers was having church. All on a sudden he started running and beating hisself and hollering and the niggers all went to shouting and saying "Thank the Lawd, Master Frank has done come through!" Master Frank after a minute say, "Yes, through the worst of 'em." He had run into a yellow jacket's nest.

One night my old man's master sent him to Sherman, Texas. He aimed to come back that night so I stayed at home with jest my baby. It went to sleep so I set down on the steps to wait and ever minute I thought I could hear Isom coming through the woods. All a sudden I heard a scream that fairly made my hair stand up. My dog that was laying out in the yard give a low growl and come and set down right by me. He kept growling real low.

Directly, right close to the house I heard that scream again. It sounded like a woman in mortal misery. I run into the house and made the dog stay outside. I locked the door and then thought what must I do. Supposing Isom did come home now and should meet that awful thing? I heard it again. It wasn't more'n a hundred yards from the house. The dog scratched on the door but I dassent open it to let him in. I knowed by this time that it was a panther screaming. I turned my table over and put it against the opening of the fireplace. I didn't aim fer that thing to come down the chimbley and git us.

Purty soon I heard it again a little mite further away—it was going on by. I heard a gun fire. Thank God, I said, somebody else heard it and was shooting at it. I set there on the side of my bed fer the rest of the night with my baby in my arms and praying that Isom wouldn't come home. He didn't come till about nine o'clock the next morning and I was that glad to see him that I jest cried and cried.

I ain't never seen many sperits but I've seen a few. One day I was laying on my bed here by myself. My son Ed was cutting wood. I'd been awful sick and I was powerful weak. I heard somebody walking real light like they was barefooted. I said, "Who's dat?"

He catch hold of my hand and he has the littlest hand I ever seen, and he say, "You been mighty sick and I want you to come and go with me to Sherman to see a doctor."

I say, "I ain't got nobody at Sherman what knows me."

He say, "You'd better come and go with me anyway."

I jest lay there fer a minute and didn't say nothing and purty soon he say, "Have you got any water?"

I told him the water was on the porch and he got up and went outside and I set in to calling Ed. He come hurrying and I asked him why he didn't lock the door when he went out and I told him to go see if he could see the little man and find out what he wanted. He went out and looked everywhere but he couldn't find him nor he couldn't even find his tracks.

I always keep a butcher-knife near me but it was between the mattress and the feather bed and I couldn't get to it. I don't guess it would have done any good though fer I guess it was jest a sperit.

The funniest thing that ever happened to me was when I was a real young gal. Master and Miss Julie was going to see one of his sisters that was sick. I went along to take care of the baby fer Miss Julie. The baby was about a year old. I had a bag of clothes and the baby to carry. I was riding a pacing mule and it was plumb gentle. I was riding along behind Master Frank and Miss Julie and I went to sleep. I lost the bag of clothes and never missed it. Purty soon I let the baby slip out of my lap and I don't know how far I went before I nearly fell off myself and jest think how I felt when I missed that baby! I turned around and went back and found the baby setting in the trail sort of crying. He wasn't hurt a mite as he fell in the grass. I got off the mule and picked him up and had to look fer a log so I could get back on again.

Jest as I got back on Master Frank rode up. He had missed me and come back to see what was wrong. I told him that I had lost the bag of clothes but I didn't say anything about losing the baby. We never did find the clothes and I sho' kept awake the rest of the way. I wasn't going to risk losing that precious baby again! I guess the reason he didn't cry much was because he was a Indian baby. He was sho' a sweet baby though.

Jest before the War people would come through the Territory stealing niggers and selling 'em in the states. Us women dassent git fur from the house. We wouldn't even go to the spring if we happened to see a strange wagon or horsebacker. One of Master Sam Love's women was stole and sold down in Texas. After freedom she made her way back to her fambly. Master Frank sent one of my brothers to Sherman on an errand. After several days the mule come back but we never did see my brother again. We didn't know whether he run off or was stole and sold.

I was glad to be free. What did I do and say? Well, I jest clapped my hands together and said, "Thank God Almighty, I'se free at last!"

I live on the forty acres that the government give me. I have been blind for nine years and don't git off my bed much. I live here with my son, Ed. Isom has been dead for over forty years. I had fifteen children, but only ten of them are living.

United States. Work Projects Administration

Oklahoma Writers' Project
Ex-Slaves

DANIEL WILLIAM LUCAS
Age 94 yrs.
Red Bird, Okla.

I remember them slave days well as it was yesterday, and when I get to remembering the very first thing comes back to me is the little log cabin where at I lived when I was a slave boy back 'fore the War.

Just like yesterday—I see that little old cabin standing on a bit of hill about a quarter-mile from the Master's brick mansion, and I see into the cabin and there's the old home-made bed with rope cords a-holding up the corn shuck bedding where on I use to sleep after putting in the day at hoeing cotton or following a slow time mule team down the corn rows 'till it got so dark the old overseer just naturally had to call it a day.

And then I see the old baker swinging in the fireplace. That cooked up the corn pone to go with the fat side meats the Master Doctor (didn't I tell you the Master was a doctor?) give us for the meals of the week day. But on a Sunday morning we always had flour bread, excepting after the War is over and then we is lucky do we get anything.

Just like yesterday—I hear the old overseer making round of the cabins every day at four, and I means in the morning, too, when the night sleep is the best, and the folkses tumbling out of the door getting ready for the fields.

All the mens dressed about the same. Just like me. Wearing the grey jeans with the blue shirt stuck in loose around the belt, brogan shoes that feels like brakes on the feet about the hot time of day when the old sun's a-grinning down like he was saying: "work, niggers, work!" And the overseer is saying the same thing, only we pays more attention to him 'cause of the whip he shakes around when the going gets kinder slow down the row.

Now I sees them getting ready for the slave auction. Many of 'em there was. The Master Doctor done owned about two hundred slaves and sometimes he sell some for to beat the bad crops.

There they'd stand on the wooden blocks, their faces greased and shiny, their arms and bodies pretty well greased too; seemed like they looked better and stronger that way, maybe some other reason, I dunno. And when the auction was over lots of the slaves would try to figger out when would the next one be and worry some afraid they'd be standing up there waiting for the buyers to punch and slap to see is they sound of limb and able to do the days work without loafing down the rows.

There's the old white preacher who tried to tell the slaves about the Lord. He had a mighty hard job sometimes, 'cause of the teaching was hard to understand. And then—then he'd just seem to be riled with anger and lay down the law of the Lord between cuss-words that all the slaves could understand. So finally I guess everybody was religionized even it was cussed into 'em right from the pulpit!

That old preacher always makes me think of haunts, 'cause every evening when I drive up the cows for milking, there's a old, old log cabin right on the way that I pass every night—and it's so haunted won't nobody pass it after the darkness covers in the daylight.

I didn't always get by 'fore then, and the sounds I hear! Like they was people inside jumping and knocking on the floor, maybe they was dancing, I dunno. But they was a light in the big room. Wasn't the moon a-shining through the windows either, 'cause sometimes I would stop at the gate and say HELLO, then out go the light and the noises would stop quick, like them haunts was a-scairt as me—and then, then I run like the old preacher's Devil is after me with all his forks.

Then along come the War. The slaves would go around from cabin to cabin telling each other about how mean and cruel was the master or the overseer, and maybe some of them would make for the North. They was the unlucky ones, 'cause lots of times they was caught.

And when the patrollers get 'em caught, they was due for a heavy licking that would last for a long time.

The slaves didn't know how to travel. The way would be marked when they'd start North, but somehow they'd get lost, 'cause they didn't know one direction from another, they was so scairt.

Just like yesterday—I remember the close of the War. Nothing exciting about it down on the plantation. Just the old overseer come around and say:

"The Yankees has whipped the Rebels and the War is over. But the Old Master don't want you to leave. He just wants you to stay right on here where at is your home. That's what the Master say is best for you to do."

That's what I do, but some of them other slaves is kinder filled up with the idea of freedom and wants to find out is it good or bad, so they leave and scatter round.

But I stays, and the Master Doctor he pays me ten dollars every month, gives me board and my sleeping place just like always, and when I gets sick there he is with the herb medicine for my ailment and I is well again.

It's long after the War before I leaves the old place. And that's when I gets married in 1885. That was my first licensed wife and we is married in Holly Springs. Her name was Josephine and we has maybe eight-ten children, I dunno.

And I is thankful they ain't none of my children born slaves and have to remember all them terrible days when we was ruled by the whip—like I remember it, just like it was yesterday.

Oklahoma Writers' Project
Ex-Slaves
[Date stamp: AUG 19 1937]

BERT LUSTER
Age 85 yrs.
Oklahoma City, Oklahoma

I'll be jest frank, I'm not for sho' when I was born, but it was in 1853. Don't know the month, but I was sho' born in 1853 in Watson County, Tennessee. You see my father was owned by Master Luster and my mother was owned by Masters Joe and Bill Asterns (father and son). I can remember when Master Astern moved from Watson County, Tennessee he brought me and my mother with him to Barnum County Seat, Texas. Master Astern owned about twelve slaves, and dey was all Astern 'cept Miriah Elmore's son Jim. He owned 'bout five or six hundred acres of ground, and de slaves raised and shucked all de corn and picked all de cotton. De whites folks lived in a big double log house and we slaves lived in log cabins. Our white folks fed us darkies! We ate nearly ever'thing dey ate. Dey ate turkey, chickens, ducks, geese, fish and we killed beef, pork, rabbits and deer. Yes, and possums too. And whenever we killed beef we tanned the hide and dere was a white man who made shoes for de white folks and us darkies. I tell you I'm not gonna lie, dem white folks was good to us darkies. We didn't have no mean overseer. Master Astern and his son jest told us niggers what to do and we did it, but 50 miles away dem niggers had a mean overseer, and dey called him "poor white trash", "old whooser", and sometime "old red neck", and he would sho' beat 'em turrible iffen dey didn't do jest like he wanted 'em to.

Seem like I can hear dem "nigger hounds" barking now. You see whenever a darky would get a permit to go off and wouldn't come back dey would put de "nigger hounds" on his trail and run dat nigger down.

De white women wove and spin our clothes. You know dey had looms, spins, and weavers. Us darkies would stay up all night sometime sep'rating cotton from the seed. When dem old darkies got sleepy dey would prop their eyes open wid straws.

Sho', we wore very fine clothes for dem days. You know dey dyed the cloth with poke berries.

We cradled de wheat on pins, caught the grain, carried it to de mill and had it ground. Sho', I ate biscuits and cornbread too. Keep telling you dat we ate.

We got de very best of care when we got sick. Don't you let nobody tell you dem white folks tried to kill out dem darkies 'cause when a darkey took sick dey would send and git de very best doctors round dat country. Dey would give us ice water when we got sick. You see we put up ice in saw dust in winter and when a slave got sick dey give him ice water, sometimes sage tea and chicken gruel. Dey wanted to keep dem darkies fat so dey could git top price for 'em. I never saw a slave sold, but my half brother's white folks let him work and buy hisself.

I was about 14, and I milked the cows, packed water, seeded cotton, churned milk up at de Big House and jest first one chore and den another. My mother cooked up at de Big House.

Dey was a lot of talk 'bout conjure but I didn't believe in it. Course dem darkies could do everything to one another, and have one another scared, but dey couldn't conjure dat overseer and stop him from beating 'em near to death. Course he didn't flog 'em till dey done sumping.

I married my woman, Nannie Wilkerson, 58 years ago. Dat was after slavery, and I love her, honest to God I does. Course in dem days we didn't buy no license, we jest got permits from old Master and jumped over a broom stick and jest got married.

I sho' did hate when de Yanks come 'cause our white folks was good to us, and jest take us right along to church with 'em. We didn't work on Sad'days or Christmas.

We raised gardens, truck patches and such for spending change.

I sho' caught hell after dem Yanks come. Befo' de war, you see de patroller rode all nite but wouldn't bother a darkey iffen he wouldn't run off. Why dem darkeys would run off I jest couldn't see.

Dose Yanks treated old master and mistress so mean. Dey took all his hams, chickens, and drove his cattle out of the pasture, but didn't bother us niggers honest. Dey drove old master Aster off'n his own plantation and we all hid in de corn field.

My mother took me to Greenville, Texas, 'cause my step-pappy was one of dem half smart niggers round dere trying to preach and de Ku Klux Klan beat him half to death.

Dere was some white folks who would take us to church wid 'em—dis dis [TR: sic] was aftah the war now—and one night we was all sitting up thar and one old woman with one leg was dah and when dem Klans shot in amongst us niggers and white folks aunt Mandy beat all of us home. Yes suh.

My first two teachers was two white men, and dem Klans shot in de hotel what dey lived in, but dey had school for us niggers jest de same. After dat, dose Klans got so bad Uncle Sam sent soljers down dere to keep peace.

After de soljers come and run de Klans out we worked hard dat fall and made good crops. 'Bout three years later I came to Indian Territory in search of educating my kids.

I landed here 46 years ago on a farm not far from now Oklahoma City. I got to be a prosperous farmer. My bale of cotton amongst 5,000 bales won the blue ribbon at Guthrie, Oklahoma, and dat bale of cotton and being a good democrat won for me a good job as a clerk on the Agriculture Board at the State Capitol. All de white folks liked me and still like me and called me "cotton king."

I have jest three chillun living. Walter is parcel post clerk here at de post office downtown. Delia Jenkins, my daughter is a housewife and Cleo Luckett, my other daughter, a common laborer.

Have been a christian 20 years. Jest got sorry for my wicked ways. I am a member of the Church of God. My wife is a member of the Church of Christ. I'm a good democrat and she is a good republican.

My fav'rite songs is: "Dark Was the Nite, and Cold the Ground" and "Couldn't Hear Nobody Pray."

I'm glad slavery is over, but I don't think dem white folks was fighting to free us niggers. God freed us. Of course, Abraham Lincoln was a pretty fine man. Don't know much about Jeff Davis. Never seen him. Yes, and Booker T. Washington. He was one of the Negro leaders. The first Negro to represent the Negroes in Washington. He was a great leader.

During slavery time never heerd of a cullud man committing 'sault on a white woman. The white and cullud all went to church together too. Niggers and white shouted alike.

I remember some of the little games we played now: "Fox in the wall", "Mollie, Mollie Bride", and "Hide and go seek."

United States. Work Projects Administration

Oklahoma Writers' Project
Ex-Slaves
[Date stamp: AUG 19 1937]

STEPHEN McCRAY
Age 88 yrs.
Oklahoma City, Okla.

I was born in Huntsville County, Alabama, right where the Scottsboro boys was in jail, in 1850.

My parents was Wash and Winnie McCray. They was the mother and father of 22 chillun. Jest five lived to be grown and the rest died at baby age. My father's mother and father was named Mandy and Peter McCray, and my mother's mother and father was Ruthie and Charlie McCray. They all had the same Master, Mister McCray, all the way thoo'.

We live in log huts and when I left home grown, I left my folks living in the same log huts. Beds was put together with ropes and called rope beds. No springs was ever heard of by white or cullud as I knows of.

All the work I ever done was pick up chips for my grandma to cook with. I was kept busy doing this all day.

The big boys went out and got rabbits, possums and fish. I would sho' lak to be in old Alabama fishing, 'cause I am a fisherman. There is sho' some pretty water in Alabama and as swift as cars run here. Water so clear and blue you can see the fish way down, and dey wouldn't bite to save your life.

Slaves had their own gardens. All got Friday and Sadday to work in garden during garden time. I liked cornbread best and I'd give a dollar to git some of the bread we had on those good old days and I ain't joking. I went in shirt tail all the time. Never had on no pants 'til I was 15 years old. No shoes, 'cept two or three winters. Never had a hat 'til I was a great big boy.

Marriage was performed by getting permission from Master and go where the woman of your choice had prepared the bed, undress and flat-footed jump a broomstick together into the bed.

Master had a brick house for hisself and the overseer. They was the only ones on the place. The overseer woke up the slaves all the way from 2 o'clock till 4 o'clock of mornings. He wasn't nothing but white trash. Nothing else in the world but that. They worked till they couldn't see how to work. I jest couldn't jedge the size of that big place, and there was a mess of slaves, not less'n three hundred.

I doesn't have no eggycation, edgecation, or ejecation, and about all I can do is spell. I jest spell till I get the pronouncements.

We had church, but iffen the white folks caught you at it, you was beat most nigh to death. We used a big pot turned down to keep our voices down. When we went to hear white preachers, he would say, "Obey your master and mistress." I am a hard shell-flint Baptist. I was baptised in Pine Bluff, Arkansas. Our baptizing song was mostly "On Jordan's Stormy Banks I Stand" and our funeral song was "Hark From The Tomb."

We had some slaves who would try to run off to the North but the white folks would catch 'em with blood hounds and beat 'em to death. Them patrollers done their work mostly at night. One night I was sleeping on cotton and the patrollers come to our house and ask for water. Happen we had plenty. They drunk a whole lot and got warm and told my father to be a good nigger and they wouldn't bother him at all. They raided till General Grant come thoo'. He sent troops out looking for Klu Klux Klanners and killed 'em jest lak killing black birds. General Grant was one of the men that caused us to set heah free today and able to talk together without being killed.

I didn't and don't believe in no conjure. No sensible person do either. We had a doctor on the place. Ever master had a doctor who waited on his slaves, but we wore asafetida or onion 'round our necks to keep off diseases. A dime was put 'round a teething baby's neck to make it tooth easy, and it sho' helped too. But today all folks done got 'bove that.

The old folks talked very little of freedom and the chillun knew nothing at all of it, and that they heard they was daresome to mention it.

Bushwhacker, nothing but poor white trash, come thoo' and killed all the little nigger chillun they could lay hands on. I was hid under the house with a big rag on my mouf many a time. Them Klu Klux after slavery sho' got enough from them soldiers to last 'em.

I was married to Kan Pry in 1884. Two chillun was born. The girl is living and the boy might be, but I don't know. My daughter works out in service.

I wish Lincoln was here now. He done more for the black face than any one in that seat. Old Jeff Davis kept slavery up till General Grant met him at the battle. Lincoln sho' snowed him under. General Grant put fire under him jest lak I'm fixing to do my pipe. Booker T. Washington was jest all right.

Every time I think of slavery and if it done the race any good, I think of the story of the coon and dog who met. The coon said to the dog "Why is it you're so fat and I am so poor, and we is both animals?" The dog said: "I lay round Master's house and let him kick me and he gives me a piece of bread right on." Said the coon to the dog: "Better then that I stay poor." Them's my sentiment. I'm lak the coon, I don't believe in 'buse.

I used to be the most wicked man in the world but a voice converted me by saying, "Friend, friend, why is you better to everybody else than you is to your self? You are sending your soul to hell." And from that day I lived like a Christian. People here don't live right and I don't lak to 'tend church. I base my Christian life on: "Believe in me, trust my work and you shall be saved, for I am God and beside me there is no other."

HANNAH McFARLAND
Age 85 yrs.
Oklahoma City, Okla.

I was born in Georgetown, South Carolina, February 29, 1853. My father was name James Gainey and my mother was name Katie Gainey. There was three chillun born to my folks doing slavery. My father was a free man, but my mother was de slave of the Sampsons, some Jews. My father was de richest Negro in South Carolina doing this time. He bought all three of we chillun for $1,000 apiece, but dem Jews jest wouldn't sell mamma. Dey was mighty sweet to her. She come home ever night and stayed with us. Doing the day a Virginian nigger woman stayed with us and she sho' was mean to we chillun. She used to beat us sumpin' terrible. You know Virginia people is mean to cullud people. My father bought her from some white folks too.

We lived in town and in a good house.

It was a good deal of confusion doing de War. I waited on the Yankees. Dey captured mamma's white people's house. Dey tried to git mamma to tell dem jest whut de white folks done done to her and all she could say was dey was good to her. Shucks, dey wouldn't sell her. She jest told them she had a free husband.

My father was a blockader. He run rafts from one place to another and sho' made a lot of money. He was drowned while doing this while I was a good size child.

Dem patrollers tied you to a whipping post iffen dey caught you out after 10 o'clock. They 'tempted to do my mother that way, but my papa sho' stopped dat. I can't say I lak white people even now, 'cause dey done done so much agin us.

I was free, but I couldn't go to school, 'cause we didn't had none. I been in Oklahoma over 40 years. Have done some traveling and could go some whar else, but I jest stays here 'cause I ain't got no desire to travel.

All we ever wore to keep off diseases was asafetida, nothing else.

I done heard more 'bout conjure in Oklahoma than I ever heerd in South Carolina. All dat stuff is in Louisiana. I didn't heah nothing 'bout the Klu Klux Klan till I come to Oklahoma neither. More devilment in Oklahoma than any place I know. South got more religion too. I jest as soon be back with the Rebels.

Bushwhackers whipped you iffen you stayed out late, and sho' nuff if dey didn't lak you.

I felt sorry for Jeff Davis when the Yankees drilled him through the streets. I saw it all. I said, "Mama, Mama, look, dey got old Jeff Davis." She said, "Be quiet, dey'll lynch you." She didn't know no better! She was a old slave nigger. I showed the Yankees where the white folks hid their silver and money and jewelry, and Mamma sho' whipped me about it too. She was no fool 'bout slavery. Slavery sho' didn't he'p us none to my belief.

I didn't care much 'bout Lincoln. It was nice of him to free us, but 'course he didn't want to.

The overseer was sho' nothing but poor white trash, the kind who didn't lak niggers and dey still don't, old devils. Don't let 'em fool you, dey don't lak a nigger a'tall.

I'm a Methodist. People ought to praise God 'cause he done done so much for dese sinners. Dey was heap more religious in my early days. I jined church in 1863. I jined the Holiness so I could git baptized and the Methodist wouldn't baptize you. After my baptism, I went back to the Methodist Church. You know my pastor, Reverend Miller, is the first Methodist preacher I ever knowed that was baptized, and that baptizes everybody.

I was married in Akin, South Carolina to Andrew Pew. We had 12 chillun. Jest one boy is my only living child today.

United States. Work Projects Administration

Oklahoma Writers' Project
Ex-Slaves

MARSHALL MACK
Age 83 yrs.
Oklahoma City, Okla.

I was born September 10, 1854. I am the second child of five. My mother was named Sylvestus Mack and my father Booker Huddleston. I do not remember my mother's master, 'cause he died before I was born. My Mistress was named Nancy Mack. She was the mother of six children, four boys and two girls. Three of dem boys went to the War and one packed and went off somewhar and nobody heard from him doing of the whole War. But soon as the War was over he come home and he never told whar he had been.

I never saw but one grown person flogged during slavery and dat was my mother. The younger son of my mistress whipped her one morning in de kitchen. His name was Jack. De slaves on Mistress' place was treated so good, all de people round and 'bout called us "Mack's Free Niggers." Dis was 14 miles northwest of Liberty, county seat of Bedford County, Virginia.

One day while de War was going on, my Mistress got a letter from her son Jim wid jest one line. Dat was "Mother: Jack's brains spattered on my gun this morning." That was all he written.

Jack Huddleston owned my father, who was his half-brother, and he was the meanest man I ever seen. He flogged my father with tobacco sticks and my mother after these floggings (which I never seen) had to pick splinters out of his back. My father had to slip off a night to come and visit us. He lived a mile and a half from our house on the south side of the Blue Ridge Mountains, and it sho' is a rocky country. He'd oversleep hisself and git up running. We would stand in our door and hear him running over them rocks til he got home. He was trying to git dere before his master called him.

It was a law among the slave-holders that if you left your master's place, you had to have a pass, for if the patroller caught you without one, he would give you 9 and 30 lashes and carry you to your master, and if he was mean, you got the same again!

On the 3-foot fireplace my mother and father cooked ash cakes and my father having to run to work, had to wash his cakes off in a spring betwixt our house and his. My mother was the cook in the Big House.

All the time we would see "nigger traders" coming through the country. I have seen men and women cuffed to 60-foot chains being took to Lynchburg, Va., to the block to be sold. Now I am talking 'bout what I know, for it would not mean one thing for me to lie. I ain't jest heard dis. My uncle John was a carpenter and always took Mistress' chillun to school in a two-horse surrey. On sech trips, the chillun learned my uncle to read and write. Dey slipped and done this, for it was a law among slave-holders that a slave not be caught wid a book.

One morning when I was on my way to de mill with

a sack of corn, I had to go down de main pike. I saw sech a fog 'til I rid close enough to see what was gwine on. I heard someone say "close up." I was told since dat it was Hood's Raid. They took every slave that could carry a gun. It was at dis time, Negroes went into de service. Lee was whipping Grant two battles to one 'til them raids, and den Grant whipped Lee two battles to one, 'cause he had Negroes in the Union Army. Dey took Negroes and all de white people's food. Dey killed chickens and picked dem on horseback. I never will forgit that time long as I live.

Ever day I had to get the mail for three families. I carried it around in a bag and each family took his'n out. I guess I was one of the first Negro mailmen.

We had church on the place and had right good meetings. Everybody went and took part in the service. We had to have passes to go off the place to the meetings.

The children wore just one garment from this time of year (spring) till the frost fell. Mistress' daughters made dese. We sure kept healthy and fat.

I will be 83 years of age September 10, 1937 and am enjoying my second eyesight. I could not see a thing hardly for some few years, but now I can read sometimes without glasses. I keep my lawn in first class shape and work all the time. I think this is 'cause I never was treated bad during slavery.

United States. Work Projects Administration

Slave Narratives

Oklahoma Writers' Project
Ex-Slaves
[Date stamp: AUG 19 1937]

ALLEN V. MANNING
Age 87
Tulsa, Okla.

I always been somewhar in the South, mostly in Texas when I was a young man, and of course us Negroes never got much of a show in court matters, but I reckon if I had of had the chance to set on a jury I would of made a mighty poor out at it.

No sir, I jest can't set in judgement on nobody, 'cause I learned when I was jest a little boy that good people and bad people—makes no difference which—jest keep on living and doing like they been taught, and I jest can't seem to blame them none for what they do iffen they been taught that way.

I was born in slavery, and I belonged to a Baptist preacher. Until I was fifteen years old I was taught that I was his own chattel-property, and he could do with me like he wanted to, but he had been taught that way too, and we both believed it. I never did hold nothing against him for being hard on Negroes sometimes, and I don't think I ever would of had any trouble even if I had of growed up and died in slavery.

The young Negroes don't know nothing 'bout that

today, and lots of them are rising up and amounting to something, and all us Negroes is proud of them. You see, it's because they been taught that they got as good a show to be something as anybody, if they tries hard.

Well, this old Negro knows one thing: they getting somewheres 'cause the young whitefolks is letting them and helping them to do it, 'cause the whitefolks has been taught the same way, and I praise God its getting to be that way, too. But it all go to show, people do like they been taught to do.

Like I say, my master was a preacher and a kind man, but he treated the Negroes jest like they treated him. He been taught that they was jest like his work hosses, and if they act like they his work hosses they git along all right. But if they don't—Oh, oh!

Like the Dixie song say, I was born "on a frosty mornin'" at the plantation in Clarke County, Mississippi, in the fall of 1850 they tell me. The old place looked the same all the time I was a child, clean up to when we pull out and leave the second year of the War.

I can shet my eyes and think about it and it seem to come right up in front of me jest like it looked. From my Pappy's cabin the Big House was off to the west, close to the big road, and most of the fields stretched off to the north. They was a big patch of woods off to the east, and no much open land between us and the Chickasawhay River. Off to the southwest a few miles was the Bucatunna Creek, and the plantation was kind of in the forks between them, a little ways east of Quitman, Mississippi.

Old Master's people been living at that place a mighty

long time, and most the houses and barns was old and been repaired time and time again, but it was a mighty pretty place. The Big House was built long, with a lot of rooms all in a row and a long porch, but it wasn't fine like a lot of the houses we seen as we passed by when we left that place to go to Louisiana.

Old Master didn't have any overseer hired, but him and his boys looked after the place and had a Negro we called the driver. We-all shore hated that old black man, but I forget his name now. That driver never was allowed to think up nothing for the slaves to do, but jest was told to make them work hard at what the master and his boys told them to do. Whitefolks had to set them at a job and then old driver would whoopity and whoopity around, and egg them and egg them until they finish up, so they can go at something else. He worked hard hisself, though, and set a mighty hard pattern for the rest to keep up with. Like I say, he been taught he didn't know how to think, so he didn't try.

Old Mistress name was Mary, and they had two daughters, Levia and Betty. Then they had three sons. The oldest was named Bill Junior, and he was plumb grown when I was a boy, but the other two, Jedson and Jim, was jest a little older then me.

Old Master didn't have but two or three single Negroes, but he had several families, and most of them was big ones. My own family was pretty good size, but three of the children was born free. Pappy's name was William and Mammy's was Lucy. My brother Joe was the oldest child and then come Adeline, Harriet, and Texana and Betty before the surrender, and then Henry, Mattie and Louisa after it.

When the War come along old Master jest didn't know what to do. He always been taught not to raise his hand up and kill nobody—no matter how come—and he jest kept holding out against all them that was talking about fighting, and he wouldn't go and fight. He been taught that it was all right to have slaves and treat them like he want to, but he been taught it was sinful to go fight and kill to keep them, and he lived up to what he been taught.

They was some Choctaw people lived 'round there, and they flew up and went right off to the War, and Mr. Trot Hand and Mr. Joe Brown that had plantations on the big road towards Quitman both went off with their grown boys right at the start, but old Master was a preacher and he jest stayed out of it. I remember one day I was sent up to the Big House and I heard old Master and some men out at the gate 'xpounding about the War. Some of the men had on soldier clothes, and they acted like they was mad. Somebody tell me later on that they was getting up a home guard because the yankees done got down in Alabama not far away, but old Master wouldn't go in with them.

Two, three days after that, it seems like, old Master come down to the quarters and say git everything bundled up and in the wagons for a long trip. The Negroes all come in and everybody pitch in to help pack up the wagons. Then old Master look around and he can't find Andy. Andy was one Negro that never did act like he been taught, and old Master's patience about wore out with him anyways.

We all know that Andy done run off again, but we didn't know where to. Leastwise all the Negroes tell old Master that. But old Master soon show us we done the work and he done the thinking! He jest goes ahead and keeps all the Negroes busy fixing up the wagons and bundling up the stuff to travel, and keeps us all in his sight all the time, and says nothing about Andy being gone.

Then that night he sends for a white man name Clements that got some blood hounds, and him and Mr. Clements takes time about staying awake and watching all the cabins to see nobody slips out of them. Everybody was afraid to stick their head out.

Early next morning we has all the wagons ready to drive right off, and old Master call Andy's brother up to him. He say, "You go down to that spring and wait, and when Andy come down to the spring to fill that cedar bucket you stole out'n the smokehouse for him to git water in you tell him to come on in here. Tell him I know he is hiding out way down the branch whar he can come up wading the water clean up to the cornfield and the melon patch, so the hounds won't git his scent, but I'm going to send the hounds down there if he don't come on in right now." Then we all knowed we was for the work and old Master was for the thinking, 'cause pretty soon Andy come on in. He'd been right whar old Master think he is.

About that time Mr. Sears come riding down the big road. He was a deacon in old Master's church, and he see us all packed up to leave and so he light at the big gate and walk up to whar we is. He ask old Master where we all lighting out for, and old Master say for Louisiana. We Negroes don't know where that is. Then old deacon say what old Master going to do with Andy, 'cause there stood Mr. Clements holding his bloodhounds and old Master had his cat-o-nine-tails in his hand.

Old Master say just watch him, and he tell Andy if he can make it to that big black gum tree down at the gate before the hounds git him he can stay right up in that tree and watch us all drive off. Then he tell Andy to git!

Poor Andy jest git hold of the bottom limbs when the blood hounds grab him and pull him down onto the ground. Time old Master and Mr. Clements git down there the hounds done tore off all Andy's clothes and bit him all over bad. He was rolling on the ground and holding his shirt up 'round his throat when Mr. Clements git there and pull the hounds off of him.

Then old Master light in on him with that cat-o-nine-tails, and I don't know how many lashes he give him, but he jest bloody all over and done fainted pretty soon. Old Deacon Sears stand it as long as he can and then he step up and grab old Master's arm and say, "Time to stop, Brother! I'm speaking in the name of Jesus!" Old Master quit then, but he still powerful mad. I don't think he believe Andy going to make that tree when he tell him that.

Then he turn on Andy's brother and give him a good beating too, and we all drive off and leave Andy setting on the ground under a tree and old Deacon standing by him. I don't know what ever become of Andy, but I reckon maybe he went and live with old Deacon Sears until he was free.

When I think back and remember it, it all seems kind of strange, but it seem like old Master and old Deacon both think the same way. They kind of understand that old Master had a right to beat his Negro all he wanted to for running off, and he had a right to set the hounds on him if he did, but he shouldn't of beat him so hard after he told him he was going let him off if he made the tree, and he ought to keep his word even if Andy was his own slave. That's the way both them white men had been taught, and that was the way they both lived.

Old Master had about five wagons on that trip down into Louisiana, but they was all full of stuff and only the old slaves and children could ride in them. I was big enough to walk most of the time, but one time I walked in the sun so long that I got sick and they put me in the wagon for most the rest of the way.

We would come to places where the people said the Yankees had been and gone, but we didn't run into any Yankees. They was most to the north of us I reckon, because we went on down to the south part of Mississippi and ferried across the big river at Baton Rouge. Then we went on to Lafayette, Louisiana, before we settled down anywhere.

All us Negroes thought that was a mighty strange place. We would hear white folks talking and we couldn't understand what they said, and lots of the Negroes talked the same way, too. It was all full of French people around Lafayette, but they had all their menfolks in the Confederate Army just the same. I seen lots of men in butternut clothes coming and going hither and yon, but they wasn't in bunches. They was mostly coming home to see their folks.

Everybody was scared all the time, and two—three times when old Master hired his Negroes out to work the man that hired them quit his place and went on west before they got the crop in. But old Master got a place and we put in a cotton crop, and I think he got some money by selling his place in Mississippi. Anyway, pretty soon after the cotton was all in he moves again and goes to a place on Simonette Lake for the winter. It aint a bit cold in that place, and we didn't have no fire 'cepting to cook, and sometimes a little charcoal fire in some crock pots that the people left on the place when they went on out to Texas.

The next spring old Master loaded up again and we struck out for Texas, when the Yankees got too close again. But Master Bill didn't go to Texas, because the Confederates done come that winter and made him go to the army. I think they took him to New Orleans, and old Master was hopping mad, but he couldn't do anything or they would make him go too, even if he was a preacher.

I think he left out of there partly because he didn't like the people at that place. They wasn't no Baptists around anywheres, they was all Catholics, and old Master didn't like them.

About that time it look like everybody in the world was going to Texas. When we would be going down the road we would have to walk along the side all the time to let the wagons go past, all loaded with folks going to Texas.

Pretty soon old Master say git the wagons loaded again, and this time we start out with some other people, going north. We go north a while and then turn west, and cross the Sabine River and go to Nachedoches, Texas. Me and my brother Joe and my sister Adeline walked nearly all the way, but my little sister Harriet and my mammy rid in a wagon. Mammy was mighty poorly, and jest when we got to the Sabine bottoms she had another baby. Old Master didn't like it 'cause it was a girl, but he named her Texana on account of where she was born and told us children to wait on Mammy good and maybe we would get a little brother next time.

But we didn't. Old Master went with a whole bunch of wagons on out to the prairie country in Coryell County and set up a farm where we just had to break the sod and didn't have to clear off much. And the next baby Mammy had the next year was a girl. We named her Betty because Mistress jest have a baby a little while before and its name was Betty.

Old Master's place was right at the corner where Coryell and McLennan and Bosque Counties come together, and we raised mostly cotton and jest a little corn for feed. He seem like he changed a lot since we left Mississippi, and seem like he paid more attention to us and looked after us better. But most the people that already live there when we git there was mighty hard on their Negroes. They was mostly hard drinkers and hard talkers, and they work and fight jest as hard as they talk, too!

One day Old Master come out from town and tell us that we all been set free, and we can go or stay jest as we wish. All of my family stay on the place and he pay us half as shares on all we make. Pretty soon the whitefolks begin to cut down on the shares, and the renters git only a third and some less, and the Negroes begin to drift out to other places, but old Master stick to the halves a year or so after that. Then he come down to a third too.

It seem like the white people can't git over us being free, and they do everything to hold us down all the time. We don't git no schools for a long time, and I never see the inside of a school. I jest grow up on hard work. And we can't go 'round where they have the voting, unless we want to ketch a whipping some night, and we have to jest keep on bowing and scraping when we are 'round white folks like we did when we was slaves. They had us down and they kept us down. But that was the way they been taught, and I don't blame them for it none, I reckon.

When I git about thirty years old I marry Betty Sadler close to Waco, and we come up to the Creek Nation forty years ago. We come to Muskogee first, and then to Tulsa about thirty seven years ago.

We had ten children but only seven are alive. Three girls and a boy live here in Tulsa and we got one boy in Muskogee and one at Frederick, Oklahoma.

I sells milk and makes my living, and I keeps so busy I don't think back on the old days much, but if anybody ask me why the Texas Negroes been kept down so much I can tell them. If they set like I did on the bank at that ferry across the Sabine, and see all that long line of covered wagons, miles and miles of them, crossing that river and going west with all they got left out of the War, it aint hard to understand.

Them whitefolks done had everything they had tore up, or had to run away from the places they lived, and they brung their Negroes out to Texas and then right away they lost them too. They always had them Negroes, and lots of them had mighty fine places back in the old states, and then they had to go out and live in sod houses and little old boxed shotguns and turn their Negroes loose. They didn't see no justice in it then, and most of them never did until they died. The folks that stayed at home and didn't straggle all over the country had their old places to live on and their old friends around them, but them Texans was different.

So I says, when they done us the way they did they was jest doing the way they was taught. I don't blame them, because anybody will do that.

Whitefolks mighty decent to me now, and I always tried to teach my children to be respectful and act like they think the whitefolks they dealing with expects them to act. That the way to git along, because some folks been taught one way and some been taught another, and folks always thinks the way they been taught.

United States. Work Projects Administration

Oklahoma Writers' Project
Ex-Slaves

BOB MAYNARD
AGE 79
23 East Choctaw
Weleetka, Oklahoma.

I was born near what is now Marlin, Texas, Falls County. My father was Robert Maynard and my mother was Chanie Maynard, both born slaves. Our Master, Gerard Branum, was a very old man and wore long white whiskers. He sho' was a fine built man, and walked straight and tall like a young man.

I was too little to do much work so my job was to carry the key basket for old Mistress. I sho' was proud of that job. The basket held the keys to the pantry, the kitchen, the linen closet, and extra keys to the rooms and smokehouse. When old Mistress started out on her rounds every morning she'd call to me to get de basket and away we'd go. I'd run errands for all the house help too, so I was kept purty busy.

The "big house" was a fine one. It was a big two-story white house made of pine lumber. There was a big porch or veranda across the front and wings on the east and west. The house faced south. There was big round white posts that went clean up to the roof and there was a big porch upstairs too. I believe the house was what you'd call colonial style. There was twelve or fifteen rooms and a big wide stairway. It was a purty place, with a yard and big trees and the house that set in a walnut and pecan grove. They was graveled walks and driveways and all along by the driveway was cedars. There was a hedge close to the house and a flower garden with purty roses, holly hocks and a lot of others I don't know the name of.

Back to the right of the house was the smokehouse, kept full of meat, and further back was the big barns. Old Master kept a spanking pair of carriage horses and several fine riding horses. He kept several pairs of mules, too, to pull the plow. He had some ox teams too.

To the left and back of the "big house" was the quarters. He owned about two thousand acres of land and three hundred slaves. He kept a white overseer and the colored overlooker was my uncle. He sho' saw that the gang worked. He saw to it that the cotton was took to the gin. They used oxen to pull the wagons full of cotton. There was two gins on the plantation. Had to have two for it was slow work to gin a bale of cotton as it was run by horse power.

Old Master raised hundreds of hogs; he raised practically all the food we et. He gave the food out to each family and they done their own cooking except during harvest. The farm hands was fed at the "big house." They was called in from the farm by a big bell.

Sunday was our only day for recreation. We went to church at our own church, and we could sing and shout jest as loud as we pleased and it didn't disturb nobody.

During the week after supper we would all set round the doors outside and sing or play music. The only musical instruments we had was a jug or big bottle, a skillet lid or frying pan that they'd hit with a stick or a bone. We had a flute too, made out of reed cane and it'd make good music. Sometimes we'd sing and dance so long and loud old Master'd have to make us stop and go to bed.

The Patrollers, Ku Kluxers or night riders come by sometimes at night to scare the niggers and make 'em behave. Sometimes the slaves would run off and the Patroller would catch 'em and have 'em whipped. I've seen that done lots of times. They was some wooden stocks (a sort of trough) and they'd put the darky in this and strap him down, take off his clothers and give him 25 to 50 licks, 'cording to what he had done.

I reckon old Master had everything his heart could wish for at this time. Old Mistress was a fine lady and she always went dressed up. She wore long trains on her skirts and I'd walk behind her and hold her train up when she made de rounds. She was awful good to me. I slept on the floor in her little boy's room, and she give me apples and candy just like she did him. Old Master gave ever chick and child good warm clothes for winter. We had store boughten shoes but the women made our clothes. For underwear we all wore 'lowers' but no shirts.

After the war started old Master took a lot of his slaves and went to Natchez, Mississippi. He thought he'd have a better chance of keeping us there I guess, and he was afraid we'd be greed [TR: freed?] and he started running with us. I remember when General Grant blowed up Vicksburg. I had a free born Uncle and Aunt who sometimes visited in the North and they'd till us how easy it was up there and it sho' made us all want to be free.

I think Abe Lincoln was next to de Lawd. He done all he could for de slaves; he set 'em free. People in the South knowed they'd lose their slaves when he was elected president. 'Fore the election he traveled all over the South and he come to our house and slept in old Mistress' bed. Didn't nobody know who he was. It was a custom to take strangers in and put them up for one night or longer, so he come to our house and he watched close. He seen how the niggers come in on Saturday and drawed four pounds of meat and a peck of meal for a week's rations. He also saw 'em whipped and sold. When he got back up north he writ old Master a letter and told him he was going to have to free his slaves, that everybody was going to have to, that the North was going to see to it. He also told him that he had visited at his house and if he doubted it to go in the room he slept in and look on the bedstead at the head and he'd see where he'd writ his name. Sho' nuff, there was his name: A. Lincoln.

Didn't none of us like Jeff Davis. We all liked Robert E. Lee, but we was glad that Grant whipped him.

When the War was over, old Master called all the darkies in and lined 'em up in a row. He told 'em they was free to go and do as they pleased. It was six months before any of us left him.

Darkies could vote in Mississippi. Fred Douglas, a colored man, came to Natchez and made political speeches for General Grant.

After the war they was a big steam boat line on the Mississippi River known as the Robert E. Lee Line. They sho' was fine boats too.

We used to have lots of Confederate money. Five cent pieces, two bit pieces, half dollar bills and half dimes. During the war old Master dug a long trench and buried all de silver ware, fine clothes, jewelry and a lot of money. I guess he dug it up, but I don't remember.

Master died three years after the War. He took it purty good, losing his niggers and all. Lots of men killed their-selves. Old Master was a good old man.

I'm getting old, I reckon. I've been married twice and am the father of 19 chillun. The oldest if 57 and my youngest is two boys, ten and twelve. I has great grand-chillun older than them two boys.

United States. Work Projects Administration

Oklahoma Writers' Project
Ex-Slaves
[Date stamp: AUG 19 1937]

JANE MONTGOMERY
Age 80 yrs.
Oklahoma City, Oklahoma

I was born March 15, 1857, in Homer, Louisiana. I claim to be 75 years old, but that's jest my way of counting. My mother was Sarah Strong and my father was Edmond Beavers. We lived in a log cabin that had jest one door. I had two sisters named Peggy and Katie. Mammy was bought from the Strong family and my pappy was bought from Beavers by Mister Eason.

We slept on wooden slabs which was jest make-shift beds. I didn't do no work in slave times 'cause I was too little. You jest had to be good and husky to work on that place. I listened and told mammy everything I heerd. I ate right side dat old white woman on the flo'. I was a little busy-body. I don't recollect eating in our quarters on Sunday and no other time.

I don't remember no possums and rabbits being on our place, 'cause when white folks killed a chicken for their selves, dey killed one for the niggers. My pappy never ate no cornbread in all his put-together. Meat was my favorite food. I never ate no dry bread without no meat.

We wore homespun clothes. My first pair of shoes was

squirrel skin. Mammy had 'em made. We wore clothes called linsey that was wool and cotton mixed.

My father was the onliest overseer. It was sho' a great big old place. My master jest seen the place on Sundays. They was jest seven Niggers on our plantation. No working late at night but we had to git up at daylight. When our day's work was done, we went to bed, but sometimes they sung. Sadday was a holiday from working on the plantation. You had Sadday to wash for yourself. We didn't do nothing on Christmas and all holidays.

Mistress never whip us and iffen master would start, mistress would git a gun and make him stop. She said, "Let ever bitch whip her own chillun." I never seen no patrollers, I jest heerd of 'em. They never come on our place. I guess they was scared to. The Klu Klux whipped niggers when so never they could catch 'em. They rid at night mostly.

I am a Baptist. I belong to Calvary Baptist Church. I was baptized in a creek. Our favorite hymn was "Dark Was the Night an' Cold the Ground." Our favorite revival hymn was "Lord I'd Come to Thee, a Sinner Undefiled." Our favorite funeral song was "Hark From the Tomb."

My family didn't believe in conjure an' all that stuff, 'though they's a heap of it was going on and still is for that matter. They had "hands" that was made up of all kinds of junk. You used 'em to make folks love you more'n they did. We used asafetida to keep off smallpox and measles. Put mole foots round a baby's neck to make him teethe easy. We used to use nine red ants tied in a sack round they neck to make 'em teethe easy and never had no trouble with 'em neither.

I think I seen a haunt once, 'cause when I looked the second time, what I seen the first time was gone.

When the War was over, mistress' son come home and he cleaned his guns on my dress tail. It sho' stunk up my dress and made me sick too. He told old mistress that niggers was free now. I went and told mammy that old Betsy's son told her the niggers was free and what did he mean. She said, "Shhhhhh!" They never did jest come out and tell us we was free. We was free in July and mammy left in September. We lived in Jordan Saline, out from Smith County. Then my mother give me to my father 'cause she was married to another man. Her and my step-father moved to Gilmore, Texas. They sent for me round 'bout Christmas and we lived on Sampers' farm.

We lived so far out, we couldn't go to school, 'though they was for us. We didn't own no land. Didn't nobody learn me to read and write.

Abe Lincoln was a good man. It was through Mr. Lincoln that God fit to free us. I don't know much 'bout Jeff Davis and don't care nothing 'bout him. Booker T. Washington built that school through God. He used to live in a cabin jest lak I done. He was sho' a great man.

I married Trole Kemp in 1883. I 'mind you they didn't marry in slavery, they jest took up. Master jest give a permit. I am the mother of 10 chillun and 5 grandchillun. Four of my chillun died young. Them what's living is doing different things sech as: writing policy, working on made work, housework, government clerk and hotel maid. One is in the pen.

United States. Work Projects Administration

Oklahoma Writers' Project
Ex-Slaves
[Date stamp: AUG 13 1937]

AMANDA OLIVER
Age 80 yrs.
Oklahoma City, Okla.

I 'membuh what my mother say—I was born November 9, 1857, in Missouri. I was 'bout eight years old, when she was sold to a master named Harrison Davis. They said he had two farms in Missouri, but when he moved to northern Texas he brought me, my mother, Uncle George, Uncle Dick and a cullud girl they said was 15 with 'im. He owned 'bout 6 acres on de edge of town near Sherman, Texas, and my mother and 'em was all de slaves he had. They said he sold off some of de folks.

We didn't have no overseers in northern Texas, but in southern Texas dey did. Dey didn't raise cotton either; but dey raised a whole lots of corn. Sometime de men would shuck corn all night long. Whenever dey was going to shuck all night de women would piece quilts while de men shuck de corn and you could hear 'em singing and shucking corn. After de cornshucking, de cullud folks would have big dances.

Master Davis lived in a big white frame house. My mother lived in the yard in a big one-room log hut with a brick chimney. De logs was "pinted" (what dey call plastered now with lime). I don't know whether young folks know much 'bout dat sort of thing now.

I slept on de floor up at de "Big House" in de white woman's room on a quilt. I'd git up in de mornings, make fires, put on de coffee, and tend to my little brother. Jest do little odd jobs sech as that.

We ate vegetables from de garden, sech as that. My favorite dish is vegetables now.

I don't remember seeing any slaves sold. My mother said dey sold 'em on de block in Kentucky where she was raised.

I don't remembuh when de War broke out, but I remembuh seeing the soldiers with de blue uniforms on. I was afraid of 'em.

Old mistress didn't tell us when he was free, but another white woman told my mother and I remembuh. One day old mistress told my mother to git to that wheel and git to work, and my mother said, "I ain't gwineter, I'm jest as free as you air." So dat very day my mother packed up all our belongings and moved us to town, Sherman, Texas. She worked awful hard, doing day work for 50¢ a day, and sometimes she'd work for food, clothes or whatever she could git.

I don't believe in conjuring though I heard lotta talk 'bout it. Sometimes I have pains and aches in my hands, feel like sometime dat somebody puts dey hands on me, but I think jest de way my nerves is.

I can't say much 'bout Abe Lincoln. He was a republican in favor of de cullud folk being free. Jeff Davis? Yeah, the boys usta sing a song 'bout 'im:

> Lincoln rides a fine hoss,
>
> Jeff Davis rides a mule,
>
> Lincoln is de President,
>
> Jeff Davis is de fool.

Booker T. Washington—I guess he is a right good man. He's for the cullud people I guess.

I been a Christian thirty some odd years. I've been here some thirty odd years. Had to come when my husband did. He died in 1902. We married in 18—I've forgot, but we went to de preacher and got married. We did more than jump over de broom stick.

In those days we went to church with de white folks. Dey had church at eleven and the cullud folks at three, but all of us had white preachers. Our church is standing right there now, at least it was de last time I was there.

I don't have a favorite song, theys so many good ones, but I like, "Bound for the Promised Land." I'm a Baptist, my mother was a Baptist, and her white folks was Baptist.

I have two daughters, Julia Goodwin and Bertha Frazier, and four grandchildren, both of 'ems been separated. Dey do housework.

United States. Work Projects Administration

Oklahoma Writers' Project
Ex-Slaves

SALOMON OLIVER
Age 78 yrs.
Tulsa, Oklahoma.

John A. Miller owned the finest plantation in Washington County, Mississippi, about 12-mile east of Greenville. I was born on this 20,000-acre plantation November 17, 1859, being one of about four hundred slave children on the place.

About three hundred negro families living in box-type cabins made it seem like a small town. Built in rows, the cabins were kept whitewashed, neat and orderly, for the Master was strict about such things. Several large barns and storage buildings were scattered around the plantation. Also, two cotton gins and two old fashioned presses, operated by horses and mules, made Miller's plantation one of the best equipped in Mississippi.

Master John was quite a character. The big plantation didn't occupy all his time. He owned a bank in Vicksburg and another in New Orleans, and only came to the plantation two or three times a year for a week or two visit.

Things happened around there mighty quick when the Master showed up. If the slaves were not being treated right—out go the white overseer. Fired! The Master was a good man and tried to hire good boss men. Master

John was bad after the slave women. A yellow child show up every once in a while. Those kind always got special privileges because the Master said he didn't want his children whipped like the rest of them slaves.

My own Mammy, Mary, was the Master's own daughter! She married Salomon Oliver (who took the name of Oliver after the War), and the Master told all the slave drivers to leave her alone and not whip her. This made the overseers jealous of her and caused trouble. John Santhers was one of the white overseers who treated her bad, and after I was born and got strong enough (I was a weakling for three-four years after birth), to do light chores he would whip me just for the fun of it. It was fun for him but not for me. I hoped to whip him when I grew up. That is the one thing I won't ever forget. He died about the end of the War so that's one thing I won't ever get to do.

My mother was high-tempered and she knew about the Master's orders not to whip her. I guess sometimes she took advantage and tried to do things that maybe wasn't right. But it did her no good and one of the white men flogged her to death. She died with scars on her back!

Father use to preach to the slaves when a crowd of them could slip off into the woods. I don't remember much about the religious things, only just what Daddy told me when I was older. He was caught several times slipping off to the woods and because he was the preacher I guess they layed on the lash a little harder trying to make him give up preaching.

Ration day was Saturday. Each person was given a peck of corn meal, four pounds of wheat flour, four pounds of pork meat, quart of molasses, one pound of sugar, the same of coffee and a plug of tobacco. Potatoes and vegetables came from the family garden and each slave family was required to cultivate a separate garden.

During the Civil War a battle was fought near the Miller plantation. The Yankees under General Grant came through the country. They burned 2,000 bales of Miller cotton. When the Yankee wagons crossed Bayou Creek the bridge gave way and quite a number of soldiers and horses were seriously injured.

For many years after the War folks would find bullets in the ground. Some of the bullets were 'twins' fastened together with a chain.

Master Miller settled my father upon a piece of land after the War and we stayed on it several years, doing well.

I moved to Muskogee in 1902, coming on to Tulsa in 1907, the same year Oklahoma was made a state. My six wives are all dead,—Liza, Lizzie, Ellen, Lula, Elizabeth and Henrietta. Six children, too. George, Anna, Salomon, Nelson, Garfield, Cosmos—all good children. They remember the Tulsa riot and don't aim ever to come back to Oklahoma.

When the riot started in 1922 (I think it was), I had a place on the corner of Pine and Owasso Streets. Two hundred of my people gathered at my place, because I was so well known everybody figured we wouldn't be molested. I was wrong. Two of my horses was shot and killed. Two of my boys, Salomon and Nelson, was wounded, one in the hip, the other in the shoulder. They wasn't bad and got well alright. Some of my people wasn't so lucky. The dead wagon hauled them away!

White men came into the negro district and gathered up the homeless. The houses were most all burned. No place to go except to the camps where armed whites kept everybody quiet. They took my clothes and all my money—$298.00—and the police couldn't do nothing about my loss when I reported it to them.

That was a terrible time, but we people are better off today that any time during the days of slavery. We have some privileges and they are worth more than all the money in the world!

Oklahoma Writers' Project
Ex-Slaves

PHYLLIS PETITE
Age 83 yrs.
Fort Gibson, Okla.

I was born in Rusk County, Texas, on a plantation about eight miles east of Belleview. There wasn't no town where I was born, but they had a church.

My mammy and pappy belonged to a part Cherokee named W. P. Thompson when I was born. He had kinfolks in the Cherokee Nation, and we all moved up here to a place on Fourteen-Mile Creek close to where Hulbert now is, 'way before I was big enough to remember anything. Then, so I been told, old master Thompson sell my pappy and mammy and one of my baby brothers and me back to one of his neighbors in Texas name of John Harnage.

Mammy's name was Letitia Thompson and pappy's was Riley Thompson. My little brother was named Johnson Thompson, but I had another brother sold to a Vann and he always call hisself Harry Vann. His Cherokee master lived on the Arkansas river close to Webber's Falls and I never did know him until we was both grown. My only sister was Patsy and she was borned after slavery and died at Wagoner, Oklahoma.

I can just remember when Master John Harnage took

us to Texas. We went in a covered wagon with oxen and camped out all along the way. Mammy done the cooking in big wash kettles and pappy done the driving of the oxen. I would set in a wagon and listen to him pop his whip and holler.

Master John took us to his plantation and it was a big one, too. You could look from the field up to the Big House and any grown body in the yard look like a little body, it was so far away.

We negroes lived in quarters not far from the Big House and ours was a single log house with a stick and dirt chimney. We cooked over the hot coals in the fireplace.

I just played around until I was about six years old I reckon, and then they put me up at the Big House with my mammy to work. She done all the cording and spinning and weaving, and I done a whole lot of sweeping and minding the baby. The baby was only about six months old I reckon. I used to stand by the cradle and rock it all day, and when I quit I would go to sleep right by the cradle sometimes before mammy would come and get me.

The Big House had great big rooms in front, and they was fixed up nice, too. I remember when old Mistress Harnage tried me out sweeping up the front rooms. They had two or three great big pictures of some old people hanging on the wall. They was full blood Indians it look like, and I was sure scared of them pictures! I would go here and there and every which-a-way, and anywheres I go them big pictures always looking straight at me and watching me sweep! I kept my eyes right on them so I could run if they moved, and old Mistress take me back to the kitchen and say I can't sweep because I miss all the dirt.

We always have good eating, like turnip greens cooked in a kettle with hog skins and crackling grease, and skinned corn, and rabbit or possum stew. I liked big fish tolerable well too, but I was afraid of the bones in the little ones.

That skinned corn aint like the boiled hominy we have today. To make it you boil some wood ashes, or have some drip lye from the hopper to put in the hot water. Let the corn boil in the lye water until the skin drops off and the eyes drop out and then wash that corn in fresh water about a dozen times, or just keep carrying water from the spring until you are wore out, like I did. Then you put the corn in a crock and set it in the spring, and you got good skinned corn as long as it last, all ready to warm up a little batch at a time.

Master had a big, long log kitchen setting away from the house, and we set a big table for the family first, and when they was gone we negroes at the house eat at that table too, but we don't use the china dishes.

The negro cook was Tilda Chisholm. She and my mammy didn't do no out-work. Aunt Tilda sure could make them corn-dodgers. Us children would catch her eating her dinner first out of the kettles and when we say something she say: "Go on child, I jest tasting that dinner."

In the summer we had cotton homespun clothes, and in winter it had wool mixed in. They was dyed with copperas and wild indigo.

My brother, Johnson Thompson, would get up behind old Master Harnage on his horse and go with him to hunt squirrels so they would go 'round on Master's side so's he could shoot them. Master's old mare was named "Old Willow", and she knowed when to stop and stand real still so he could shoot.

His children was just all over the place! He had two houses full of them! I only remember Bell, Ida, Maley, Mary and Will, but they was plenty more I don't remember.

That old horn blowed 'way before daylight, and all the field negroes had to be out in the row by the time of sun up. House negroes got up too, because old Master always up to see everybody get out to work.

Old Master Harnage bought and sold slaves most all the time, and some of the new negroes always acted up and needed a licking. The worst ones got beat up good, too! They didn't have no jail to put slaves in because when the Masters got done licking them they didn't need no jail.

My husband was George Petite. He tell me his mammy was sold away from him when he was a little boy. He looked down a long lane after her just as long as he could see her, and cried after her. He went down to the big road and set down by his mammy's barefooted tracks in the sand and set there until it got dark, and then he come on back to the quarters.

I just saw one slave try to get away right in hand. They caught him with bloodhounds and brung him back in. The hounds had nearly tore him up, and he was sick a long time. I don't remember his name, but he wasn't one of the old regular negroes.

In Texas we had a church where we could go. I think it was a white church and they just let the negroes have it when they got a preacher sometimes. My mammy took me sometimes, and she loved to sing them salvation songs.

We used to carry news from one plantation to the other I reckon, 'cause mammy would tell about things going on some other plantation and I know she never been there.

Christmas morning we always got some brown sugar candy or some molasses to pull, and we children was up bright and early to get that 'lasses pull, I tell you! And in the winter we played skeeting on the ice when the water froze over. No, I don't mean skating. That's when you got iron skates, and we didn't have them things. We just get a running start and jump on the ice and skeet as far as we could go, and then run some more.

I nearly busted my head open, and brother Johnson said: "Try it again," but after that I was scared to skeet any more.

Mammy say we was down in Texas to get away from the War, but I didn't see any war and any soldiers. But one day old Master stay after he eat breakfast and when us negroes come in to eat he say: "After today I ain't your master any more. You all as free as I am." We just stand and look and don't know what to say about it.

After while pappy got a wagon and some oxen to drive for a white man who was coming to the Cherokee Nation because he had folks here. His name was Dave Mounts and he had a boy named John.

We come with them and stopped at Fort Gibson where my own grand mammy was cooking for the soldiers at the garrison. Her name was Phyllis Brewer and I was named after her. She had a good Cherokee master. My mammy was born on his place.

We stayed with her about a week and then we moved out on Four Mile Creek to live. She died on Fourteen-Mile Creek about a year later.

When we first went to Four Mile Creek I seen negro women chopping wood and asked them who they work for and I found out they didn't know they was free yet.

After a while my pappy and mammy both died, and I was took care of by my aunt Elsie Vann. She took my brother Johnson too, but I don't know who took Harry Vann.

I was married to George Petite, and I had on a white underdress and black high-top shoes, and a large cream colored hat, and on top of all I had a blue wool dress with tassels all around the bottom of it. That dress was for me to eat the terrible supper in. That what we called the wedding supper because we eat too much of it. Just danced all night, too! I was at Mandy Foster's house in Fort Gibson, and the preacher was Reverend Barrows, I had that dress a long time, but its gone now. I still got the little sun bonnet I wore to church in Texas.

We had six children, but all are dead but George, Tish, and Annie now.

Yes, they tell me Abraham Lincoln set me free, and I love to look at his picture on the wall in the school house at Four Mile branch where they have church. My grand mammy kind of help start that church, and I think everybody ought to belong to some church.

I want to say again my Master Harnage was Indian, but he was a good man and mighty good to us slaves, and you can see I am more than six feet high, and they say I weighs over a hundred and sixty, even if my hair is snow white.

United States. Work Projects Administration

Oklahoma Writers' Project
Ex-Slaves

MATILDA POE
Age 80 yrs.
McAlester, Okla.

I was born in Indian Territory on de plantation of Isaac Love. He was old Master, and Henry Love was young Master. Isaac Love was a full blood Chickasaw Indian but his wife was a white woman.

Old Master was sure good to his slaves. The young niggers never done no heavy work till dey was fully grown. Dey would carry water to de men in de field and do other light jobs 'round de place.

De Big House set way back from de road 'bout a quarter of a mile. It was a two-story log house, and the rooms was awful big and they was purty furniture in it. The furniture in de parlor was red plush and I loved to slip in and rub my hand over it, it was so soft like. The house was made of square logs and de cracks was filled out even with the edges of de logs. It was white washed and my but it was purty. They was a long gallery clean across de front of de house and big posts to support de roof. Back a ways from de house was de kitchen and nearby was de smokehouse. Old Master kept it well filled with meat, lard and molasses all de time. He seen to it that we always had plenty to eat. The old women done all de cooking in big iron pots that hung over the fire. De slaves was all served together.

The slave quarters was about two hundred yards back of de Big House. Our furniture was made of oak 'cepting de chairs, and dey was made out of hackberry. I still have a chair dat belonged to my mammy.

The boys didn't wear no britches in de summer time. Dey just wore long shirts. De girls wore homespun dresses, either blue or gray.

Old Master never hired no overseer for his slaves, but he looked after 'em hisself. He punished dem hisself too. He had to go away one time and he hired a white man to oversee while he was gone. The only orders he left was to keep dem busy. Granny Lucy was awful old but he made her go to the field. She couldn't hold out to work so he ups and whips her. He beat her scandalous. He cut her back so bad she couldn't wear her dress. Old Master come home and my, he was mad when he see Granny Lucy. He told de man to leave and iffen he ever set foot on his ground again he's shoot him, sure!

Old Master had a big plantation and a hundred or more slaves. Dey always got up at daylight and de men went out and fed de horses. When de bell rang dey was ready to eat. After breakfast dey took de teams and went out to plow. Dey come in 'bout half past 'leven and at twelve de bell rung agin. Dey eat their dinner and back to plowing dey went. 'Bout five o'clock dey come in again, and den they'd talk, sing and jig dance till bedtime.

Old Master never punished his niggers 'cepting dey was sassy or lazy. He never sold his slaves neither. A owner once sold several babies to traders. Dey stopped at our plantation to stay awhile. My mammy and de other women had to take care of dem babies for two days, and teach dem to nuss a bottle or drink from a glass. Dat was awful, dem little children crying for they mothers. Sometimes dey sold de mothers away from they husbands and children.

Master wasn't a believer in church but he let us have church. My we'd have happy times singing an shouting. They'd have church when dey had a preacher and prayer meeting when dey didn't.

Slaves didn't leave de plantation much on 'count of de Patrollers. De patroller was low white trash what jest wanted a excuse to shoot niggers. I don't think I ever saw one but I heard lots of 'em.

I don't believe in luck charms and things of the such. Iffen you is in trouble, there ain't nothing gonna save you but de Good Lawd. I heard of folks keeping all kind of things for good luck charms. When I was a child different people gave me buttons to string and we called them our charm string and wore 'em round our necks. If we was mean dey would tell us "Old Raw Head and Bloody Bones" would git us. Grand mammy told us ghost stories after supper, but I don't remember any of dem.

I never did know I was a slave, 'cause I couldn't tell I wasn't free. I always had a good time, didn't have to work much, and allus had something to eat and wear and that was better than it is with me now.

When de War was over old Master told us we was free. Mammy she say, "Well, I'm heading for Texas." I went out and old Master ask me to bring him a coal of fire to light his pipe. I went after it and mammy left pretty soon. My pappy wouldn't leave old Master right then but old Master told us we was free to go where we pleased, so me an' pappy left and went to Texas where my mammy was. We never saw old Master any more. We stayed a while in Texas and then come back to de Indian Territory.

Abe Lincoln was a good man, everybody liked him. See, I've got his picture. Jeff Davis was a good man too, he just made a mistake. I like Mr. Roosevelt, too.

Oklahoma Writers' Project
Ex-Slaves

HENRY F. PYLES
Age 81 yrs.
Tulsa, Okla.

Little pinch o' pepper——

Little bunch o' wool——

Mumbledy—Mumbledy——

Two, three Pammy Christy beans——

Little piece o' rusty iron——

Mumbledy—Mumbledy——

Wrop it in a rag and tie it wid hair,

Two fum a hoss an' one fum a mare——

Mumbledy, Mumbledy, Mumbledy——

Wet it in whiskey

Boughten wid silver;

Dat make you wash so hard your sweat pop out,

And he come to pass, sho'!

That's how the niggers say old Bab Russ used to make the hoodoo "hands" he made for the young bucks and wenches, but I don't know, 'cause I was too trusting to look inside de one he make for me, and anyways I lose it, and it no good nohow!

Old Bab Russ live about two mile from me, and I went to him one night at midnight and ask him to make me de hand. I was a young strapper about sixteen years old, and thinking about wenches pretty hard and wanting something to help me out wid the one I liked best.

Old Bab Russ charge me four bits for dat hand, and I had to give four bits more for a pint of whiskey to wet it wid, and it wasn't no good nohow!

Course dat was five-six years after de War. I wasn't yet quite eleven when de War close. Most all the niggers was farming on de shares and whole lots of them was still working for their old Master yet. Old Bab come in there from deep South Carolina two-three years befo', and live all by hisself. De gal I was worrying about had come wid her old pappy and mammy to pick cotton on de place, and dey was staying in one of de cabins in the "settlement", but dey didn't live there all de time.

I don't know whether I believed in conjure much or not in dem days, but anyways I tried it that once and it stirred up sech a rumpus everybody called me "Hand" after that until after I was married and had a pack of children.

Old Bab Russ was coal black, and he could talk African or some other unknown tongue, and all the young bucks and wenches was mortal 'fraid of him!

Well sir, I took dat hand he made for me and set out to try it on dat gal. She never had give me a friendly look even, and when I would speak to her polite she just hang her head and say nothing!

We was all picking cotton, and I come along up behind

her and decided to use my "Hand." I had bought me a pint of whiskey to wet the hand wid, but I was scared to take out of my pocket and let the other niggers see it, so I jest set down in de cotton row and taken a big mouthful. I figgered to hold it in my mouth until I catched up wid that gal and then blow it on the hand jest before I tech her on the arm and speak to her.

Well, I take me a big mouthful, but it was so hot and scaldy it jest slip right on down my throat! Then I had to take another, and when I was gitting up I kind of stumbled and it slip down, too!

Then I see all the others get way on ahead, and I took another big mouthful—the last in the bottle—and drap the bottle under a big stalk and start picking fast and holding the whiskey in my mouth this time. I missed about half the cotton I guess, but at last I catch up with de rest and git close up behind dat purty gal. Then I started to speak to her, but forgot I had de whiskey in mouth and I lost most of it down my neck and all over my chin, and then I strangled a little on the rest, so as when I went to squirt it on de "hand" I didn't have nothing left to squirt but a little spit.

That make me a little nervous right then, but anyways I step up behind dat gal and lay my hand on her arm and speak polite and start to say something, but I finish up what I start to say laying on my neck with my nose shoved up under a cotton stalk about four rows away!

De way that gal lam me across the head was a caution! We was in new ground, and she jest pick up a piece of old root and whopped me right in de neck with it!

That raise sech a laugh on me that I never say nothing to her for three-four days, but after while I gets myself wound up to go see her at her home. I didn't know how she going to act, but I jest took my foot in my hand and went on over.

Her old pappy and mammy was asleep in the back of the room on a pallet, and we set in front of the fireplace on our hunches and jest looked at the fire and punched it up a little. It wasn't cold, but de malary fog was thick all through de bottoms.

After while I could smell the whiskey soaked up in dat "hand" I had in my pocket, and I was scared she could smell it too. So I jest reached in my pocket and teched it for luck, then I reached over and teched her arm. She jerked it back so quick she knocked over the churn and spilled buttermilk all over de floor! Dat make de old folks mad, and dey grumble and holler and told de gal, "Send dat black rapscallion on out of here!" But I didn't go.

I kept on moving over closer and she kept on backing away, but after while I reach over and put my hand on her knee. All I was going to do was say something but I shore forgot what it was the next minnit, 'cause she jest whinnied lak a scared hoss and give me a big push. I was settin straddledy-legged on the floor, and that push sent me on my head in the hot ashes in the fur corner of the chimney.

Then the old man jump up and make for me and I make for the door! It was dark, all 'cepting the light from the chimney, and I fumble all up and down the door jamb before I find de latch pin. The old man shorely git me if he hadn't stumble over the eating table and whop his hand right down in de dish of fresh made butter. That make him so mad he jest stand and holler and cuss.

I git de pin loose and jerk de door open so quick and hard I knock de powder gourd down what was hanging over it, and my feet git caught in the string. The stopper gits knocked out, and when I untangle it from my feet and throw it back in de house it fall in the fireplace.

I was running all de time, but I hear dat gourd go "Blammity Blam!" and then all de yelling, but I didn't go back to see how dey git the hot coals all put out what was scattered all over de cabin!

I done drap dat "hand" and I never did see it again. Never did see the gal but two-three times after that, and we never mention about dat night. Her old pappy was too old to work, so I never did see him neither, but she must of told about it because all the young bucks called me "Hand" after that for a long time.

Old Bab kept on trying to work his conjure with the old niggers, but the young ones didn't pay him much mind cause they was hearing about the Gospel and de Lord Jesus Christ. We was all free then, and we could go and come without a pass, and they was always some kind of church meeting going on close enough to go to. Our niggers never did hear about de Lord Jesus until after we was free, but lots of niggers on de other plantations had masters that told them all about him, and some of dem niggers was pretty good at preaching. Then de good church people in de North was sending white preachers amongst us all the time too. Most of de young niggers was Christians by that time.

One day old Bab was hoeing in a field and got in a squabble about something with a young gal name Polly, same name as his wife. After while he git so mad he reach up with his fingers and wet them on his tongue and point straight up and say, "Now you got a trick on you! Dere's a heavy trick on you now! Iffen you don't change your mind you going pass on before de sun go down!"

All de young niggers looked like they want to giggle but afraid to, and the old ones start begging old Bab to take the trick off, but that Polly git her dander up and take in after him with a hoe!

She knocked him down, and he jest laid there kicking his feet in the air and trying to keep her from hitting him in the head!

Well, that kind of broke up Bab's charm, so he set out to be a preacher. The Northern whites was paying some of the Negro preachers, so he tried to be one too. He didn't know nothing about de Bible but to shout loud, so the preacher board at Red Mound never would give him a paper to preach. Then he had to go back to tricking and trancing again.

One day he come in at dinner and told his wife to git him something to eat. She told him they aint nothing but some buttermilk, and he says give me some of that. He hollered around till she fix him a big ash cake and he ate that and she made him another and he ate that. Then he drunk the rest of de gallon of buttermilk and went out and laid down on a tobacco scaffold in de yard and nearly died.

After while he jest stiffened out and looked like he

was dead, and nobody couldn't wake him up. 'Bout forty niggers gathered round and tried but it done no good. Old mammy Polly got scared and sent after the white judge, old Squire Wilson, and he tried, and then the white preacher Reverend Dennison tried and old man Gorman tried. He was a infidel, but that didn't do no good.

By that time it was getting dark, and every nigger in a square mile was there, looking on and acting scared. Me and my partner who was a little bit cripple but mighty smart come up to see what all the rumpus was about, and we was jest the age to do anything.

He whispered to me to let him start it off and then me finish it while he got a head running start. I ast him what he talking about.

Then he fooled round the house and got a little ball of cotton and soaked it in kerosene from a lamp. It was a brass lamp with a hole and a stopper in the side of the bowl. Wonder he didn't burn his fool head off! Then he sidle up close and stuck dat cotton 'tween old Bab's toes. Old Bab had the biggest feet I ever see, too.

'Bout that time I lit a corn shuck in de lamp and run out in de yard and stuck it to de cotton and jest kept right on running!

My partner had a big start but I catch up wid him and we lay down in de bresh and listened to everybody hollering and old Bab hollering louder than anybody. Old Bab moved away after that.

All that foolishness happen after the War, but before de War while I was a little boy they wasn't much foolishness went on I warrant you.

I was born on de 15th of August in 1856, and belonged to Mister Addison Pyles. He lived in town, in Jackson, Tennessee, and was a old man when de War broke. He had a nephew named Irvin T. Pyles he raised from a baby, and Mister Irvin kept a store at de corner of de roads at our plantation. The plantation covered about 300 or 400 acres I reckon, and they had about 25 slaves counting de children.

The plantation was about 9 miles north of Red Mound, close to Lexington, Tennessee, and about a mile and a half from Parker's Crossroads where they had a big battle in de War.

They wasn't no white overseer on the place, except Mister Irvin, and he stayed in de store or in town and didn't bother about the farm work. We had a Negro overlooker who was my stepdaddy. His name was Jordan, and he run away wid de Yankees about de middle of de War and was in a Negro Yankee regiment. After he left we jest worked on as usual because we was afraid not to. Several of de men got away like that but he was de only one that got in de army.

They was a big house in de middle of de place and a settlement of Negro cabins behind and around it. We called it de settlement, but on other plantations where white folks lived there too they called it de quarters. We always kept this big house clean and ready, and sometimes de white folks come out from town and stay a few days and hunt and fish and look over de crops.

We all worked at farm work. Cotton and corn and tobacco mostly. We all laid off Sunday after noontime, but we didn't have no church nor preaching and we didn't hear anything 'bout Jesus much until after de emancipation.

I reckon old Master wasn't very religious, 'cause he never tell us 'bout the Holy Word. He jest said to behave ourselves and tell him when we wanted to marry, and not have but one wife.

We had little garden patches and cotton patches we could work on Sunday and what de stuff brung we could sell and keep the money. Old Master let us have what we made that way on Sunday. We could buy ribbons and hand soap and coal oil and such at de store. Master Irvin was always honest 'bout continuing de money, too.

We didn't have no carders and spinners nor no weavers on de plantation. They cost too much money to buy just for 25 niggers, and they cost a lot more than field niggers. So we got our clothes sent out to us from in town, and sometimes we was give cloth from de store to make our clothes out of.

We got de shorts and seconds from de mill when we had wheat ground, and so we had good wheat bread as well as corn pone, and de big smokehouse was on de place and we had all de meat we wanted to eat. Old Master sent out after de meat he wanted every day or so and we kept him in garden sass that way too.

We was right between de forks of Big Beaver and Little Beaver and we could go fishing without getting far off de place. We couldn't go far away without a pass, though, and they wasn't nobody on the place to write us a pass, so we couldn't go to meeting and dances and sech.

But de niggers on de other plantations could get

passes to come to our place, and so we had parties sometimes there at our place. We always had them on Sundays, 'cause in the evening we would be too tired to work if we set up, and the other masters wouldn't give passes to their niggers to come over in de evening.

We had a white doctor lived at de next plantation, and old Master had a contract with old Dr. Brown to look after us. He had a beard as long as your arm. He come for all kinds of misery except bornings. Then we had a midwife who was a white woman lived down below us. They was poor people renting or living on war land. Nearly all de white folks in that country been there a long time and their old people got de land from de government for fighting in the Revolutionary War. Most all was from North Carolina—way back. I think old Master's pappy was from dere in de first place.

Old Master had two sons named Newton and Willis. Newton was in de War and was killed, and Willis went to war later and was sick a long time and come home early. Old Master was too old to go.

There was two daughters, Mary, de oldest, married a Holmes, and Miss Laura never did marry I don't think.

My mammy's name was Jane, and she was born on de 10th day of May in 1836. I know de dates 'cause old Master kept his book on all his niggers de same as on his own family. Mammy was the nurse of all de children but I think old Master sent her to de plantation about the time I was born. I don't think I had any pappy. I think I was jest one of them things that happened sometimes in slavery days, but I know old Master didn't have nothing to do with it—I'm too black.

Mammy married a man named Jordan when I was a little baby. He was the overlooker and went off to de Yankees, when dey come for foraging through dat country de first time.

He served in de Negro regiment in de battle at Fort Piller and a lot of Sesesh was killed in dat battle, so when de War was over and Jordan come back home he was a changed nigger and all de whites and a lot of de niggers hated him. All 'cepting old Master, and he never said a word out of de way to him. Jest told him to come on and work on de place as long as he wanted to.

But Jordan had a hard time, and he brung it on his self I reckon.

'Bout de first thing, he went down to Wildersville Schoolhouse, about a mile from Wildersville, to a nigger and carpet bagger convention and took me and mammy along. That was de first picnic and de first brass band I ever see. De band men was all white men and they still had on their blue soldier clothes.

Lots of de niggers there had been in de Union army too, and they had on parts of their army clothes. They took them out from under their coats and their wagon seats an put them on for de picnic.

There was a saloon over in Wildersville, and a lot of them went over there but they was scared to go in, most of them. But a colored delegate named Taylor and my pappy went in and ordered a drink. The bartender didn't pay them no mind.

Then a white man named Billy Britt walked up and throwed a glass of whiskey in Jordan's face and cussed him for being in de Yankee army. Then a white man from the North named Pearson took up the fight and him and Jordan jumped on Billy Britt, but de crowd stopped them and told pappy to git on back to whar he come from.

He got elected a delegate at de convention and went on down to Nashville and helped nominate Brownlow for governor. Then he couldn't come back home for a while, but finally he did.

Old Master was uneasy about de way things was going on, and he come out to de farm and stayed in de big house a while.

One day in broad daylight he was on de gallery and down de road come 'bout 20 bushwhackers in Sesesh clothes on horses and rid up to de gate. Old Master knowed all of them, and Captain Clay Taylor, who had been de master of de nigger delegate, was at the head of them.

They had Jordan Pyles tied with a rope and walked along on de ground betwixt two horses.

"Whar you taking my nigger?", Old Master say. He run down off de gallery and out in de road.

"He ain't your nigger no more—you know that", old Captain Taylor holler back.

"He jest as much my nigger as that Taylor nigger was your nigger, and you ain't laid hands on him! Now you jest have pity on my nigger!"

"Your nigger Jordan been in de Yankee army, and he was in de battle at Fort Piller and help kill our white folks, and you know it!" Old Captain Taylor say, and argue on like that, but old Master jest take hold his bridle and shake his head.

"No, Clay", he say, "that boy maybe didn't kill Confederates, but you and him both know my two boys killed plenty Yankees, and you forgot I lost one of my boys in de War. Ain't that enough to pay for letting my nigger alone?"

And old Captain Taylor give the word to turn Jordan loose, and they rid on down de road.

That's one reason my stepdaddy never did leave old Master's place, and I stayed on dere till I was grown and had children.

The Yankees come through past our place three-four times, and one time they had a big battle jest a mile and a half away at Parker's Crossroads.

I was in de field hoeing, and I remember I hadn't watered the cows we had hid way down in de woods, so I started down to water them when I first heard de shooting.

We had de stock hid down in de woods and all de corn and stuff hid too, 'cause the Yankees and the Sesesh had been riding through quite a lot, and either one take anything they needed iffen they found it.

First I hear something way off say "Br-r-rump!" Then again, and again. Then something sound like popcorn beginning to pop real slow. Then it git faster and I start for de settlement and de big house.

All Master's folks was staying at de big house then, and couldn't git back to town 'count of de soldiers, so they all put on they good clothes, with de hoop skirts and little sunshades and the lace pantaloons and got in the buggy to go see de battle!

They rid off and it wasn't long till all the niggers was following behind. We all got to a hill 'bout a half a mile from the crossroads and stopped when we couldn't see nothing but thick smoke all over de whole place.

We could see men on horses come in and out of de smoke, going this way and that way, and then some Yankees on horses broke through de woods right close to us and scattered off down through de field. One of de white officers rid up close and yelled at us and took off his hat, but I couldn't hear nothing he said.

Then he rid on and catch up with his men. They had stopped and was turning off to one side. He looked back and waved his hat again for us to git away from that, and jest then he clapped his hand to his belly and fell off his hoss.

Our white folks turned their buggy round and made it for home and no mistake! The niggers wasn't fur behind neither!

They fit on back toward our plantation, and some of the fighting was inside it at one corner. For three-four days after that they was burying soldiers 'round there, and some of de graves was on our old place.

Long time afterwards people come and moved all them to other graveyards at Shiloh and Corinth and other places. They was about a hundred killed all around there.

After de War I married Molly Timberlake and we lived

on there 'til 1902, when we come to Indian Territory at Haskell. They wasn't no Haskell there then, and I helped to build dat town, doing carpenter work and the like.

We had two boys, Bill and Jim Dick, and eight daughters, Effie, Ida, Etta, Eva, Jessie, Tommie, Bennie and Timmie. Her real name is Timberlake after her mammy. They all went to school and graduated in the high schools.

My wife has been dead about ten years.

United States. Work Projects Administration

Oklahoma Writers' Project
Ex-Slaves
10-13-37
[Date stamp: NOV 5 1937]

CHANEY RICHARDSON
Age 90 years
Fort Gibson, Okla.

I was born in the old Caney settlement southeast of Tahlequah on the banks of Caney Creek. Off to the north we could see the big old ridge of Sugar Mountain when the sun shine on him first thing in the morning when we all getting up.

I didn't know nothing else but some kind of war until I was a grown woman, because when I first can remember my old Master, Charley Rogers, was always on the lookout for somebody or other he was lined up against in the big feud.

My master and all the rest of the folks was Cherokees, and they'd been killing each other off in the feud ever since long before I was borned, and jest because old Master have a big farm and three-four families of Negroes them other Cherokees keep on pestering his stuff all the time. Us children was always afeared to go any place less'n some of the grown folks was along.

We didn't know what we was a-feared of, but we heard the Master and Mistress keep talking 'bout "another Party killing" and we stuck close to the place.

Old Mistress' name was Nancy Rogers, but I was a orphan after I was a big girl and I called her "Aunt" and "Mamma" like I did when I was little. You see my own mammy was the house woman and I was raised in the house, and I heard the little children call old mistress "mamma" and so I did too. She never did make me stop.

My pappy and mammy and us children lived in a one-room log cabin close to the creek bank and jest a little piece from old Master's house.

My pappy's name was Joe Tucker and my mammy's name was Ruth Tucker. They belonged to a man named Tucker before I was born and he sold them to Master Charley Rogers and he just let them go on by the same name if they wanted to, because last name didn't mean nothing to a slave anyways. The folks jest called my pappy "Charley Rogers' boy Joe."

I already had two sisters, Mary and Mandy, when I was born, and purty soon I had a baby brother, Louis. Mammy worked at the Big House and took me along every day. When I was a little bigger I would help hold the hank when she done the spinning and old Mistress done a lot of the weaving and some knitting. She jest set by the window and knit most all of the time.

When we weave the cloth we had a big loom out on the gallery, and Miss Nancy tell us how to do it.

Mammy eat at our own cabin, and we had lots of game meat and fish the boys get in the Caney Creek. Mammy bring down deer meat and wild turkey sometimes, that the Indian boys git on Sugar Mountain.

Then we had corn bread, dried bean bread and green

stuff out'n Master's patch. Mammy make the bean bread when we git short of corn meal and nobody going to the mill right away. She take and bile the beans and mash them up in some meal and that make it go a long ways.

The slaves didn't have no garden 'cause they work the old Master's garden and make enough for everybody to have some anyway.

When I was about 10 years old that feud got so bad the Indians was always talking about getting their horses and cattle killed and their slaves harmed. I was too little to know how bad it was until one morning my own mammy went off somewhere down the road to git some stuff to dye cloth and she didn't come back.

Lots of the young Indian bucks on both sides of the feud would ride around the woods at night, and old Master got powerful oneasy about my mammy and had all the neighbors and slaves out looking for her, but nobody find her.

It was about a week later that two Indian men rid up and ast old master wasn't his gal Ruth gone. He says yes, and they take one of the slaves along with a wagon to show where they seen her.

They find her in some bushes where she'd been getting bark to set the dyes, and she been dead all the time. Somebody done hit her in the head with a club and shot her through and through with a bullet too. She was so swole up they couldn't lift her up and jest had to make a deep hole right along side of her and roll her in it she was so bad mortified.

Old Master nearly go crazy he was so mad, and the

young Cherokee men ride the woods every night for about a month, but they never catch on to who done it.

I think old Master sell the children or give them out to somebody then, because I never see my sisters and brother for a long time after the Civil War, and for me, I have to go live with a new mistress that was a Cherokee neighbor. Her name was Hannah Ross, and she raised me until I was grown.

I was her home girl, and she and me done a lot of spinning and weaving too. I helped the cook and carried water and milked. I carried the water in a home-made pegging set on my head. Them peggings was kind of buckets made out of staves set around a bottom and didn't have no handle.

I can remember weaving with Miss Hannah Ross. She would weave a strip of white and one of yellow and one of brown to make it pretty. She had a reel that would pop every time it got to a half skein so she would know to stop and fill it up again. We used copperas and some kind of bark she bought at the store to dye with. It was cotton clothes winter and summer for the slaves, too, I'll tell you.

When the Civil War come along we seen lots of white soldiers in them brown butternut suits all over the place, and about all the Indian men was in it too. Old master Charley Rogers' boy Charley went along too. Then pretty soon—it seem like about a year—a lot of the Cherokee men come back home and say they not going back to the War with that General Cooper and some of them go off the Federal side because the captain go to the Federal side too.

Somebody come along and tell me my own pappy have to go in the war and I think they say he on the Copper side, and then after while Miss Hannah tell me he git kilt over in Arkansas.

I was so grieved all the time I don't remember much what went on, but I know pretty soon my Cherokee folks had all the stuff they had et up by the soldiers and they was jest a few wagons and mules left.

All the slaves was piled in together and some of the grown ones walking, and they took us way down across the big river and kept us in the bottoms a long time until the War was over.

We lived in a kind of a camp, but I was too little to know where they got the grub to feed us with. Most all the Negro men was off somewhere in the War.

Then one day they had to bust up the camp and some Federal soldiers go with us and we all start back home. We git to a place where all the houses is burned down and I ask what is that place. Miss Hannah say: "Skullyville, child. That's where they had part of the War."

All the slaves was set out when we git to Fort Gibson, and the soldiers say we all free now. They give us grub and clothes to the Negroes at that place. It wasn't no town but a fort place and a patch of big trees.

Miss Hannah take me to her place and I work there until I was grown. I didn't git any money that I seen, but I got a good place to stay.

Pretty soon I married Ran Lovely and we lived in a double log house here at Fort Gibson. Then my second husband was Henry Richardson, but he's been dead for years, too. We had six children, but they all dead but one.

I didn't want slavery to be over with, mostly because we had the War I reckon. All that trouble made me the loss of my mammy and pappy, and I was always treated good when I was a slave. When it was over I had rather be at home like I was. None of the Cherokees ever whipped us, and my mistress give me some mighty fine rules to live by to git along in this world, too.

The Cherokee didn't have no jail for Negroes and no jail for themselves either. If a man done a crime he come back to take his punishment without being locked up.

None of the Negroes ran away when I was a child that I know of. We all had plenty to eat. The Negroes didn't have no school and so I can't read and write, but they did have a school after the War, I hear. But we had a church made out of a brush arbor and we would sing good songs in Cherokee sometimes.

I always got Sunday off to play, and at night I could go git a piece of sugar or something to eat before I went to bed and Mistress didn't care.

We played bread-and-butter and the boys played hide the switch. The one found the switch got to whip the one he wanted to.

When I got sick they give me some kind of tea from weeds, and if I et too many roasting ears and swole up they biled gourds and give me the liquor off'n them to make me throw up.

I've been a good church-goer all my life until I git too

feeble, and I still understand and talk Cherokee language and love to hear songs and parts of the Bible in it because it make me think about the time I was a little girl before my mammy and pappy leave me.

United States. Work Projects Administration

Oklahoma Writers' Project
Ex-Slaves
[Date stamp: AUG 16 1937]

RED RICHARDSON
Age 75 yrs.
Oklahoma City, Oklahoma

I was born July 21, 1862, at Grimes County, Texas. Smith Richardson was my father's name, and Eliza Richardson my mother's. My father came from Virginia. My mother she was born in Texas.

We lived in so many places round there I can't tell jest what, but we lived in a log house most of the time. We slept on the flo' on pallets on one quilt. We ate cornbread, beans, vegetables, and got to drink plenty milk. We ate rabbits, fish, possums and such as that but we didn't get no chicken. I don't have no fav'rite food, I don't guess.

We wore shirts, long shirts slit up the side. I didn't know what pants was until I was 14. In Grimes County it ain't even cold these days, and I never wore no shoes. I married in a suit made of broad cloth. It had a tail on the coat.

Master Ben Hadley, and Mistress Minnie Hadley, they had three sons: Josh, Henry and Charley. Didn't have no overseer. We had to call all white folks, poor or rich, Mr. Master and Mistress. Master Hadley owned 'bout 2,000 acres. He had a big number of slaves. They used to wake 'em up early in the mornings by ringing a large bell. They said they used to whip 'em, drive 'em, and sell 'em away from their chillun,—I'd hear my old folks talk about it. Say they wasn't no such a thing as going to jail. The master stood good for anything his nigger done. If the master's nigger killed 'im another nigger, the old master stood good.

They never had no schools for the Negro chillun. I can't remember the date of the first school—its in a book someplace—but anyway I went to one of the first schools that was established for the education of Negro chillun.

You know Mr. Negro always was a church man, but he don't mean nothing. I don't have no fav'rite spiritual. All of them's good ones. Whenever they'd baptise they'd sing:

"Harp From the Tune the Domeful Sound."

Which starts like this:

"Come live in man and view this ground

where we must sho'ly lie."

I'm a member of Tabernacle Baptist Church myself, and I think all people should be religious 'cause Jesus died for us all.

The patrollers used to run after me but I'd jump 'em. They used to have a permit to go from one plantation to another. You had to go to old master and say, "I want to go to such and such a place." And if you had a permit they didn't bother you. The pateroller would stop you and say, "Where you going? You got a permit to go to such and such a place?" You'd say, yes suh, and show that pass.

Den he wouldn't bother you and iffen he did old master would git on 'em.

When 10 o'clock come which was bed time the slaves would go to their cabins and some of 'em would go stealing chickens, hogs, steal sweet potatoes, and cook and eat 'em. Jest git in to all kind of devilment.

Old master would give 'em Sadday afternoon off, and they'd have them Sadday night breakdowns. We played a few games such as marbles, mumble peg, and cards—jest anything to pass off the time. Heahs one of the games we'd play an' I sho did like it too:

> She is my sweetheart as I stand,
>
> Come and stand beside of me,
>
> Kiss her sweet and;
>
> Hug her near.

On Christmas they'd make egg nog, drink whiskey and kiss their girls.

Some wore charms to ward off the devil, but I don't believe in such. I do believe in voodoo like this: People can put propositions up to you and fool you. Don't believe in ghost. Tried to see 'em but I never could.

Old master didn't turn my father loose and tell 'em we was free. They didn't turn us loose 'til they got the second threat from President Lincoln. Good old Lincoln; they wasn't nothing like 'im. Booker T. Washington was one of the finest Negro Educators in the world, but old Jefferson Davis was against the cullud man.

I think since slavery is all over, it has been a benefit to the cullud man. He's got more freedom now.

United States. Work Projects Administration

Oklahoma Writer's Project
Ex-Slaves

BETTY ROBERTSON
Age 93 yrs.
Fort Gibson, Oklahoma

I was born close to Webber's Falls, in the Canadian District of the Cherokee Nation, in the same year that my pappy was blowed up and killed in the big boat accident that killed my old Master.

I never did see my daddy excepting when I was a baby and I only know what my mammy told me about him. He come from across the water when he was a little boy, and was grown when old Master Joseph Vann bought him, so he never did learn to talk much Cherokee. My mammy was a Cherokee slave, and talked it good. My husband was a Cherokee born negro, too, and when he got mad he forgit all the English he knowed.

Old Master Joe had a mighty big farm and several families of negroes, and he was a powerful rich man. Pappy's name was Kalet Vann, and mammy's name was Sally. My brothers was name Sone and Frank. I had one brother and one sister sold when I was little and I don't remember the names. My other sisters was Polly, Ruth and Liddie. I had to work in the kitchen when I was a gal, and they was ten or twelve children smaller than me for me to look after, too. Sometime Young Master Joe and the other boys give me a piece of money and say I worked for it, and I reckon

I did for I have to cook five or six times a day. Some of the Master's family was always going down to the river and back, and every time they come in I have to fix something to eat. Old Mistress had a good cookin' stove, but most Cherokees had only a big fireplace and pot hooks. We had meat, bread, rice, potatoes and plenty of fish and chicken. The spring time give us plenty of green corn and beans too. I couldn't buy anything in slavery time, so I jest give the piece of money to the Vann children. I got all the clothes I need from old Mistress, and in winter I had high top shoes with brass caps on the toe. In the summer I wear them on Sunday, too. I wore loom cloth clothes, dyed in copperas what the old negro women and the old Cherokee women made.

The slaves had a pretty easy time I think. Young Master Vann never very hard on us and he never whupped us, and old Mistress was a widow woman and a good Christian and always kind. I sure did love her. Maybe old Master Joe Vann was harder, I don't know, but that was before my time. Young Master never whip his slaves, but if they don't mind good he sell them off sometimes. He sold one of my brothers and one sister because they kept running off. They wasn't very big either, but one day two Cherokees rode up and talked a long time, then young Master came to the cabin and said they were sold because mammy couldn't make them mind him. They got on the horses behind the men and went off.

Old Master Joe had a big steam boat he called the Lucy Walker, and he run it up and down the Arkansas and the Mississippi and the Ohio river, old Mistress say. He went clean to Louisville, Kentucky, and back. My pappy was a kind of a boss of the negroes that run the boat, and they all belong to old Master Joe. Some had been in a big runaway and had been brung back, and wasn't so good, so he keep them on the boat all the time mostly. Mistress say old Master and my pappy on the boat somewhere close to Louisville and the boiler bust and tear the boat up. Some niggers say my pappy kept hollering, "Run it to the bank! Run it to the bank!" but it sunk and him and old Master died.

Old Master Joe was a big man in the Cherokees, I hear, and was good to his negroes before I was born. My pappy run away one time, four or five years before I was born, mammy tell me, and at that time a whole lot of Cherokee slaves run off at once. They got over in the Creek country and stood off the Cherokee officers that went to git them, but pretty soon they give up and come home. Mammy say they was lots of excitement on old Master's place and all the negroes mighty scared, but he didn't sell my pappy off. He jest kept him and he was a good negro after that. He had to work on the boat, though, and never got to come home but once in a long while.

Young Master Joe let us have singing and be baptized if we want to, but I wasn't baptized till after the War. But we couldn't learn to read or have a book, and the Cherokee folks was afraid to tell us about the letters and figgers because they have a law you go to jail and a big fine if you show a slave about the letters.

When the War come they have a big battle away west of us, but I never see any battles. Lots of soldiers around all the time though.

One day young Master come to the cabins and say we all free and can't stay there less'n we want to go on working for him just like we'd been, for our feed and clothes. Mammy got a wagon and we traveled around a few days and go to Fort Gibson. When we git to Fort Gibson they was a lot of negroes there, and they had a camp meeting and I was baptized. It was in the Grand River close to the ford, and winter time. Snow on the ground and the water was muddy and all full of pieces of ice. The place was all woods, and the Cherokees and the soldiers all come down to see the baptizing.

We settled down a little ways above Fort Gibson. Mammy had the wagon and two oxen, and we worked a good size patch there until she died, and then I git married to Cal Robertson to have somebody to take care of me. Cal Robertson was eighty-nine years old when I married him forty years ago, right on this porch. I had on my old clothes for the wedding, and I aint had any good clothes since I was a little slave girl. Then I had clean warm clothes and I had to keep them clean, too!

I got my allotment as a Cherokee Freedman, and so did Cal, but we lived here at this place because we was too old to work the land ourselves. In slavery time the Cherokee negroes do like anybody else when they is a death—jest listen to a chapter in the Bible and all cry. We had a good song I remember. It was "Don't Call the Roll, Jesus, Because I'm Coming Home." The only song I remember from the soldiers was: "Hang Jeff Davis to a Sour Apple Tree", and I remember that because they said he used to be at Fort Gibson one time. I don't know what he done after that.

I don't know about Robert Lee, but I know about Lee's Creek.

I been a good Christian ever since I was baptized, but I keep a little charm here on my neck anyways, to keep me from having the nose bleed. Its got a buckeye and a lead bullet in it. I had a silver dime on it, too, for a long time, but I took it off and got me a box of snuff. I'm glad the War's over and I am free to meet God like anybody else, and my grandchildren can learn to read and write.

United States. Work Projects Administration

Oklahoma Writers' Project
Ex-slaves
[Date stamp: AUG 18 1937]

HARRIET ROBINSON
Age 95 yrs.
500 Block N. Fonshill
Oklahoma City, Oklahoma.

I was born September 1, 1842, in Bastrop, Texas, on Colorado River. My pappy was named Harvey Wheeler and my mammy was named Carolina Sims. My brothers and sisters was named Alex, Taylor, Mary, Cicero, Tennessee, Sarah, Jeff, Ella and Nora. We lived in cedar log houses with dirt floors and double chimneys, and doors hung on wooden hinges. One side of our beds was bored in the walls and had one leg on the other. Them white folks give each nigger family a blanket in winter.

I nussed 3 white chillun, Lulu, Helen Augusta, and Lola Sims. I done this before that War that set us free. We kids use to make extra money by toting gravel in our aprons. They'd give us dimes and silver nickles.

Our clothes was wool and cotton mixed. We had red rustic shoes, soles one-half inch thick. They'd go a-whick a-whack. The mens had pants wid one seam and a right-hand pocket. Boys wore shirts.

We ate hominy, mush, grits and pone bread for the

most part. Many of them ate out of one tray with wooden spoons. All vittles for field hands was fixed together.

Women broke in mules throwed 'em down and roped 'em. They'd do it better'n men. While mammy made some hominy one day both my foots was scalded and when they clipped them blisters, they jest put some cotton round them and catched all dat yellow water and made me a yellow dress out of it. This was 'way back yonder in slavery, before the War.

Whenever white folks had a baby born den all de old niggers had to come thoo the room and the master would be over 'hind the bed and he'd say, "Here's a new little mistress or master you got to work for." You had to say, "Yessuh Master" and bow real low or the overseer would crack you. Them was slavery days, dog days.

I remember in slavery time we had stages. Them devilish things had jest as many wrecks as cars do today. Only thing, we jest didn't have as many.

My mammy belonged to Master Colonel Sam Sims and his old mean wife Julia. My pappy belonged to Master Meke Smith and his good wife Harriett. She was sho' a good woman. I was named after her. Master Sam and Master Meke was partners. Ever year them rich men would send so many wagons to New Mexico for different things. It took 6 months to go and come.

Slaves was punished by whip and starving. Decker was sho' a mean slave-holder. He lived close to us. Master Sam didn't never whip me, but Miss Julia whipped me every day in the mawning. During the war she beat us so terrible. She say, "Your master's out fighting and losing blood trying to save you from them Yankees, so you kin git your'n here." Miss Julia would take me by my ears and butt my head against the wall. She wanted to whip my mother, but old Master told her, naw sir. When his father done give my mammy to Master Sam, he told him not to beat her, and iffen he got to whar he jest had to, jest bring her back and place her in his yard from whar he got her.

White folks didn't 'low you to read or write. Them what did know come from Virginny. Mistress Julia used to drill her chillun in spelling any words. At every word them chillun missed, she gived me a lick 'cross the head for it. Meanest woman I ever seen in my whole life.

This skin I got now, it ain't my first skin. That was burnt off when I was a little child. Mistress used to have a fire made on the fireplace and she made me scour the brass round it and my skin jest blistered. I jest had to keep pulling it off'n me.

We didn't had no church, though my pappy was a preacher. He preached in the quarters. Our baptizing song was "On Jordan's Stormy Bank I stand" and "Hark From The Tomb." Now all dat was before the War. We had all our funerals at the graveyard. Everybody, chillun and all picked up a clod of dirt and throwed in on top the coffin to help fill up the grave.

Taling 'bout niggers running away, didn't my step-pappy run away? Didn't my uncle Gabe run away? The frost would jest bite they toes most nigh off too, whiles they was gone. They put Uncle Isom (my step-pappy) in jail and while's he was in there he killed a white guardman. Then they put in the paper, "A nigger to kill", and our Master seen it and bought him. He was a double-strengthed man, he was so strong. He'd run off so help you God. They had the blood hounds after him once and he caught the hound what was leading and beat the rest of the dogs. The white folks run up on him before he knowed it and made them dogs eat his ear plumb out. But don't you know he got away anyhow. One morning I was sweeping out the hall in the big house and somebody come a-knocking on the front door and I goes to the door. There was Uncle Isom wid rags all on his head. He said, "Tell ole master heah I am." I goes to Master's door and says, "Master Colonel Sam, Uncle Isom said heah he am." He say, "Go 'round to the kitchen and tell black mammy to give you breakfast." When he was thoo' eating they give him 300 lashes and, bless my soul, he run off again.

When we went to a party the nigger fiddlers would play a chune dat went lak this:

> I fooled Ole Mastah 7 years
>
> Fooled the overseer three;
>
> Hand me down my banjo
>
> And I'll tickle your bel-lee.

We had the same doctors the white folks had and we wore asafetida and garlic and onions to keep from taking all them ailments.

I 'member the battle being fit. The white folks buried all the jewelry and silver and all the gold in the Blue Ridge Mountains, in Orange, Texas. Master made all us niggers come together and git ready to leave 'cause the Yankees was coming. We took a steamer. Now this was in slavery time, sho' 'nuff slavery. Then we got on a steamship and pulled out to Galveston. Then he told the captain to feed we niggers. We was on the bay, not the ocean. We left Galveston and went on trains for Houston.

One, my sister Liza, was mulatto and Master Colonel Sims' son had 3 chillun by her. We never seen her no more after her last child was born. I found out though that she was in Canada.

After the War, Master Colonel Sims went to git the mail and so he call Daniel Ivory, the overseer, and say to him, "Go round to all the quarters and tell all the niggers to come up, I got a paper to read to 'em. They're free now, so you kin git you another job, 'cause I ain't got no more niggers which is my own." Niggers come up from the cabins nappy-headed, jest lak they gwine to the field. Master Colonel Sims say, "Caroline (that's my mammy), you is free as me. Pa said bring you back and I'se gwina do jest that. So you go on and work and I'll pay you and your three oldest chillun $10.00 a month a head and $4.00 fer Harriet," that's me, and then he turned to the rest and say "Now all you'uns will receive $10.00 a head till the crops is laid by." Don't you know before he got half way thoo', over half them niggers was gone.

Them Klu Klux Klans come and ask for water with the false stomachs and make lak they was drinking three bucketsful. They done some terrible things, but God seen it all and marked it down.

We didn't had no law, we had "bureau." Why, in them days iffen somebody stole anything from you, they had to pay you and not the Law. Now they done turned that round and you don't git nothing.

One day whiles master was gone hunting, Mistress Julia told her brother to give Miss Harriett (me) a free whipping. She was a nigger killer. Master Colonel Sam come home and he said, "You infernal sons o' bitches don't you know there is 300 Yankees camped out here and iffen they knowed you'd whipped this nigger the way you done done, they'd kill all us. Iffen they find it out, I'll kill all you all." Old rich devils, I'm here, but they is gone.

God choosed Abraham Lincoln to free us. It took one of them to free us so's they couldn't say nothing.

Doing one 'lection they sung:

> Clark et the watermelon
>
> J. D. Giddings et the vine!
>
> Clark gone to Congress
>
> An' J. D. Giddings left behind.

They hung Jeff Davis up a sour apple tree. They say he was a president, but he wasn't, he was a big senator man.

Booker T. Washington was all right in his way, I guess, but Bruce and Fred Douglass, or big mens jest sold us back to the white folks.

I married Haywood Telford and had 13 head of chillun by him. My oldest daughter is the mammy of 14. All my chillun but four done gone to heaven before me.

I jined the church in Chapel Hill, Texas. I am born of the Spirit of God sho' nuff. I played with him seven years and would go right on dancing at Christmas time. Now I got religion. Everybody oughta live right, though you won't have no friends iffen you do.

Our overseer was a poor man. Had us up before day and lak-a-that. He was paid to be the head of punishment. I jest didn't like to think of them old slavery days, dogs' days.

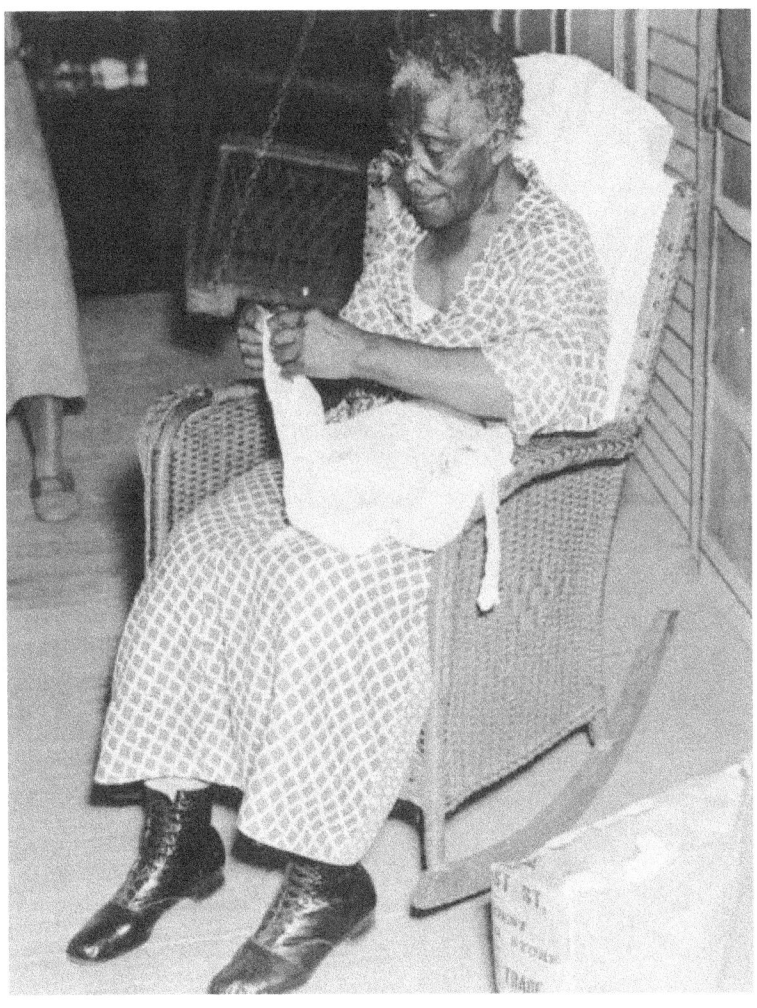

United States. Work Projects Administration

Oklahoma Writers' Project
Ex-Slaves
[HW: (photo)]
[Date stamp: AUG 16 1937]

KATIE ROWE
Age 88 yrs.
Tulsa, Oklahoma

I can set on de gallery, whar de sunlight shine bright, and sew a powerful fine seam when my grandchillun wants a special purty dress for de school doings, but I ain't worth much for nothing else I reckon.

These same old eyes seen powerful lot of tribulations in my time, and when I shets 'em now I can see lots of l'il chillun jest lak my grandchillun, toting hoes bigger dan dey is, and dey pore little black hands and legs bleeding whar dey scratched by de brambledy weeds, and whar dey got whuppings 'cause dey didn't git out all de work de overseer set out for 'em.

I was one of dem little slave gals my own self, and I never seen nothing but work and tribulations till I was a grown up woman, jest about.

De niggers had hard traveling on de plantation whar I was born and raised, 'cause old Master live in town and jest had de overseer on de place, but iffen he had lived out dar hisself I speck it been as bad, 'cause he was a hard driver his own self.

He git biling mad when de Yankees have dat big battle at Pea Ridge and scatter de 'Federates all down through our country all bleeding and tied up and hungry, and he jest mount on his hoss and ride out to de plantation whar we all hoeing corn.

He ride up and tell old man Saunders—dat de overseer—to bunch us all up round de lead row man—dat my own uncle Sandy—and den he tell us de law!

"You niggers been seeing de 'Federate soldiers coming by here looking purty raggedy and hurt and wore out," he say, "but dat no sign dey licked!

"Dem Yankees ain't gwine git dis fur, but iffen dey do you all ain't gwine git free by 'em, 'cause I gwine free you befo' dat. When dey git here dey going find you already free, 'cause I gwine line you up on de bank of Bois d' Arc Creek and free you wid my shotgun! Anybody miss jest one lick wid de hoe, or one step in de line, or one clap of dat bell, or one toot of de horn, and he gwine be free and talking to de debil long befo' he ever see a pair of blue britches!"

Dat de way he talk to us, and dat de way he act wid us all de time.

We live in de log quarters on de plantation, not far from Washington, Arkansas, close to Bois d' Arc Creek, in de edge of de Little River bottom.

Old Master's name was Dr. Isaac Jones, and he live in de town, whar he keep four, five house niggers, but he have about 200 on de plantation, big and little, and old man Saunders oversee 'em at de time of de War. Old Mistress name was Betty, and she had a daughter name Betty about grown, and then they was three boys, Tom, Bryan, and Bob, but they was too young to go to de War. I never did see 'em but once or twice 'til after de War.

Old Master didn't go to de War, 'cause he was a doctor and de onliest one left in Washington, and purty soon he was dead anyhow.

Next fall after he ride out and tell us dat he gwine shoot us befo' he let us free he come out to see how his steam gin doing. De gin box was a little old thing 'bout as big as a bedstead, wid a long belt running through de side of de gin house out to de engine and boiler in de yard. De boiler burn cord wood, and it have a little crack in it whar de nigger ginner been trying to fix it.

Old Master come out, hopping mad 'cause de gin shet down, and ast de ginner, old Brown, what de matter. Old Brown say de boiler weak and it liable to bust, but old Master jump down off'n his hoss and go 'round to de boiler and say, "Cuss fire to your black heart! Dat boiler all right! Throw on some cordwood, cuss fire to your heart!"

Old Brown start to de wood pile grumbling to hisself and old Master stoop down to look at de boiler again, and it blow right up and him standing right dar!

Old Master was blowed all to pieces, and dey jest find little bitsy chunks of his clothes and parts of him to bury.

De wood pile blow down, and old Brown land way off in de woods, but he wasn't killed.

Two wagons of cotton blowed over, and de mules run away, and all de niggers was scared nearly to death 'cause we knowed de overseer gwine be a lot worse, now dat old Master gone.

Before de War when Master was a young man de slaves didn't have it so hard, my mammy tell me. Her name was Fanny and her old mammy name was Nanny. Grandma Nanny was alive during de War yet.

How she come in de Jones family was dis way: old Mistress was jest a little girl, and her older brother bought Nanny and give her to her. I think his name was Little John, anyways we called him Master Little John. He drawed up a paper what say dat Nanny allus belong to Miss Betty and all de chillun Nanny ever have belong to her, too, and nobody can't take 'em for a debt and things like dat. When Miss Betty marry, old Master he can't sell Nanny or any of her chillun neither.

Dat paper hold good too, and grandmammy tell me about one time it hold good and keep my own mammy on de place.

Grandmammy say mammy was jest a little gal and was playing out in de road wid three, four other little chillun when a white man and old Master rid up. The white man had a paper about some kind of a debt, and old Master say take his pick of de nigger chillun and give him back de paper.

Jest as Grandmammy go to de cabin door and hear him say dat de man git off his hoss and pick up my mammy and put her up in front of him and start to ride off down de road.

Pretty soon Mr. Little John come riding up and say something to old Master, and see grandmammy standing in de yard screaming and crying. He jest job de spur in his hoss and go kiting off down de road after dat white man.

Mammy say he ketch up wid him jest as he git to Bois d' Arc Creek and start to wade de hoss across. Mr. Little John holler to him to come back wid dat little nigger 'cause de paper don't kiver dat child, 'cause she old Mistress' own child, and when de man jest ride on, Mr. Little John throw his big old long hoss-pistol down on him and make him come back.

De man hopping mad, but he have to give over my mammy and take one de other chillun on de debt paper.

Old Master allus kind of techy 'bout old Mistress having niggers he can't trade or sell, and one day he have his whole family and some more white folks out at de plantation. He showing 'em all de quarters when we all come in from de field in de evening, and he call all de niggers up to let de folks see 'em.

He make grandmammy and mammy and me stand to one side and den he say to the other niggers, "Dese niggers belong to my wife but you belong to me, and I'm de only one you is to call Master.

"Dis is Tom, and Bryan, and Bob, and Miss Betty, and you is to call 'em dat, and don't you ever call one of 'em Young Master or Young Mistress, cuss fire to your black hearts!" All de other white folks look kind of funny, and old Mistress look 'shamed of old Master.

My own pappy was in dat bunch, too. His name was Frank, and after de War he took de name of Frank Henderson, 'cause he was born under dat name, but I allus went by Jones, de name I was born under.

Long about de middle of de War, after old Master was killed, de soldiers begin coming 'round de place and camping. Dey was Southern soldiers and dey say dey have to take de mules and most de corn to git along on. Jest go in de barns and cribs and take anything dey want, and us niggers didn't have no sweet 'taters nor Irish 'taters to eat on when dey gone neither.

One bunch come and stay in de woods across de road from de overseer's house, and dey was all on hosses. Dey lead de hosses down to Bois d' Arc Creek every morning at daylight and late every evening to git water. When we going to de field and when we coming in we allus see dem leading big bunches of hosses.

Dey bugle go jest 'bout de time our old horn blow in de morning and when we come in dey eating supper, and we smell it and sho' git hungry!

Before old Master died he sold off a whole lot of hosses and cattle, and some niggers too. He had de sales on de plantation, and white men from around dar come to bid, and some traders come. He had a big stump whar he made de niggers stand while dey was being sold, and de men and boys had to strip off to de waist to show dey muscle and iffen dey had any scars or hurt places, but de women and gals didn't have to strip to de waist.

De white men come up and look in de slave's mouth jest lak he was a mule or a hoss.

After old Master go, de overseer hold one sale, but mostly he jest trade wid de traders what come by. He make de niggers git on de stump, through. De traders all had big bunches of slaves and dey have 'em all strung out in a line going down de road. Some had wagons and de chillun could ride, but not many. Dey didn't chain or tie 'em 'cause dey didn't have no place dey could run to anyway.

I seen chillun sold off and de mammy not sold, and, sometimes de mammy sold and a little baby kept on de place and give to another woman to raise. Dem white folks didn't care nothing 'bout how de slaves grieved when dey tore up a family.

Old man Saunders was de hardest overseer of anybody. He would git mad and give a whipping some time and de slave wouldn't even know what it was about.

My uncle Sandy was de lead row nigger, and he was a good nigger and never would tech a drap of likker. One night some de niggers git hold of some likker somehow, and dey leave de jug half full on de step of Sandy's cabin. Next morning old man Saunders come out in de field so mad he was pale.

He jest go to de lead row and tell Sandy to go wid him, and start toward de woods along Bois d' Arc Creek wid Sandy follering behind. De overseer always carry a big heavy stick, but we didn't know he was so mad, and dey jest went off in de woods.

Purty soon we hear Sandy hollering and we know old overseer pouring in on, den de overseer come back by his self and go on up to de house.

Come late evening he come and see what we done in de day's work, and go back to de quarters wid us all. Then he git to mammy's cabin, whar grandmammy live too, he say to grandmammy, "I sent Sandy down in de woods to hunt a hoss, he gwine come in hungry purty soon. You better make him a extra hoe cake," and he kind of laugh and go on to his house.

Jest soon as he gone we all tell grandmammy we think he got a whipping, and sho' nuff he didn't come in.

De next day some white boys find uncle Sandy whar dat overseer done killed him and throwed him in a little pond, and dey never done nothing to old man Saunders at all!

When he go to whip a nigger he make him strip to de waist, and he take a cat-o-nine tails and bring de blisters, and den bust de blisters wid a wide strap of leather fastened to a stick handle. I seen de blood running out'n many a back, all de way from de neck to de waist!

Many de time a nigger git blistered and cut up so dat we have to git a sheet and grease it wid lard and wrap 'em up in it, and dey have to wear a greasy cloth wrapped around dey body under de shirt for three-four days after dey git a big whipping!

Later on in de War de Yankees come in all around us and camp, and de overseer git sweet as honey in de comb! Nobody git a whipping all de time de Yankees dar!

Dey come and took all de meat and corn and 'taters dey want too, and dey tell us, "Why don't you poor darkeys take all de meat and molasses you want? You made it and it's your's much as anybody's!" But we know dey soon be gone, and den we git a whipping iffen we do. Some niggers run off and went wid de Yankees, but dey had to work jest as hard for dem, and dey didn't eat so good and often wid de soldiers.

I never forget de day we was set free!

Dat morning we all go to de cotton field early, and den a house nigger come out from old Mistress on a hoss and say she want de overseer to come into town, and he leave and go in. After while de old horn blow up at de overseer's house, and we all stop and listen, 'cause it de wrong time of day for de horn.

We start chopping again, and dar go de horn again.

De lead row nigger holler "Hold up!" And we all stop again. "We better go on in. Dat our horn," he holler at de head nigger, and de head nigger think so too, but he say he afraid we catch de devil from de overseer iffen we quit widout him dar, and de lead row man say maybe he back from town and blowing de horn hisself, so we line up and go in.

When we git to de quarters we see all de old ones and de chillun up in de overseer's yard, so we go on up dar. De overseer setting on de end of de gallery wid a paper in his hand, and when we all come up he say come and stand close to de gallery. Den he call off everybody's name and see we all dar.

Setting on de gallery in a hide-bottom chair was a man we never see before. He had on a big broad black hat lak de Yankees wore but it din't have no yaller string on it lak most de Yankees had, and he was in store clothes dat wasn't homespun or jeans, and dey was black. His hair was plumb gray and so was his beard, and it come way down here on his chest, but he didn't look lak he was very old, 'cause his face was kind of fleshy and healthy looking. I think we all been sold off in a bunch, and I notice some kind of smiling, and I think they sho' glad of it.

De man say, "You darkies know what day dis is?" He talk kind, and smile.

We all don't know of course, and we jest stand dar and grin. Pretty soon he ask again and de head man say, No, we don't know.

"Well dis de fourth day of June, and dis is 1865, and I want you all to 'member de date, 'cause you allus going 'member de day. Today you is free, Jest lak I is, and Mr. Saunders and your Mistress and all us white people," de man say.

"I come to tell you", he say, "and I wants to be sho' you all understand, 'cause you don't have to git up and go by de horn no more. You is your own bosses now, and you don't have to have no passes to go and come."

We never did have no passes, nohow, but we knowed lots of other niggers on other plantations got 'em.

"I wants to bless you and hope you always is happy, and tell you got all de right and lief [TR: sic] dat any white people got", de man say, and den he git on his hoss and ride off.

We all jest watch him go on down de road, and den we go up to Mr. Saunders and ask him what he want us to do. He jest grunt and say do lak we dam please, he reckon, but git off dat place to do it, less'n any of us wants to stay and make de crop for half of what we make.

None of us know whar to go, so we all stay, and he

split up de fields and show us which part we got to work in, and we go on lak we was, and make de crop and git it in, but dey ain't no more horn after dat day. Some de niggers lazy and don't git in de field early, and dey git it took away from 'em, but dey plead around and git it back and work better de rest of dat year.

But we all gits fooled on dat first go-out! When de crop all in we don't git half! Old Mistress sick in town, and de overseer was still on de place and he charge us half de crop for de quarters and de mules and tools and grub!

Den he leave, and we gits another white man, and he sets up a book, and give us half de next year, and take out for what we use up, but we all got something left over after dat first go-out.

Old Mistress never git well after she lose all her niggers, and one day de white boss tell us she jest drap over dead setting in her chair, and we know her heart jest broke.

Next year de chillun sell off most de place and we scatter off, and I and mammy go into Little Rock and do work in de town. Grandmammy done dead.

I git married to John White in Little Rock, but he died and we didn't have no chillun. Den in four, five years I marry Billy Rowe. He was a Cherokee citizen and he had belonged to a Cherokee name Dave Rowe, and lived east of Tahlequah before de War. We married in Little Rock, but he had land in de Cherokee Nation, and we come to east of Tahlequah and lived 'til he died, and den I come to Tulsa to live wid my youngest daughter.

Billy Rowe and me had three chillun, Ellie, John, and Lula. Lula married a Thomas, and it's her I lives with.

Lots of old people lak me say dat dey was happy in slavery, and dat dey had de worst tribulations after freedom, but I knows dey didn't have no white master and overseer lak we all had on our place. Dey both dead now I reckon, and dey no use talking 'bout de dead, but I know I been gone long ago iffen dat white man Saunder didn't lose his hold on me.

It was de fourth day of June in 1865 I begins to live, and I gwine take de picture of dat old man in de big black hat and long whiskers, setting on de gallery and talking kind to us, clean into my grave wid me.

No, bless God, I ain't never seen no more black boys bleeding all up and down de back under a cat o' nine tails, and I never go by no cabin and hear no poor nigger groaning, all wrapped up in a lardy sheet no more!

I hear my chillun read about General Lee, and I know he was a good man, I didn't know nothing about him den, but I know now he wasn't fighting for dat kind of white folks.

Maybe dey dat kind still yet, but dey don't show it up no more, and I got lots of white friends too. All my chillun and grandchillun been to school, and dey git along good, and I know we living in a better world, what dey ain't nobody "cussing fire to my black heart!"

I sho' thank de good Lawd I got to see it.

Oklahoma Writers' Project
Ex-Slaves

MORRIS SHEPPARD
Age 85 yrs.
Fort Gibson, Okla.

Old Master tell me I was borned in November 1852, at de old home place about five miles east of Webber's Falls, mebbe kind of northeast, not far from de east bank of de Illinois River.

Master's name was Joe Sheppard, and he was a Cherokee Indian. Tall and slim and handsome. He had black eyes and mustache but his hair was iron gray, and everybody liked him because he was so good-natured and kind.

I don't remember old Mistress' name. My mammy was a Crossland negro before she come to belong to Master Joe and marry my pappy, and I think she come wid old Mistress and belong to her. Old Mistress was small and mighty pretty too, and she was only half Cherokee. She inherit about half a dozen slaves, and say dey was her own and old Master can't sell one unless she give him leave to do it.

Dey only had two families of slaves wid about twenty in all, and dey only worked about fifty acres, so we sure did work every foot of it good. We git three or four crops of different things out of dat farm every year, and something growing on dat place winter and summer.

Pappy's name was Caesar Sheppard and Mammy's name was Easter. Dey was both raised 'round Webber's Falls somewhere. I had two brothers, Silas and George, dat belong to Mr. George Holt in Webber's Falls town. I got a pass and went to see dem sometimes, and dey was both treated mighty fine.

The Big House was a double log wid a big hall and a stone chimney but no porches, wid two rooms at each end, one top side of de other. I thought it was mighty big and fine.

Us slaves lived in log cabins dat only had one room and no windows so we kept de doors open most of de time. We had home-made wooden beds wid rope springs, and de little ones slept on trundle beds dat was home made too.

At night dem trundles was jest all over de floor, and in de morning we shove dem back under de big beds to git dem out'n de way. No nails in none of dem nor in de chairs and tables. Nails cost big money and old Master's blacksmith wouldn't make none 'cepting a few for old Master now and den, so we used wooden dowels to put things together.

They was so many of us for dat little field we never did have to work hard. Up at five o'clock and back in sometimes about de middle of de evening, long before sundown, unless they was a crop to git in before it rain or something like dat.

When crop was laid by de slaves jest work 'round at dis and dat and keep tol'able busy. I never did have much of a job, jest tending de calves mostly. We had about twenty calves and I would take dem out and graze 'em while some grown-up negro was grazing de cows so as to keep de cows milk. I had me a good blaze-faced horse for dat.

One time old Master and another man come and took some calves off and Pappy say old Master taking dem off to sell. I didn't know what "sell" meant and I ast Pappy, "Is he going to bring 'em back when he git through selling them?" I never did see no money neither, until time of de War or a little before.

Master Joe was sure a good provider, and we always had plenty of corn pone, sow belly and greens, sweet potatoes, cow peas and cane molasses. We even had brown sugar and cane molasses most of de time before de War. Sometimes coffee, too.

De clothes wasn't no worry neither. Everything we had was made by my folks. My aunt done de carding and spinning and my mammy done de weaving and cutting and sewing, and my pappy could make cowhide shoes wid wooden pegs. Dey was for bad winter only.

Old Master bought de cotton in Ft. Smith because he didn't raise no cotton, but he had a few sheep and we had wool-mix for winter.

Everything was stripedy 'cause Mammy like to make it fancy. She dye wid copperas and walnut and wild indigo and things like dat and make pretty cloth. I wore a stripedy shirt till I was about eleven years old, and den one day while we was down in de Choctaw Country old Mistress see me and nearly fall off'n her horse! She holler, "Easter, you go right now and make dat big buck of a boy some britches!"

We never put on de shoes until about late November when de frost begin to hit regular and split our feet up, and den when it git good and cold and de crop all gathered in anyways, they is nothing to do 'cepting hog killing and a lot of wood chopping, and you don't git cold doing dem two things.

De hog killing mean we gits lots of spare-ribs and chitlings, and somebody always git sick eating too much of dat fresh pork. I always pick a whole passel of muskatines for old Master and he make up sour wine, and dat helps out when we git the bowel complaint from eating dat fresh pork.

If somebody bad sick he git de doctor right quick, and he don't let no negroes mess around wid no poultices and teas and sech things like cupping-horns neither!

Us Cherokee slaves seen lots of green corn shootings and de like of dat, but we never had no games of our own. We was too tired when we come in to play any games. We had to have a pass to go any place to have singing or praying, and den they was always a bunch of patrollers around to watch everything we done. Dey would come up in a bunch of about nine men on horses, and look at all our passes, and if a negro didn't have no pass dey wore him out good and made him go home. Dey didn't let us have much enjoyment.

Right after de War de Cherokees that had been wid the South kind of pestered the freedmen some, but I was so small dey never bothered me; jest de grown ones. Old

Master and Mistress kept on asking me did de night riders persecute me any but dey never did. Dey told me some of dem was bad on negroes but I never did see none of dem night riding like some said dey did.

Old Master had some kind of business in Fort Smith, I think, 'cause he used to ride in to dat town 'bout every day on his horse. He would start at de crack of daylight and not git home till way after dark. When he get home he call my uncle in and ask about what we done all day and tell him what we better do de next day. My uncle Joe was de slave boss and he tell us what de Master say do.

When dat Civil War come along I was a pretty big boy and I 'remember it good as anybody. Uncle Joe tell us all to lay low and work hard and nobody bother us, and he would look after us. He sure stood good with de Cherokee neighbors we had, and dey all liked him. There was Mr. Jim Collins, and Mr. Bell, and Mr. Dave Franklin, and Mr. Jim Sutton and Mr. Blackburn that lived around close to us and dey all had slaves. Dey was all wid the South, but dey was a lot of dem Pin Indians all up on de Illinois River and dey was wid de North and dey taken it out on de slave owners a lot before de War and during it too.

Dey would come in de night and hamstring de horses and maybe set fire to de barn, and two of 'em named Joab Scarrel and Tom Starr killed my pappy one night just before de War broke out.

I don't know what dey done it for, only to be mean, and I guess they was drunk.

Them Pins was after Master all de time for a while at de first of de War, and he was afraid to ride into Fort

Smith much. Dey come to de house one time when he was gone to Fort Smith and us children told dem he was at Honey Springs, but they knowed better and when he got home he said somebody shot at him and bushwhacked him all the way from Wilson's Rock to dem Wildhorse Mountains, but he run his horse like de devil was setting on his tail and dey never did hit him. He never seen them neither. We told him 'bout de Pins coming for him and he just laughed.

When de War come old Master seen he was going into trouble and he sold off most of de slaves. In de second year of de War he sold my mammy and my aunt dat was Uncle Joe's wife and my two brothers and my little sister. Mammy went to a mean old man named Peper Goodman and he took her off down de river, and pretty soon Mistress tell me she died 'cause she can't stand de rough treatment.

When Mammy went old Mistress took me to de Big House to help her, and she was kind to me like I was part of her own family. I never forget when they sold off some more negroes at de same time, too, and put dem all in a pen for de trader to come and look at.

He never come until the next day, so dey had to sleep in dat pen in a pile like hogs.

It wasn't my Master done dat. He done already sold 'em to a man and it was dat man was waiting for de trader. It made my Master mad, but dey didn't belong to him no more and he couldn't say nothing.

The man put dem on a block and sold 'em to a man dat had come in on a steamboat, and he took dem off on it when de freshet come down and de boat could go back to Fort Smith. It was tied up at de dock at Webber's Falls about a week and we went down and talked to my aunt and brothers and sister. De brothers was Sam and Eli. Old Mistress cried jest like any of de rest of us when de boat pull out with dem on it.

Pretty soon all de young Cherokee menfolks all gone off to de War, and de Pins was riding 'round all de time, and it aint safe to be in dat part around Webber's Falls, so old Master take us all to Fort Smith where they was a lot of Confederate soldiers.

We camp at dat place a while and old Mistress stay in de town wid some kinfolks. Den old Master get three wagons and ox teams and take us all way down on Red River in de Choctaw Nation.

We went by Webber's Falls and filled de wagons. We left de furniture and only took grub and tools and bedding and clothes, 'cause they wasn't very big wagons and was only single-yoke.

We went on a place in de Red River bottoms close to Shawneetown and not far from de place where all de wagons crossed over to go into Texas. We was at dat place two years and made two little crops.

One night a runaway negro come across from Texas and he had de blood hounds after him. His britches was all muddy and tore where de hounds had cut him up in de legs when he clumb a tree in de bottoms. He come to our house and Mistress said for us negroes to give him something to eat and we did.

Then up come de man from Texas with de hounds and

wid him was young Mr. Joe Vann and my uncle that belong to young Joe. Dey called young Mr. Joe "Little Joe Vann" even after he was grown on account of when he was a little boy before his pappy was killed. His pappy was old Captain "Rich Joe" Vann, and he been dead ever since long before de War. My uncle belong to old Captain Joe nearly all his life.

Mistress try to get de man to tell her who de negro belong to so she can buy him, but de man say he can't sell him and he take him on back to Texas wid a chain around his two ankles. Dat was one poor negro dat never got away to de North, and I was sorry for him 'cause I know he must have had a mean master, but none of us Sheppard negroes, I mean the grown ones, tried to git away.

I never seen any fighting in de War, but I seen soldiers in de South army doing a lot of blacksmithing 'long side de road one day. Dey was fixing wagons and shoeing horses.

After de War was over, old Master tell me I am free but he will look out after me 'cause I am just a little negro and I aint got no sense. I know he is right, too.

Well, I go ahead and make me a crop of corn all by myself and then I don't know what to do wid it. I was afraid I would get cheated out of it 'cause I can't figure and read, so I tell old Master about it and he bought it off'n me.

We never had no school in slavery and it was agin the law for anybody to even show a negro de letters and figures, so no Cherokee slave could read.

We all come back to de old place and find de negro cabins and barns burned down and de fences all gone and de field in crab grass and cockleburrs. But de Big House aint hurt 'cepting it need a new roof. De furniture is all gone, and some said de soldiers burned it up for firewood. Some officers stayed in de house for a while and tore everything up or took it off.

Master give me over to de National Freedmen's Bureau and I was bound out to a Cherokee woman name Lizzie McGee. Then one day one of my uncles named Wash Sheppard come and tried to git me to go live wid him. He say he wanted to git de family all together agin.

He had run off after he was sold and joined de North army and discharged at Fort Scott in Kansas, and he said lots of freedmen was living close to each other up by Coffeyville in de Coo-ee-scoo-ee District.

I wouldn't go, so he sent Isaac and Joe Vann dat had been two of old Captain Joe's negroes to talk to me. Isaac had been Young Joe's driver, and he told me all about how rich Master Joe was and how he would look after us negroes. Dey kept after me 'bout a year, but I didn't go anyways.

But later on I got a freedman's allotment up in dat part close to Coffeyville, and I lived in Coffeyville a while but I didn't like it in Kansas.

I lost my land trying to live honest and pay my debts. I raised eleven children just on de sweat of my hands and none of dem ever tasted anything dat was stole.

When I left Mrs. McGee's I worked about three years for Mr. Sterling Scott and Mr. Roddy Reese. Mr. Reese had a big flock of peafowls dat had belonged to Mr. Scott and I had to take care of dem.

Whitefolks, I would have to tromp seven miles to Mr. Scott's house two or three times a week to bring back some old peafowl dat had got out and gone back to de old place!

Poor old Master and Mistress only lived a few years after de War. Master went plumb blind after he move back to Webber's Falls and so he move up on de Illinois River 'bout three miles from de Arkansas, and there old Mistress take de white swelling and die and den he die pretty soon. I went to see dem lots of times and they was always glad to see me.

I would stay around about a week and help 'em, and dey would try to git me to take something but I never would. Dey didn't have much and couldn't make anymore and dem so old. Old Mistress had inherited some property from her pappy and dey had de slave money and when dey turned everything into good money after de War dat stuff only come to about six thousand dollars in good money, she told me. Dat just about lasted 'em through until dey died, I reckon.

By and by I married Nancy Hildebrand what lived on Greenleaf Creek, 'bout four miles northwest of Gore. She had belonged to Joe Hildebrand and he was kin to old Steve Hildebrand dat owned de mill on Flint Creek up in de Going Snake District. She was raised up at dat mill, but she was borned in Tennessee before dey come out to de Nation. Her master was white but he had married into de Nation and so she got a freedmen's allotment too. She had some land close to Catoosa and some down on Greenleaf Creek.

We was married at my home in Coffeyville, and she

bore me eleven children and then went on to her reward. A long time ago I came to live wid my daughter Emma here at dis place, but my wife just died last year. She was eighty three.

I reckon I wasn't cut out on de church pattern, but I raised my children right. We never had no church in slavery, and no schooling, and you had better not be caught wid a book in your hand even, so I never did go to church hardly any.

Wife belong to de church and all de children too, and I think all should look after saving their souls so as to drive de nail in, and den go about de earth spreading kindness and hoeing de row clean so as to clinch dat nail and make dem safe for Glory.

Of course I hear about Abraham Lincoln and he was a great man, but I was told mostly by my children when dey come home from school about him. I always think of my old Master as de one dat freed me, and anyways Abraham Lincoln and none of his North people didn't look after me and buy my crop right after I was free like old Master did. Dat was de time dat was de hardest and everything was dark and confusion.

United States. Work Projects Administration

Oklahoma Writers' Project
Ex-Slaves
[Date stamp: AUG 16 1937]

ANDREW SIMMS
Age 80
Sapulpa, Okla.

My parents come over on a slave ship from Africa about twenty year before I was born on the William Driver plantation down in Florida. My folks didn't know each other in Africa but my old Mammy told me she was captured by Negro slave hunters over there and brought to some coast town where the white buyers took her and carried her to America.

She was kinder a young gal then and was sold to some white folks when the boat landed here. Dunno who they was. The same thing happen to my pappy. Must have been about the same time from the way they tells it. Maybe they was on the [HW: same] boat, I dunno.

They was traded around and then mammy was sold to William Driver. The plantation was down in Florida. Another white folks had a plantation close by. Mister Simms was the owner. Bill Simms—that's the name pappy kept after the War.

Somehow or other mammy and pappy meets 'round the place and the first thing happens they is in love. That's what mammy say. And the next thing happen is me. They didn't get married. The Master's say it is alright for them to have a baby. They never gets married, even after the War. Just jumped the broomstick and goes to living with somebody else I reckon.

Then when I was four year old along come the War and Master Driver takes up his slaves and leaves the Florida country and goes way out to Texas. Mammy goes along, I goes along, all the children goes along. I don't remember nothing about the trip but I hears mammy talk about it when I gets older.

Texas, that was the place, down near Fairfield. That's where I learn to do the chores. But the work was easy for the Master was kind as old Mammy herself and he never give me no hard jobs that would wear me down. All the slaves on our place was treated good. All the time. They didn't whip. The Master feeds all the slaves on good clean foods and lean meats so's they be strong and healthy.

Master Driver had four children, Mary, Julia, Frank and George. Every one of them children kind and good just the old Master. They was never mean and could I find some of 'em now hard times would leave me on the run! They'd help this old man get catched up on his eating!

Makes me think of the old song we use to sing:

> Don't mind working from Sun to Sun,
>
> Iffen you give me my dinner—
>
> When the dinner time comes!

Nowadays I gets me something to eat when I can catch it. The trouble is sometimes I don't catch! But that ain't telling about the slave days.

In them times it was mostly the overseers and the drivers who was the mean ones. They caused all the misery. There was other whitefolks caused troubles too. Sneak around where there was lots of the black children on the plantation and steal them. Take them poor children away off and sell them.

There wasn't any Sunday Schooling. There was no place to learn to read and write—no big brick schools like they is now. The old Master say we can teach ourselves but we can't do it. Old Elam Bowman owned the place next door to Mister Driver. If he catch his slaves toying with the pencil, why, he cut off one of their fingers. Then I reckon they lost interest in education and get their mind back on the hoe and plow like he say for them to do.

I didn't see no fighting during of the War. If they was any Yankees soldiering around the country I don't remember nothing of it.

Long time after the War is over, about 1885, I meets a gal named Angeline. We courts pretty fast and gets married. The wedding was a sure enough affair with the preacher saying the words just like the whitefolks marriage. We is sure married.

The best thing we do after that is raise us a family. One of them old fashioned families. Big 'uns! Seventeen children does we have and twelve of them still living. Wants to know they names? I ain't never forgets a one! There was Lucy, Bill, Ebbie, Cora, Minnie, George, Frank, Kizzie, Necie, Andrew, Joe, Sammie, David, Fannie, Jacob, Bob and Myrtle.

All good children. Just like their old pappy who's tried

to care for 'em just like the old Master takes care of their old daddy when he was a boy on that plantation down Texas way.

When the age comes on a man I reckon religion gets kind of meanful. Thinks about it more'n when he's young and busy in the fields. I believes in the Bible and what it says to do. Some of the Colored folks takes to the voodoo. I don't believe in it. Neither does I believe in the fortune telling or charms. I aims to live by the Bible and leave the rabbit foots alone!

Oklahoma Writers' Project
Ex-Slaves
10-19-38
718 words

LIZA SMITH
Age 91
Muskogee, Oklahoma

Both my mammy and pappy was brought from Africa on a slave boat and sold on de Richmond (Va.) slave market. What year dey come over I don't know. My mammy was Jane Mason, belonging to Frank Mason; pappy was Frank Smith, belonging to a master wid de same name. I mean, my pappy took his Master's name, and den after my folks married mammy took de name of Smith, but she stayed on wid de Masons and never did belong to my pappy's master. Den, after Frank Mason took all his slaves out of de Virginia county, mammy met up wid another man, Ben Humphries, and married him.

In Richmond, dat's where I was born, 'bout 1847, de Master said; and dat make me more dan 90-year old dis good year. I had two brothers named Webb and Norman, a half-brother Charley, and two half-sisters, Mealey and Ann. Me, I was born a slave and so was my son. His father, Toney, was one of de Mason slave boys; de Master said I was 'bout 13-year old when de boy was born.

Frank Mason was a young man when de War started, living wid his mother. Dey had lots of slaves, maybe a hundred, and dey always try to take good care of 'em; even after de War was over he worried 'bout trying to get us settled so's we wouldn't starve. De Master had overseer, but dere was no whuppings.

All de way from Richmond to a place dey call Waco, Texas, we traveled by ox-wagon and boats, and den de Master figures we all be better off over in Arkansas and goes to Pine Bluff.

What wid all de running 'round de slaves was kept clean and always wid plenty to eat and good clothes to wear. De Master was a plenty rich man and done what his mother, Mrs. Betsy Mason, told him when we all left de Big Mansion, way back dere in Richmond. De Mistress said, "Frank, you watch over dem Negroes cause dey's good men and women; keep dem clean!" Dat's what he done, up until we was freed, and den times was so hard nobody wanted us many Negroes around, and de work was scarce, too. Hard times! Folks don't know what hard times is.

When a Negro get sick de master would send out for herbs and roots. Den one of de slaves who knew how to cook and mix 'em up for medicine use would give de doses. All de men and women wore charms, something like beads, and if dey was any good or not I don't know, but we didn't have no bad diseases like after dey set us free.

I was at Pine Bluff when de Yankees was shooting all over de place. De fighting got so hot we all had to leave; dat's the way it was all de time for us during de War—running away to some place or de next place, and we was all glad when it stopped and we could settle down in a place.

We was back at Waco when de peace come, but Master Frank was away from home when dat happen. It was on a Sunday when he got back and called all de slaves up in de yard and counted all of dem, young and old.

The first thing he said was, "You men and women is all free! I'm going back to my own mammy in old Virginia, but I ain't going back until all de old people is settled in cabins and de young folks fix up wid tents!"

Den he kinder stopped talking. Seem now like he was too excited to talk, or maybe he was feeling bad and worried 'bout what he going to do wid all of us. Pretty soon he said, "You men and women, can't none of you tell anybody I ain't always been a good master. Old folks, have I ever treated you mean?" He asked. Everybody shout, "No, sir!" And Master Frank smiled; den he told us he was going 'round and find places for us to live.

He went to see Jim Tinsley, who owned some slaves, about keeping us. Tinsley said he had cabins and could fix up tents for extra ones, if his own Negroes was willing to share up with us. Dat was the way it worked out. We stayed on dere for a while, but times was so hard we finally get dirty and ragged like all de Tinsley Negroes. But Master Frank figure he done the best he could for us.

After he go back to Virginia we never hear no more of him, but every day I still pray if he has any folks in Richmond dey will find me someway before I die. Is dere someway I could find dem, you s'pose?

United States. Work Projects Administration

Oklahoma Writers' Project
Ex-Slaves
[Date Stamp: Aug 12 1937]

LOU SMITH
Age 83 yrs.
Platter, Okla.

Sho', I remembers de slavery days! I was a little gal but I can tell you lots of things about dem days. My job was nussing de younguns. I took keer of them from daylight to dark. I'd have to sing them to sleep too. I'd sing:

> "By-lo Baby Bunting
>
> Daddy's gone a-hunting
>
> To get a rabbit skin
>
> To wrap Baby Bunting in."

Sometimes I'd sing:

> "Rock-a-bye baby, in a tree top
>
> When de wind blows your cradle'll rock.
>
> When de bough breaks de crad'll fall
>
> Down comes baby cradle'n all."

My father was Jackson Longacre and he was born in Mississippi. My mother, Caroline, was born in South Carolina. Both of them was born slaves. My father belonged to Huriah Longacre. He had a big plantation and lots of niggers. He put up a lot of his slaves as security on a debt and he took sick and died so they put them all on de block and sold them. My father and his mother (my grandma) was sold together. My old Mistress bought my grandmother and old Mistress' sister bought my grandma's sister. These white women agreed that they would never go off so far that the two slave women couldn't see each other. They allus kept this promise. A Mr. Covington offered old Master $700 for me when I was about ten years old, but he wouldn't sell me. He didn't need to for he was rich as cream and my, how good he was to us.

Young Master married Miss Jo Arnold and old Master sent me and my mother over to live with them. I was small when I was took out of old man McWilliams' yard. It was his wife that bought my grandmother and my father. My mother's folks had always belonged to his family. They all moved to Texas and we all lived there until after the surrender.

Miss Jo wasn't a good Mistress and mother and me wasn't happy. When young Master was there he made her treat us good but when he was gone she made our lives a misery to us. She was what we called a "low-brow." She never had been used to slaves and she treated us like dogs. She said us kids didn't need to wear any clothes and one day she told us we could jest take'em off as it cost too much to clothe us. I was jest a little child but I knowed I oughten to go without my clothes. We wore little enough as it was. In summer we just wore one garment, a sort of slip without any sleeves. Well, anyway she made me take off my clothes and I just crept off and cried. Purty soon young Master come home.

He wanted to know what on earth I was doing without

my dress on. I told him, and my goodness, but he raised the roof. He told her if she didn't treat us better he was going to take us back to old Master. I never did have any more good times 'cepting when I'd get to go to visit at old Master's. None of our family could be sold and that was why old Master just loaned us to young Master. When old Master died, dey put all our names in a hat and all the chilluns draw out a name. This was done to 'vide us niggers satisfactory. Young Master drawed my mother's name and they all agreed that I should go with her, so back we went to Miss Jo. She wouldn't feed us niggers. She'd make me set in a corner like a little dog. I got so hungry and howled so loud they had to feed me. When the surrender come, I was eleven years old, and they told us we was free. I ran off and hid in the plum orchard and I said over'n over, "I'se free, I'se free; I ain't never going back to Miss Jo." My mother come out and got me and in a few days my father came and lived with us. He worked for young Master and the crops was divided with him. Miss Jo died and we lived on there. My mother took over the charge of the house and the chillun for young Master and we was all purty happy after that.

They was a white man come into our settlement and bought a plantation and some slaves. My, but he treated them bad. He owned a boy about fifteen years old. One day he sent him on a errand. On the way home he got off his mule and set down in the shade of a tree to rest. He fell asleep and the mule went home. When he woke up he was scared to go home and he stayed out in de woods for several days. Finally they caught him and took him home and his master beat him nearly to death. He then dug a hole and put him in it and piled corn shucks all around him. This nearly killed him 'cause his body was cut up so with the whip. One of the niggers slipped off and went to the jining plantation and told about the way the boy was being treated and a bunch of white men came over and made him take the child out and doctor his wounds. This man lived there about ten years and he was so mean to his slaves 'til all the white men round who owned niggers finally went to him and told him they would just give him so long to sell out and leave. They made him sell his slaves to people there in the community, and he went back north.

My mother told me that he owned a woman who was the mother of several chillun and when her babies would get about a year or two of age he'd sell them and it would break her heart. She never got to keep them. When her fourth baby was born and was about two months old she just studied all the time about how she would have to give it up and one day she said, "I just decided I'm not going to let old Master sell this baby; he just ain't going to do it." She got up and give it something out of a bottle and purty soon it was dead. 'Course didn't nobody tell on her or he'd of beat her nearly to death. There wasn't many folks that was mean to their slaves.

Old Master's boys played with the nigger boys all the time. They'd go swimming, fishing and hunting together. One of his boys name was Robert but everybody called him Bud. They all would catch rabbits and mark them and turn them loose. One day a boy come along with a rabbit he had caught in a trap. Old Master's boy noticed that it had Bud's mark on it and they made him turn it loose.

Old Master was his own overseer, but my daddy was the overlooker. He was purty hard on them too, as they had to work just like they never got tired. The women had to do housework, spinning, sewing and work in the fields too. My mother was housewoman and she could keep herself looking nice. My, she went around with her hair and clothes all Jenny-Lynned-up all the time until we went to live with Miss Jo. She took all the spirit out of poor mother and me too.

I remember she allus kept our cabin as clean and neat as a pin. When other niggers come to visit her they would say, "My you are Buckry Niggers (meaning we tried to live like white folks)."

I love to think of when we lived with old Master. We had a good time. Our cabin was nice and had a chimbley in it. Mother would cook and serve our breakfast at home every morning and dinner and supper on Sundays. We'd have biscuit every Sunday morning for our breakfast. That was something to look forward to.

We all went to church every Sunday. We would go to the white folks church in the morning and to our church in the evening. Bill McWilliams, old Master's oldest boy, didn't take much stock in church. He owned a nigger named Bird, who preached for us. Bill said, "Bird, you can't preach, you can't read, how on earth can you get a text out of the Bible when you can't even read? How'n hell can a man preach that don't know nothing?" Bird told him the Lord had called him to preach and he'd put the things in his mouth that he ought to say. One night Bill went to church and Bird preached the hair-raisingest sermon you ever heard. Bill told him all right to go and preach, and he gave Bird a horse and set him free to go anywhere he wanted to and preach.

Old Master and old Mistress lived in grand style. Bob

was the driver of their carriage. My, but he was always slick and shiny. He'd set up in front with his white shirt and black clothes. He looked like a black martin (bird) with a white breast. The nurse set in the back with the chillun. Old Master and Mistress set together in the front seat.

Old Master and Mistress would come down to the quarters to eat Christmas dinners sometimes and also birthday dinners. It was sho' a big day when they done that. They'd eat first, and the niggers would sing and dance to entertain them. Old Master would walk 'round through the quarters talking to the ones that was sick or too old to work. He was awful kind. I never knowed him to whip much. Once he whipped a woman for stealing. She and mother had to spin and weave. She couldn't or didn't work as fast as Ma and wouldn't have as much to show for her days work. She'd steal hanks of Ma's thread so she couldn't do more work than she did. She'd also steal old Master's tobacco. He caught up with her and whipped her.

I never saw any niggers on the block but I remember once they had a sale in town and I seen them pass our house in gangs, the little ones in wagons and others walking. I've seen slaves who run away from their masters and they'd have to work in the field with a big ball and chain on their leg. They'd hoe out to the end of the chain and then drag it up a piece and hoe on to the end of the row.

Times was awful hard during the War. We actually suffered for some salt. We'd go to the smoke house where meat had been salted down for years, dig a hole in the ground and fill it with water. After it would stand for a while we'd dip the water up carefully and strain it and cook our food in it. We parched corn and meal for coffee. We used syrup for sugar. Some folks parched okra for coffee. When the War was over you'd see men, women and chillun walk out of their cabins with a bundle under their arms. All going by in droves, just going nowhere in particular. My mother and father didn't join them; we stayed on at the plantation. I run off and got married when I was twenty. Ma never did want me to get married. My husband died five years ago. I never had no chillun.

I reckon I'm a mite superstitious. If a man comes to your house first on New Years you will have good luck; if a woman is your first visitor you'll have bad luck. When I was a young woman I knowed I'd be left alone in my old age. I seen it in my sleep. I dreamed I spit every tooth in my head right out in my hand and something tell me I would be a widow. That's a bad thing to dream about, losing your teeth.

Once my sister was at my house. She had a little baby and we was setting on the porch. They was a big pine tree in front of the house, and we seen something that looked like a big bird light in the tree. She begun to cry and say that's a sign my baby is going to die. Sho' nuff it just lived two weeks. Another time a big owl lit in a tree near a house and we heard it holler. The baby died that night. It was already sick, we's setting up with it.

I don't know where they's hants or not but I'se sho heard things I couldn't see.

We allus has made our own medicines. We used herbs and roots. If you'll take poke root and cut it in small pieces and string it and put it 'round a baby's neck it will cut teeth easy. A tea made out of dog fennel or corn shucks will cure chills and malaria. It'll make 'em throw up. We used to take button snake root, black snake root, chips of anvil iron and whiskey and make a tonic to cure consumption. It would cure it too.

Oklahoma Writers' Project
Ex-Slaves
10-13-37
[Date stamp: NOV 5 1937]

JAMES SOUTHALL
Age 82 years,
Oklahoma City, Okla.

I was born in Clarksville, Tenn. My father was Wesley and my mother was Hagar Southall. Our owner was Dr. John Southall, an old man. Father always belonged to him but he bought my mother when she was a young girl and raised her. She never knew anything 'bout her people but my father's mother lived with us in de quarter's at Master Southall's. Master John never sold any of his slaves.

We was known as "Free Niggers." Master said he didn't believe it was right to own human beings just because dey was black, and he freed all his slaves long before de War. He give 'em all freedom papers and told dem dat dey was as free as he was and could go anywhere dey wanted. Dey didn't have no where to go so we all stayed on wid him. It was nice though to know we could go where we pleased 'thout having to get a pass and could come back when we pleased even if we didn't take advantage of it.

He told his slaves dat dey could stay on at his farm but dey would have to work and make a living for deyselves and families. Old Master managed de farm and bought all de food and clothes for us all. Everybody had to work, but dey had a good time.

We had good clothes, plenty of food and good cabins. We had what was known as Georgia bedsteads. Dey was wooden bedsteads wid holes bored in de side pieces and in de foot and head-boards. Ropes was laced back and forth across and this took de place of both slats and springs. De ropes would git loose and we had what was called a "following-pin" to tighten 'em wid. We'd take a block of wood wid a notch in it and catch de rope and hold it till de following-pin could be driven in and den we'd twist de ropes tight again. We had grass or cotton beds and we slept good, too.

We had tin plates but no knives or forks so we et with our fingers. Old Master was a doctor and we had good attention when we was sick. We had no wish to take advantage of our freedom for we was a lot better off even than we is now and we knowed it. We never had to worry about anything.

De quarters was about a half mile from de "Big House" as we called Master John's house. It really wasn't such a big house as it had only four or five rooms in it. It was a common boxed house, painted white and wid a long gallery across de front. Maybe it was de gallery dat made it look so big to us. We liked to set on de steps at night and listen to Master John talk and to hear old Mistress and de girls sing. Sometimes we'd join in wid dem and fairly make de woods ring. Everybody thought dey was crazy to let us have so much freedom but dey wasn't nothing any of us black folks wouldn't a-done for that family.

He never employed any overseers as he done his own overseeing. He'd tell de older hands what he wanted done and dey would see it was done. We was never punished. Just iffen dey didn't work dey didn't have nothing to eat and wear and de hands what did work wouldn't divide wid 'em iffen dey didn't work. Old Master sho' was wise fer he knowed iffen we was ever set free dat we would have to work and he sure didn't bide no laziness in his hands. Dey got up 'bout four o'clock in de morning and was at work as soon as dey could see. Dey would work and sing as happy as you please.

We used to hear stories 'bout how slaves was punished but we never saw any of it. Dey would punish 'em by whupping 'em or by making 'em stand on one foot for a long time, tie 'em up by de thumbs as high as dey could reach and by making 'em do hard tasks and by going without food for two-three days.

Niggers was very religious and dey had church often. Dey would annoy de white folks wid shouting and singing and praying and dey would take cooking pots and put over dey mouths so de white folks couldn't hear 'em. Dey would dig holes in de ground too, and lie down when dey prayed.

Old Master let us have church in de homes. We had prayer-meeting every Wednesday night. All our cullud preachers could read de Bible. He let dem teach us how to read iffen we wanted to learn.

In de evening when we was through wid our work dey would gather at one of de cabins and visit and sing or dance. We'd pop corn, eat walnuts, peanuts, hickory nuts, and tell ghost stories. We didn't have any music instruments so de music we danced by wasn't so very good. Everybody sang and one or two would beat on tin pans or beat bones together.

Us boys played marbles. I got to be a professional. I could hit de middler ever time. We made a square and put a marble in each corner and one in de middle and got off several feet from de ring and shot at de marbles. Iffen you hit de middler you got de game. I could beat 'em all.

Old Master kept us through de War. We saw Yankee soldiers come through in droves lak Coxsey's Army. We wasn't afraid for ourselves but we was afraid dey would catch old Master or one of de boys when dey would come home on a furlough. We'd hep 'em git away and just swear dat dey hadn't been home a-tall.

After de war we stayed until old Master died. It broke us all up for we knowed we had lost de best friend dat we ever had or ever would have. He was a sort of father to all of us. Old Mistress went to live with her daughter and we started wandering 'round. Some folks from de North come down and made de cullud folks move on. I guess dey was afraid dat we'd hep our masters rebuild dey homes again. We lived in a sort of bondage for a long time.

De white folks in de South as well as de cullud folks lost de best friend dey had when Abe Lincoln was killed. He was God's man and it was a great loss when he died.

God created us all free and equal. Somewhere along de road we lost out.

Cullud folks would have been better off iffen dey had been left alone in Africa. We'd a-had better opportunities. We should have some compensation fer what we have suffered. Yes, we could be sent back and we'd like it if dey would help us to get started out again. Dat's where our forefathers come from.

I learned a long time ago dat dey was nothing to charms. How could a rabbit's foot bring me good luck? De Bible teaches me better'n dat. I believes in dreams though. I've seen de end of time in my dreams. Saw de great trouble we going through right now, years ago in a dream. It's clear in my mind how de world is coming to a end.

I believe all Christians should all join up together as dat makes 'em stronger. I believe in praying fer what we want and need. I'm a licensed preacher in de Baptist church. I've been a member for forty years but have just been a licensed preacher about ten years.

United States. Work Projects Administration

Slave Narratives

Oklahoma Writers' Project
Ex-Slaves

BEAUREGARD TENNEYSON
Age 87 yrs.
West Tulsa, Okla.

My mother and father just about stocked Jess Tenneyson's plantation with slaves. That's a fact. The old folks had one big family—twenty-three Children was the number. With the old folks that make twenty-five (there were only five more slaves), so I reckon they done mighty well by Master Jess.

The Master done well by them, too. Master Jess and Mistress Lula was Christian peoples. They raised their two sons, Henry and George, the same way.

There was so many of us children I don't remember all the names. Three of the boys was named after good southern gentlemen who soldiered in the War. Price, Lee and Beaugard. Beaugard is me. Proud of that name just like I'm proud of the Master's name.

My folks named Patrick and Harriett. Mother worked round the house And father was the field boss. They was close by the Master all the time.

The plantation was down in Craig County, Texas. Nine hundred acre it was. They raise everything, but mostly corn and cotton. Big times when come the harvest. Master fix up a cotton gin right on the place. It was an old-fashioned press. Six horses run it with two boys tromping down the cotton with their feets.

In the fall time was the best of all. Come cotton picking time, all the master from miles around send in their best pickers—and how they'd work, sometimes pick the whole crop in one day! The one who picked the most win a prize. Then come noon and the big feast, and at night come the dancing.

Something like that when the corn was ready. All the folks have the biggest time. Log rollings. Clearing the new ground for planting. Cutting the trees, burning the bresh, making ready for the plow. The best worker wins hisself a prize at these log rollings, too.

Them kind of good times makes me think of Christmas. Didn't have no Christmas tree, but they set up a long pine table in the house and that plank table was covered with presents and none of the Negroes was ever forgot on that day.

Master Jess didn't work his slaves like other white folks done. Wasn't no four o'clock wake-up horns and the field work started at seven o'clock. Quitting time was five o'clock—just about union hours nowadays. The Master believed in plenty of rest for the slaves and they work better that way, too.

One of my brother took care of the Master's horse while on the plantation. When the Master join in with rebels that horse went along. So did brother. Master need them both and my brother mighty pleased when he get to go.

When Master come back from the War and tell us that

brother is dead, he said brother was the best boy in all the army.

The Tenneyson slaves wasn't bothered with patrollers, neither the Klan. The Master said we was all good Negroes—nobody going to bother a good Negro.

We was taught to work and have good manners. And to be honest. Just doing them three things will keep anybody out of trouble.

United States. Work Projects Administration

Oklahoma Writers' Project
Ex-Slaves

WILLIAM WALTERS
Age 85 yrs.
Tulsa, Oklahoma.

Mammy Ann (that was my mother) was owned by Mistress Betsy, and lived on the Bradford plantation in Relsford County, Tennessee, when I was born in 1852.

My daddy, Jim Walters, then lived in Nashville, where my mammy carried me when she ran away from the Mistress after the Rebs and Yanks started to fight. My daddy died in Nashville in 1875.

We were runaway slaves. The slipper-offers were often captured, but Mammy Ann and her little boy William (that's me) escaped the sharp eyes of the patrollers and found refuge with a family of northern symphatizers living in Nashville.

Nashville was a fort town, filled with trenches and barricades. Right across the road from where we stayed was a vacant block used by the Rebs as an emergency place for treating the wounded.

I remember the boom of cannons one whole day, and I heard the rumble of army wagons as they crossed through the town. But there was nothing to see as the fog of powder smoke became thicker with every blast of Sesesh cannon.

When the smoke fog cleared away I watched the wounded being carried to the clearing across the road—fighting men with arms shot off, legs gone, faces blood smeared—some of them just laying there cussing God and Man with their dying breath!

Those were awful times. Yet I have heard many of the older Negroes say the old days were better.

Such talk always seemed to me but an expression of sentiment for some good old master, or else the older Negroes were just too handicapped with ignorance to recognize the benefits of liberty or the opportunities of freedom.

But I've always been proud of my freedom, and proud of my old mother who faced death for her freedom and mine when she escaped from the Bradford plantation a long time before freedom came to the Negro race as a whole.

Oklahoma Writers' Project
Ex-Slaves
570 words
10-19-1938

MARY FRANCES WEBB
Grand daughter of Sarah Vest, aged 92, (deceased) McAlester, Okla.

I've heard my grandmother tell a lot of her experiences during slavery. She remembered things well as she was a grown woman at the time of the War of the Rebellion.

Her home was at Sedalia, Mo., and her owner was Baxter West, a prominent farmer and politician. He was very kind and good to his slaves. He provided them with plenty of food and good clothes. He would go to town and buy six or eight bolts of cloth at a time and the women could pick out two dresses apiece off it. These would be their dresses for dressing up. They wove the cloth for their everyday clothes.

The men wore jeans suits in winter. He bought shoes for all his slaves, young and old. He had about twenty slaves counting the children.

My grandmother was a field hand. She plowed and hoed the crops in the summer and spring, and in the winter she sawed and cut cord wood just like a man. She said it didn't hurt her as she was as strong as an ox.

She could spin and weave and sew. She helped make all the cloth for their clothes and in the spring one of the jobs for the women was to weave hats for the men. They used oat-straw, grass, and cane which had been split and dried and soaked in hot water until it was pliant, and they wove it into hats. The women wore a cloth tied around their head.

They didn't have many matches so they always kept a log heap burning to keep a fire. It was a common thing for a neighbor to come in to borrow a coal of fire as their fire had died out.

On wash days all the neighbors would send several of their women to the creek to do the family wash. They all had a regular picnic of it as they would wash and spread the clothes on the bushes and low branches of the trees to dry. They would get to spend the day together.

They had no tubs or wash boards. They had a large flat block of wood and a wooden paddle. They'd spread the wet garment on the block, spread soap on it and paddle the garment till it was clean. They would rinse the clothes in the creek. Their soap was made from lye, dripped from ashes, and meat scraps.

The slaves had no lamps in their cabins. In winter they would pile wood on the fire in their fireplace and have the light from the fire.

The colored men went with their master to the army. They made regular soldiers and endured the same hardships that the white soldiers did. They told of one battle when so many men were killed that a little stream seemed to be running pure blood as the water was so bloody.

After the war the slaves returned home with their masters and some of the older ones stayed on with them and helped them to rebuild their farms. None of them seemed to think it strange that they had been fighting on the wrong side in the army as they were following their white folks.

Those who stayed with their old master were taught to read and write and were taught to handle their own business and to help themselves in every way possible to take their place in life.

United States. Work Projects Administration

Oklahoma Writers' Project
Ex-Slaves
10-14-37
[Date stamp: NOV 5 1937]

EASTER WELLS
Age 83
Colbert, Okla.

I was born in Arkansas, in 1854, but we moved to Texas in 1855. I've heard 'em tell about de trip to Texas. De grown folks rode in wagons and carts but de chaps all walked dat was big enuff. De men walked and toted their guns and hunted all de way. Dey had plenty of fresh game to eat.

My mother's name was Nellie Bell. I had one sister, Liza. I never saw my father; in fact, I never heard my mammy say anything about him and I don't guess I ever asked her anything about him for I never thought anything about not having a father. I guess he belonged to another family and when we moved away he was left behind and he didn't try to find us after de War.

My mammy and my sister and me belonged to young Master Jason Bell. We was his onliest slaves and as he wasn't married and lived at home wid his parents we was worked and bossed by his father, Cap'n William Bell and his wife, Miss Mary.

After we moved to Texas, old Master built a big double log house, weather-boarded on de inside and out. It was painted white. Dey was a long gallery clean across de front of de house and a big open hall between de two front rooms. Dey was three rooms on each side of de hall and a wide gallery across de back. De kitchen set back from de house and dey was a board walk leading to it. Vines was planted 'round de gallery and on each side of de walk in de summer time. De house was on a hill and set back from de big road about a quarter of a mile and dey was big oak and pine trees all 'round de yard. We had purty flowers, too.

We had good quarters. Dey was log cabins, but de logs was peeled and square-adzed and put together with white plaster and had shuttered windows and pine floors. Our furniture was home made but it was good and made our cabins comfortable.

Old Master give us our allowance of staple food and it had to run us, too. We could raise our own gardens and in dat way we had purty plenty to eat. Dey took good care of us sick or well and old Mistress was awful good to us.

My mammy was de cook. I remember old Master had some purty strict rules and one of 'em was iffen you burnt de bread you had to eat it. One day mammy burnt de bread. She was awful busy and forgot it and it burnt purty bad. She knowed dat old Master would be mad and she'd be punished so she got some grub and her bonnet and she lit out. She hid in de woods and cane brakes for two weeks and dey couldn't find her either. One of de women slipped food out to her. Finally she come home and old Master give her a whipping but he didn't hurt her none. He was glad to git her back. She told us dat she could'a slipped off to de North but she didn't want to leave us children. She was afraid young Master would be mad and sell us and we'd a-had a hard time so she come back. I don't know whether she ever burnt de bread any more or not.

Once one of de men got his 'lowance and he decided he'd have de meat all cooked at once so he come to our cabin and got mammy to cook it for him. She cooked it and he took it home. One day he was at work and a dog got in and et de meat all up. He didn't have much food for de rest of de week. He had to make out wid parched corn.

We all kept parched corn all de time and went 'round eating it. It was good to fill you up iffen you was hungry and was nourishing, too.

When de niggers cooked in dere own cabins dey put de food in a sort of tray or trough and everybody et together. Dey didn't have no dishes. We allus ate at de Big House as mammy had to do de cooking for de family.

I never had to work hard as old Master wanted us to grow up strong. He'd have mammy boil Jerusalem Oak and make a tea for us to drink to cure us of worms and we'd run races and get exercise so we would be healthy.

Old Mistress and old Master had three children. Dey was two children dead between Master Jason and Miss Jane. Dey was a little girl 'bout my age, named Arline. We played together all de time. We used to set on de steps at night and old Mistress would tell us about de stars. She'd tell us and show us de Big Dipper, Little Dipper, Milky Way, Ellen's Yard, Job's Coffin, and de Seven Sisters. I can show 'em to you and tell you all about 'em yet.

I scared Arline and made her fall and break her leg twice. One time we was on de porch after dark one night and I told her dat I heard something and I made like I could see it and she couldn't so she got scared and run and hung her toe in a crack and fell off de high porch and broke her leg. Another time while de War was going on we was dressed up in long dresses playing grown-ups. We had playhouses under some big castor-bean bushes. We climbed up on de fence and jest for fun I told her dat I seen some Yankees coming. She started to run and got tangled up in her long dress and fell and broke her leg again. It nigh broke my heart for I loved her and she loved me and she didn't tell on me either time. I used to visit her after she was married and we'd sure have a good visit talking 'bout de things we used to do. We was separated when we was about fifteen and didn't see [HW: each] other any more till we was both married and had children. I went to visit her at Bryant, Brazos County, Texas and I ain't seen her since. I don't know whether she is still living or not.

I 'members hearing a man say dat once he was a nigger trader. He'd buy and trade or sell 'em like they was stock. He become a Christian and never sold any more.

Our young Master went to de War and got wounded and come home and died. Old Master den took full charge of us and when de War ended he kept us because he said we didn't have no folks and he said as our owner was dead we wasn't free. Mother died about a year after de War, and some white folks took my sister but I was afraid to go. Old Master told me iffen I left him he would cut my ears off end I'd starve and I don't know what all he did tell me he'd do. I must a-been a fool but I was afraid to try it.

I had so much work to do and I never did git to go anywhere. I reckon he was afraid to let me go off de place for fear some one would tell me what a fool I was, so I never did git to go anywhere but had to work all de time. I was de only one to work and old Mistress and de girls never had done no work and didn't know much about it. I had a harder time den when we was slaves.

I got to wanting to see my sister so I made up my mind to run off. One of old Master's motherless nephews lived with him and I got him to go with me one night to the potato bank and I got me a lap full of potatoes to eat so I wouldn't starve like old Master said I would. Dis white boy went nearly to a house where some white folks lived. I went to de house and told 'em I wanted to go to where my sister was and dey let me stay fer a few days and sent me on to my sister.

I saw old Master lots of times after I run away but he wasn't mad at me. I heard him tell de white folks dat I lived wid dat he raised me and I sure wouldn't steal nor tell a lie. I used to steal brown sugar lumps when mammy would be cooking but he didn't know 'bout dat.

On holidays we used to allus have big dinners, 'specially on Christmas, and we allus had egg-nog.

We allus had hog-jowl and peas on New Years Day 'cause iffen you'd have dat on New Years Day you'd have good luck all de year.

Iffen you have money on New Years' Day you will have money all de year.

My husband, Lewis Wells, lived to be one-hundred and seven years old. He died five years ago. He could see witches, spirits and ghosts but I never could. Dere are a few things dat I've noticed and dey never fail.

Dogs howling and scritch owls hollering is allus a warning. My mother was sick and we didn't think she was much sick. A dog howled and howled right outside de house. Old Master say, "Nellie gonna die." Sure nuff she died dat night.

Another time a gentle old mule we had got after de children and run 'em to do house and den he lay down and wallow and wallow. One of our children was dead 'fore a week.

One of our neighbors say his dog been gone 'bout a week. He was walking and met de dog and it lay down and stretch out on de ground and measure a grave wid his body. He made him git up and he went home jest as fast as he could. When he got dere one of his children was dead.

Iffen my left eye quiver I know I'm gwineter cry and iffen both my eyes quiver I know I gwinter laugh till I cry. I don't like for my eyes to quiver.

We has allus made our own medicine. Iffen we hadn't we never could astood de chills and fevers. We made a tea out'n bitter weeds and bathed in it to cure malaria. We also made bread pills and soaked 'em in dis tea and swallowed 'em. After bathing in dis tea we'd go to bed and kiver up and sweat de malaria out.

Horse mint and palm of crystal (Castor-bean) and bullnettle root boiled together will make a cure fer swelling. Jest bathe de swollen part in dis hot tea.

Anvil dust and apple vinegar will cure dropsy. One tea cup of anvil dust to a quart of vinegar. Shake up well and bathe in it. It sure will cure de worse kind of a case.

God worked through Abraham Lincoln and he answered de prayers of dem dat was wearing de burden of slavery. We cullud folks all love and honor Abraham Lincoln's memory and don't you think we ought to?

I love to hear good singing. My favorite songs are: "Am I A Soldier Of The Cross", an "How Can I Live In Sin and Doubt My Savior's Love." I belongs to de Baptist church.

United States. Work Projects Administration

Oklahoma Writers' Project
Ex-Slaves
Revision of story sent in 8-13-37.

JOHN WHITE
Age 121 years
Sand Springs, Okla.

Of all my Mammy's children I am the first born and the longest living. The others all gone to join Mammy. She was named Mary White, the same name as her Mistress, the wife of my first master, James White.

About my pappy. I never hear his name and I never see him, not even when I was the least child around the old Master's place 'way back there in Georgia more'n one-hundred twenty years ago!

Mammy try to make it clear to me about my daddy. She married like the most of the slaves in them days.

He was a slave on another plantation. One day he come for to borrow something from Master White. He sees a likely looking gal, and the way it work out that gal was to be my Mammy. After that he got a paper saying it was all right for him to be off his own plantation. He come a'courting over to Master White's. After a while he talks with the Master. Says he wants to marry the gal, Mary. The Master says it's all right if it's all right with Mary and the other white folks. He finds out it is and they makes ready for the wedding.

Mary says a preacher wedding is the best but Master say he can marry them just as good. There wasn't no Bible, just an old Almanac. Master White read something out of that. That's all and they was married. The wedding was over!

Every night he gets a leave paper from his Master and come over to be with his wife, Mary. The next morning he leaves her to work in the fields. Then one night Mammy says he don't come home. The next night is the same, and the next. From then on Mammy don't see him no more—never find out what happen to my pappy.

When I was born Mammy named me John, John White. She tells me I was the blackest 'white' boy she ever see. I stays with her till I was eleven year old. The Master wrote down in the book when I was born, April 10, 1816, and I know it's right. Mammy told me so, and Master told me when I was eleven and he sold me to Sarah Davenport.

Mistress Sarah lived in Texas. Master White always selling and trading to folks all over the country. I hates to leave on account of Mammy and the good way Master White fared the slaves—they was good people. Mammy cry but I has to go just the same. The tears are on my face a long time after the leaving. I was hoping all the time to see Mammy again, but that's the last time.

We travels and travels on the stage coach. Once we cross the Big River (Mississippi) on the boat and pick up with the horses on the other side. A new outfit and we rides some more. Seems like we going to wear out all the horses before we gets to the place.

The Davenport plantation was way north of Linden, Texas, up in the Red River country. That's where I stayed for thirty-eight year. There I was drug through the hackles by the meanest master that ever lived. The Mistress was the best white woman I ever knew but Master Presley used his whip all the time, reason or no reason, and I got scars to remember by!

I remembers the house. A heavy log house with a gallery clear across the front. The kitchen was back of the house. I work in there and I live in there. It wasn't built so good as the Master's house. The cold winds in the winter go through the cracks between the logs like the walls was somewheres else, and I shivers with the misery all the time.

The cooking got to be my job. The washing too. Washday come around and I fills the tub with clothes. Puts the tub on my head and walks half a mile to the spring where I washes the clothes. Sometimes I run out of soap. Then I make ash soap right by the spring. I learns to be careful about streaks in the clothes. I learns by the bull whip. One day the Master finds a soapy streak in his shirt. Then he finds me.

The Military Road goes by the place and the Master drives me down the road and ties me to a tree. First he tears off the old shirt and then he throws the bull whip to me. When he is tired of beating me more torture is a-coming. The salt water cure. It don't cure nothing but that's what the white folks called it. "Here's at you," the Master say, and slap the salt water into the bleeding cuts.

"Here's at you!" The blisters burst every time he slap me with the brine.

Then I was loosened to stagger back into the kitchen. The Mistress couldn't do nothing about it 'cept to lay on the grease thick, with a kind word to help stop the misery.

Ration time was Saturday night. Every slave get enough fat pork, corn meal and such to last out the week. I reckon the Master figure it to the last bite because they was no leavings over. Most likely the shortage catch them!

Sometimes they'd borrow, sometimes I'd slip somethings from out the kitchen. The single women folks was bad that way. I favors them with something extra from the kitchen. Then they favors me—at night when the overseer thinks everybody asleep in they own places!

I was always back to my kitchen bed long before the overseer give the get-up-knock. I hear the knock, he hear me answer. Then he blow the horn and shout the loud call, ARE YOU UP, and everybody know it was four o'clock and pour out of the cabins ready for the chores.

Sometimes the white folks go around the slave quarters for the night. Not on the Davenport plantation, but some others close around. The slaves talked about it amongst themselves.

After a while they'd be a new baby. Yellow. When the child got old enough for chore work the master would sell him (or her). No difference was it his own flesh and blood—if the price was right!

I traffic with lots of the women, but never marries. Not even when I was free after the War. I sees too many married troubles to mess up with such doings!

Sometimes the master sent me alone to the grinding mill. Load in the yellow corn, hitch in the oxen, I was ready to go. I gets me fixed up with a pass and takes to the road.

That was the trip I like best. On the way was a still. Off in the bresh. If the still was lonely I stop, not on the way to but on the way back. Mighty good whiskey, too! Maybe I drinks too much, then I was sorry.

Not that I swipe the whiskey, just sorry because I gets sick! Then I figures a woods camp meeting will steady me up and I goes.

The preacher meet me and want to know how is my feelings. I says I is low with the misery and he say to join up with the Lord.

I never join because he don't talk about the Lord. Just about the Master and Mistress. How the slaves must obey around the plantation—how the white folks know what is good for the slaves. Nothing about obeying the Lord and working for him.

I reckon the old preacher was worrying more about the bull whip than he was the Bible, else he say something about the Lord! But I always obeys the Lord—that's why I is still living!

The slaves would pray for to get out of bondage. Some of them say the Lord told them to run away. Get to the

North. Cross the Red River. Over there would be folks to guide them to the Free State (Kansas).

The Lord never tell me to run away. I never tried it, maybe, because mostly they was caught by patrollers and fetched back for a flogging—and I had whippings enough already!

Before the Civil War was the fighting with Mexico. Some of the troops on they way south passed on the Military Road. Wasn't any fighting around Linden or Jefferson during the time.

They was lots of traveling on the Military Road. Most of the time you could see covered wagons pulled by mules and horses, and sometimes a crawling string of wagons with oxen on the pulling end.

From up in Arkansas come the stage coach along the road. To San Antonio. The drivers bring news the Mexicans just about all killed off and the white folks say Texas was going to join the Union. The country's going to be run different they say, but I never see no difference. Maybe, because I ain't white folks.

Wasn't many Mexicans around the old plantation. Come and go. Lots of Indians. Cherokees and Choctaws. Living in mud huts and cabin shacks. I never see them bother the whites, it was the other way around.

During the Civil War, when the Red River was bank high with muddy water, the Yankee's made a target of Jefferson. That was a small town down south of Linden.

Down the river come a flat barge with cannon fastened to the deck. The Yankee soldiers stopped across the river from Jefferson and the shooting started.

When the cannon went to popping the folks went arunning—hard to tell who run the fastest, the whites or the blacks! Almost the town was wiped out. Buildings was smashed and big trees cut through with the cannon balls.

And all the time the Yankee drums was a-beating and the soldiers singing:

We'll hang Jeff Davis on a sour apple tree,

As we go marching on!

Before the Civil War everybody had money. The white folks, not the negroes. Sometimes the master take me to the town stores. They was full of money. Cigar boxes on the counter, boxes on the shelf, all filled with money. Not the crinkley paper kind, but hard, jingley gold and silver! Not like these scarce times!

After the War I stay on the plantation 'til a soldier man tells me of the freedom. The master never tell us—negroes working just like before the War.

That's when I leave the first time. Slip off, saying nothing, to Jefferson. There I found some good white folks going to New Orleans. First place we go is Shreveport, by wagon. They took me because I fix up with them to do the cooking.

On to the Big River (Mississippi) and boards a river steamboat for New Orleans. Lots of negroes going down there—to work on the canal.

The whole town was built on logs covered with dirt.

Trying to raise itself right out of the swamp. Sometimes the water get high and folks run for the hills. When I got there almost was I ready to leave.

I like Texas the best. Back to Jefferson is where I go. Fifteen-twenty mile below Linden. Almost the first person I see was Master Davenport.

He says, "Black rascal, you is coming with me." And I do. He tried to keep his slaves and just laugh when I tell him about the freedom. I worked for food and quarters 'til his meanness come cropping out again.

That wasn't long and he threatened me with the whip and the buck and gag. The buck and gag was maybe worse. I got to feeling that iron stick in my mouth, fastened around my head with chains, pressing hard on my tongue. No drinking, no eating, no talking!

So I slip off again. That night I goes through Linden. Crawling on my hands and knees! Keeping in the dark spots, hiding from the whites, 'til I pass the last house, then my feets hurries me to Jefferson, where I gets a ride to Arkansas.

In Russelville is where I stop. There I worked around in the yards, cutting the grass, fancying the flower beds, and earned a little money for clothes and eats, with some of it spent for good whiskey.

That was the reason I left Arkansas. Whiskey. The law got after me to tell where was a man's whiskey still. I just leave so's I won't have to tell.

But while I was making a little money in Russelville,

I lose out on some big money, account some white folks beat me to it.

I was out in the hills west of town, walking along the banks of a little creek, when I heard a voice. Queer like. I called out who is that talking and I hears it again.

"Go to the white oak tree and you will find Ninety Thousand Dollars!" That's what I hear. I look around, nobody in sight, but I see the tree. A big white oak tree standing taller than all the rest 'round about.

Under the tree was a grave. An old grave. I scratch around but finds no money and thinks of getting some help.

I done some work for a white man in town and told him about the voice. He promised to go with me, but the next day he took two white mens and dug around the tree. Then he says they was nothing to find.

To this day I know better. I know wherever they's a ghost, money is around someplace! That's what the ghost comes back for.

Somebody dies and leaves buried money. The ghost watches over it 'til it sees somebody it likes. Then ghost shows himself—lets know he's around. Sometimes the ghost tells where is the money buried, like that time at Russelville.

That ain't the only ghost I've seen or heard. I see one around the yard where I is living now. A woman. Some of these times she'll tell me where the buried money is.

Maybe the ghost woman thinks I is too old to dig. But

I been a-digging all these long years. For a bite to eat and a sleep-under cover.

I reckon pretty soon she's going to tell where to dig. When she does, then old Uncle John won't have to dig for the eats no more!

Oklahoma Writers' Project
Ex-Slaves
[HW: (photo)]
[Date stamp: AUG 16 1937]

CHARLEY WILLIAMS
Age 94 yrs.
Tulsa, Okla.

Iffen I could see better out'n my old eyes, and I had me something to work with and de feebleness in my back and head would let me 'lone, I would have me plenty to eat in de kitchen all de time, and plenty tobaccy in my pipe, too, bless God!

And dey wouldn't be no rain trickling through de holes in de roof, and no planks all fell out'n de flo' on de gallery neither, 'cause dis one old nigger knows everything about making all he need to git along! Old Master done showed him how to git along in dis world, jest as long as he live on a plantation, but living in de town is a different way of living, and all you got to have is a silver dime to lay down for everything you want, and I don't git de dime very often.

But I aint give up! Nothing like dat! On de days when I don't feel so feeble and trembly I jest keep patching 'round de place. I got to keep patching so as to keep it whar it will hold de winter out, in case I git to see another winter.

Iffen I don't, it don't grieve me none, 'cause I wants

to see old Master again anyways. I reckon maybe I'll jest go up an ask him what he want me to do, and he'll tell me, and iffen I don't know how he'll show me how, and I'll try to do it to please him. And when I git it done I wants to hear him grumble like he used to and say, "Charley, you ain't got no sense but you is a good boy. Dis here ain't very good but it'll do, I reckon. Git yourself a little piece o' dat brown sugar, but don't let no niggers see you eating it—if you do I'll whup your black behind!"

Dat ain't de way it going be in Heaven, I reckon, but I can't set here on dis old rottendy gallery and think of no way I better like to have it!

I was a great big hulking buck of a boy when de War come along and bust up everything, and I can 'member back when everybody was living peaceful and happy, and nobody never had no notion about no war.

I was borned on the 'leventh of January, in 1843, and was old enough to vote when I got my freedom, but I didn't take no stock in all dat politics and goings on at dat time, and I didn't vote till a long time after old Master passed away, but I was big enough before de War to remember everything pretty plain.

Old Master name was John Williams, and old Mistress name was Miss Betty, and she was a Campbell before she married. Young Missy was named Betty after her mommy, and Young Master was named Frank, but I don't know who after. Our overseer was Mr. Simmons, and he was mighty smart and had a lot of patience, but he wouldn't take no talk nor foolishness. He didn't whup nobody very often, but he only had to whup 'em jest one time! He never did whup a nigger at de time the nigger done something, but he would wait till evening and have old Master come and watch him do it. He never whupped very hard 'cept when he had told a nigger about something and promised a whupping next time and the nigger done it again. Then that nigger got what he had been hearing 'bout!

De plantation was about as big as any. I think it had about three hundred acres, and it was about two miles northwest of Monroe, Louisiana. Then he had another one not so big, two—three miles south of the big one, kind of down in the woodsy part along the White river bottoms. He had another overseer on that place and a big passel of niggers, but I never did go down to that one. That was where he raised most of his corn and shoats, and lots of sorghum cane.

Our plantation was up on higher ground, and it was more open country, but still they was lots of woods all around and lots of the plantations had been whacked right out of de new ground and was full of stumps. Master's place was more open, though, and all in the fields was good plowing.

The big road runned right along past our plantation, and it come from Shreveport and run into Monroe. There wasn't any town at Monroe in them days, jest a little cross roads place with a general store and a big hide house. I think there was about two big hide houses, and you could smell that place a mile before you got into it. Old Master had a part in de store, I think.

De hide houses was jest long sheds, all open along de sides and kivered over wid cypress clapboards.

Down below de hide houses and de store was jest a little settlement of one or two houses, but they was a school for white boys. Somebody said there was a place where they had been an old fort, but I never did see it.

Everything boughten we got come from Shreveport, and was brung in by the stage and the freighters, and that was only a little coffee or gunpowder, or some needles for the sewing, or some strap iron for the blacksmith, or something like dat. We made and raised everything else we needed right on the place.

I never did even see any quinine till after I was free. My mammy knowed jest what root to go out and pull up to knock de chills right out'n me. And de bellyache and de running off de same way, too.

Our plantation was a lot different from some I seen other places, like way east of there, around Vicksburg. Some of them was fixed up fancier but dey didn't have no more comforts than we had.

Old Master come out into that country when he was a young man, and they didn't have even so much then as they had when I was a boy. I think he come from Alabama or Tennessee, and way back his people had come from Virginia, or maybe North Carolina, 'cause he knowed all about tobacco on the place. Cotton and tobacco was de long crops on his big place, and of course lots of horses and cattle and mules.

De big house was made out'n square hewed logs, and chinked wid little rocks and daubed wid white clay, and kivered wid cypress clapboards. I remember one time we put on a new roof, and de niggers hauled up de cypress logs and sawed dem and frowed out de clapboards by hand.

De house had two setting rooms on one side and a big kitchen room on de other, wid a wide passage in between, and den about was de sleeping rooms. They wasn't no stairways 'cepting on de outside. Steps run up to de sleeping rooms on one side from de passageway and on de other side from clean outside de house. Jest one big chimbley was all he had, and it was on de kitchen end, and we done all de cooking in a fireplace dat was purty nigh as wide as de whole room.

In de sleeping rooms day wasn't no fires 'cepting in brazers made out of clay, and we toted up charcoal to burn in 'em when it was cold mornings in de winter. Dey kept warm wide de bed clothes and de knitten clothes dey had.

Master never did make a big gallery on de house, but our white folks would set out in de yard under de big trees in de shade. They was long benches made out'n hewed logs and all padded wid gray moss and corn shuck padding, and dey set pretty soft. All de furniture in de house was home-made, too. De beds had square posts as big around as my shank and de frame was mortised into 'em, and holes bored in de frame and home-made rope laced in to make it springy. Den a great big mattress full of goose feathers and two—three comforts as thick as my foot wid carded wool inside! Dey didn't need no fireplaces!

De quarters was a little piece from de big house, and dey run along both sides of de road dat go to de fields. All one-room log cabins, but dey was good and warm, and every one had a little open shed at de side whar we sleep in de summer to keep cool.

They was two or three wells at de quarters for water, and some good springs in de branch at de back of de fields. You could ketch a fish now and den in dat branch, but Young Master used to do his fishing in White River, and take a nigger or two along to do de work at his camp.

It wasn't very fancy at de Big House, but it was mighty pretty jest de same, wid de gray moss hanging from de big trees, and de cool green grass all over de yard, and I can shet my old eyes and see it jest like it was before de War come along and bust it up.

I can see old Master setting out under a big tree smoking one of his long cheroots his tobacco nigger made by hand, and fanning hisself wid his big wide hat another nigger platted out'n young inside corn shucks for him, and I can hear him holler at a big bunch of white geeses what's gitting in his flower beds and see 'em string off behind de old gander towards de big road.

When de day begin to crack de whole plantation break out wid all kinds of noises, and you could tell what going on by de kind of noise you hear.

Come de daybreak you hear de guinea fowls start potracking down at de edge of de woods lot, and den de roosters all start up 'round de barn and de ducks finally wake up and jine in. You can smell de sow belly frying down at the cabins in de "row", to go wid de hoecake and de buttermilk.

Den purty soon de wind rise a little, and you can hear a old bell donging way on some plantation a mile or two off, and den more bells at other places and maybe a horn, and purty soon younder go old Master's old ram horn wid a long toot and den some short toots, and here come de overseer down de row of cabins, hollering right and left, and picking de ham out'n his teeth wid a long shiny goose quill pick.

Bells and horns! Bells for dis and horns for dat! All we knowed was go and come by de bells and horns!

Old ram horn blow to send us all to de field. We all line up, about seventy-five field niggers, and go by de tool shed and git our hoes, or maybe go hitch up de mules to de plows and lay de plows out on de side so de overseer can see iffen de points is shart. Any plow gits broke or de point gits bungled up on de rocks it goes to de blacksmith nigger, den we all git on down in de field.

Den de anvil start dangling in de blacksmith shop: "Tank! Deling-ding! Tank! Deling-ding!", and dat ole bull tongue gitting straightened out!

Course you can't hear de shoemaker awling and pegging, and de card spinners, and de old mammy sewing by hand, but maybe you can hear de old loom going "frump, frump", and you know it all right iffen your clothes do be wearing out, 'cause you gwine git new britches purty soon!

We had about a hundred niggers on dat place, young and old, and about twenty on de little place down below. We could make about every kind of thing but coffee and gunpowder dat our whitefolks and us needed.

When we needs a hat we gits inside cornshucks and

weave one out, and makes horse collars de same way. Jest tie two little soft shucks together and begin plaiting.

All de cloth 'cepting de Mistress' Sunday dresses come from de sheep to de carders and de spinners and de weaver, den we dye it wid "butternut" and hickory bark and indigo and other things and set it wid copperas. Leather tanned on de place made de shoes, and I never see a store boughten wagon wheel 'cepting among de stages and de freighters along de big road.

We made purty, long back-combs out'n cow horn, and knitting needles out'n second hickory. Split a young hickory and put in a big wedge to prize it open, then cut it down and let it season, and you got good bent grain for wagon hames and chair rockers and such.

It was jest like dat until I was grown, and den one day come a neighbor man and say we in de War.

Little while young Master Frank ride over to Vicksburg and jine de Sesesh army, but old Master jest go on lak nothing happen, and we all don't hear nothing more until long come some Sesesh soldiers and take most old Master's hosses and all his wagons.

I bin working on de tobacco, and when I come back to de barns everything was gone. I would go into de woods and git good hickory and burn it till it was all coals and put it out wid water to make hickory charcoal for curing de tobacco. I had me some charcoal in de fire trenches under de curing houses, all full of new tobacco, and overseer come and say bundle all de tobacco up and he going take it to Shreveport and sell it befo' de soldiers take it too.

After de hosses all gone and most de cattle and de cotton and de tobacco gone too, here come de Yankees and spread out all over de whole country. Dey had a big camp down below our plantation.

One evening a big bunch of Yankee officers come up to de Big House and old Master set out de brandy in de yard and dey act purty nice. Next day de whole bunch leave on out of dat part.

When de hosses and stuff all go old Master sold all de slaves but about four, but he kept my pappy and mammy and my brother Jimmie and my sister Betty. She was named after old Mistress. Pappy's name was Charley and mammy's was Sally. De niggers he kept didn't have much work without any hosses and wagons, but de blacksmith started in fixing up more wagons and he kept them hid in de woods till they was all fixed.

Den along come some more Yankees, and dey tore everything we had up, and old Master was afeared to shoot at them on account his womenfolks, so he tried to sneak the fambly out but they kotched him and brung him back to de plantation.

We niggers didn't know dat he was gone until we seen de Yankees bringing dem back. De Yankees had done took charge of everything and was camping in de big yard, and us was all down at de quarters scared to death, but dey was jest letting us alone.

It was night when de white folks tried to go away, and still night when de Yankees brung dem back, and a house nigger come down to de quarters wid three—four mens in blue clothes and told us to come up to de Big House.

De Yankees didn't seem to be mad wid old Master, but jest laughed and talked wid him, but he didn't take de jokes any too good.

Den dey asked him could he dance and he said no, and dey told him to dance or make us dance. Dar he stood inside a big ring of dem mens in blue clothes, wid dey brass buttons shining in de light from de fire dey had in front of de tents, and he jest stood and said nothing, and it look lak he wasn't wanting to tell us to dance.

So some of us young bucks jest step up and say we was good dancers, and we start shuffling while de rest of de niggers pat.

Some nigger women go back to de quarters and git de gourd fiddles and de clapping bones made out'n beef ribs, and bring dem back so we could have some music. We git all warmed up and dance lak we never did dance befo'! I speck we invent some new steps dat night!

We act lak we dancing for de Yankees, but we trying to please Master and old Mistress more than anything, and purty soon he begin to smile a little and we all feel a lot better.

Next day de Yankees move on away from our place, and old Master start gitting ready to move out. We git de wagons we hid, and de whole passel of us leaves out for Shreveport. Jest left de old place standing like it was.

In Shreveport old Master git his cotton and tobacco money what he been afraid to have sent back to de plantation when he sell his stuff, and we strike out north through Arkansas.

Dat was de awfullest trip any man ever make! We had to hide from everybody until we find out if dey Yankees or Sesesh, and we go along little old back roads and up one mountain and down another, through de woods all de way.

After a long time we git to the Missouri line, and kind of cut off through de corner of dat state into Kansas. I don't know how we ever git across some of dem rivers but we did. Dey nearly always would be some soldiers around de fords, and dey would help us find de best crossing. Sometimes we had to unload de wagons and dry out de stuff what all got wet, and camp a day or two to fix up again.

Purty soon we git to Fort Scott, and that was whar de roads forked ever whichaways. One went on north and one east and one went down into de Indian country. It was full of soldiers coming and going back and forth to Arkansas and Fort Gibson.

We took de road on west through Kansas, and made for Colorado Springs.

Fort Scott was all run down, and the old places whar dey used to have de soldiers was all fell in in most places. Jest old rackety walls and leaky roofs, and a big pole fence made out'n poles sot in de ground all tied together, but it was falling down too.

They was lots of wagons all around what belong to de army, hauling stuff for de soldiers, and some folks told old Master he couldn't make us niggers go wid him, but we said we wanted to anyways, so we jest went on west across Kansas.

When we got away on west we come to a fork, and de best road went kinda south into Mexico, and we come to a little place called Clayton, Mexico whar we camped a while and then went north.

Dat place is in New Mexico now, but old Master jest called it Mexico. Somebody showed me whar it is on de map, and it look lak it a long ways off'n our road to Colorado Springs, but I guess de road jest wind off down dat ways at de time we went over it. It was jest two or three houses made out'n mud at dat time, and a store whar de soldiers and de Indians come and done trading.

About dat time old Master sell off some of de stuff he been taking along, 'cause de wagons loaded too heavy for de mountains and he figger he better have de money than some of de stuff, I reckon.

On de way north it was a funny country. We jest climb all day long gitting up one side of one bunch of mountains, and all de nigger men have to push on de wheels while de mules pull and den scotch de wheels while de mules rest. Everybody but de whitefolks has to walk most de time.

Down in de valleys it was warm like in Louisiana, but it seem lak de sun aint so hot on de head, but it look lak every time night come it ketch us up on top of one of dem mountains, and it almost as cold as in de winter time!

All de niggers had shoes and plenty warm clothes and we wrop up at night in everything we can git.

We git to Fort Scott again, and den de Yankee officers come and ask all us niggers iffen we want to leave old

Master and stay dar and work, 'cause we all free now. Old Master say we can do what we please about it.

A few of de niggers stay dar in Fort Scott, but most of us say we gwine stay wid old Master, and we don't care iffen we is free or not.

When we git back to Monroe to de old place us niggers git a big surprise. We didn't hear about it, but some old Master's kinfolks back in Virginia done come out dar an fix de place up and kept it for him while we in Colorado, and it look 'bout as good as when we left it.

He cut it up in chunks and put us niggers out on it on de halves, but he had to sell part of it to git de money to git us mules and tools and found to run on. Den after while he had to sell some more, and he seem lak he git old mighty fast.

Young Master bin in de big battles in Virginia, and he git hit, and den he git sick, and when he come home he jest lak a old man he was so feeble.

About dat time they was a lot of people coming into dat country from de North, and dey kept telling de niggers dat de thing for dem to do was to be free, and come and go whar dey please.

Dey try to git de darkeys to go and vote but none us folks took much stock by what dey say. Old Master tell us plenty time to mix in de politics when de younguns git educated and know what to do.

Jest de same he never mind iffen we go to de dances and de singing and sech. He allus lent us a wagon iffen we want to borry one to go in, too.

Some de niggers what work for de white folks from de North act purty uppity and big, and come pestering 'round de dance places and try to talk up ructions amongst us, but it don't last long.

De Ku Kluckers start riding 'round at night, and dey pass de word dat de darkeys got to have a pass to go and come and to stay at de dances. Dey have to git de pass from de white folks dey work for, and passes writ from de Northern people wouldn't do no good. Dat de way de Kluckers keep the darkies in line.

De Kluckers jest ride up to de dance ground and look at everybody's passes, and iffen some darkey dar widout a pass or got a pass from de wrong man dey run him home, and iffen he talk big and won't go home dey whop him and make him go.

Any nigger out on de road after dark liable to run across de Kluckers, and he better have a good pass! All de dances got to bust up at about 'leven o'clock, too.

One time I seen three-four Kluckers on hosses, all wrapped up in white, and dey was making a black boy git home. Dey was riding hosses and he was trotting down de road ahead of 'em. Ever time he stop and start talking dey pop de whip at his heels and he start trotting on. He was so made he was crying, but he was gitting on down de road jest de same.

I seen 'em coming and I gits out my pass young Master writ so I could show it, but when dey ride by one in front jest turns in his saddle and look back at tother men and nod his head, and they jest ride on by widout stopping to see my pass. Dat man knowed me, I reckon. I looks to see iffen I knowed de hoss, but de Kluckers sometime swapped dey hosses 'round amongst 'em, so de hoss maybe wasn't hisn.

Dey wasn't very bad 'cause de niggers 'round dar wasn't bad, but I hear plenty of darkeys git whopped in other places 'cause dey act up and say dey don't have to take off dey hats in de white stores and such.

Any nigger dat behave hisself and don't go running 'round late at night and drinking never had no trouble wid de Kluckers.

Young Mistress go off and git married, but I don't remember de name 'cause she live off somewhar else, and de next year, I think it was, my pappy and mammy go on a place about five miles away owned by a man named Mr. Bumpus, and I go 'long wid my sister Betty and brother Jimmie to help 'em.

I live around dat place and never marry till old mammy and pappy both gone, and Jimmie and Betty both married and I was gitting about forty year old myself, and den I go up in Kansas and work around till I git married at last.

I was in Fort Scott, and I married Mathilda Black in 1900, and she is 73 years old now and was born in Tennessee. We went to Pittsburg, Kansas, and lived from 1907 to 1913 when we come to Tulsa.

Young Master's children writ to me once in a while and told me how dey gitting 'long up to about twenty year ago, and den I never heard no more about 'em. I never had no children, and it look lak my wife going outlive me, so my mainest hope when I goes on is seeing

Mammy and Pappy and old Master. Old overseer, I speck, was too devilish mean to be thar!

'Course I loves my Lord Jesus same as anybody, but you see I never hear much about Him until I was grown, and it seem lak you got to hear about religion when you little to soak it up and put much by it. Nobody could read de Bible when I was a boy, and dey wasn't no white preachers talked to de niggers. We had meeting sometimes, but de nigger preacher jest talk about bein a good nigger and "doing to please de Master," and I allus thought he meant to please old Master, and I allus wanted to do dat anyways.

So dat de reason I allus remember de time old Master pass on.

It was about two years after de War, and old Master been mighty porely all de time. One day we was working in de Bumpus field and a nigger come on a mule and say old Mistress like to have us go over to de old place 'cause old Master mighty low and calling mine and Pappy's and Mammy's name. Old man Bumpus say go right ahead.

When we git to de Big House old Master setting propped up in de bed and you can see he mighty low and out'n his head.

He been talking about gitting de oats stacked, 'cause it seem to him lak it gitting gloomy-dark, and it gwine to rain, and hail gwine to ketch de oats in de shocks. Some nigger come running up to de back door wid an old horn old Mistress sent him out to hunt up, and he blowed it so old Master could hear it.

Den purty soon de doctor come to de door and say old

Master wants de bell rung 'cause de slaves should ought to be in from de fields, 'cause it gitting too dark to work. Somebody git a wagon tire and beat on it like a bell ringing, right outside old Master's window, and den we all go up on de porch and peep in. Every body was snuffling kind of quiet, 'cause we can't help it.

We hear old Master say, "Dat's all right, Simmons. I don't want my niggers working in de rain. Go down to de quarters and see dey all dried off good. Dey ain't got no sense but dey all good niggers." Everybody around de bed was crying, and we all was crying too.

Den old Mistress come to de door and say we can go in and look at him if we want to. He was still setting propped up, but he was gone.

I stayed in Louisiana a long time after dat, but I didn't care nothing about it, and it look lak I'm staying a long time past my time in dis world, 'cause I don't care much about staying no longer only I hates to leave Mathilda.

But any time de Lord want me I'm ready, and I likes to think when He ready He going tell old Master to ring de bell for me to come on in.

United States. Work Projects Administration

Oklahoma Writers' Project
Ex-Slaves

SARAH WILSON
Age 87 yrs.
Fort Gibson, Okla.

I was a Cherokee slave and now I am a Cherokee freedwoman, and besides that I am a quarter Cherokee my own self. And this is the way it is.

I was born in 1850 along the Arkansas river about half way between Fort Smith and old Fort Coffee and the Skullyville boat landing on the river. The farm place was on the north side of the river on the old wagon road what run from Fort Smith out to Fort Gibson, and that old road was like you couldn't hardly call a road when I first remember seeing it. The ox teams bog down to they bellies in some places, and the wagon wheel mighty nigh bust on the big rocks in some places.

I remember seeing soldiers coming along that old road lots of times, and freighting wagons, and wagons what we all know carry mostly wiskey, and that was breaking the law, too! Them soldiers catch the man with that whiskey they sure put him up for a long time, less'n he put some silver in they hands. That's what my Uncle Nick say. That Uncle Nick a mean Negro, and he ought to know about that.

Like I tell you, I am quarter Cherokee. My mammy was

named Adeline and she belong to old Master Ben Johnson. Old Master Ben bring my grandmammy out to that Sequoyah district way back when they call it Arkansas, mammy tell me, and God only know who my mammy's pa is, but mine was old Master Ben's boy, Ned Johnson.

Old Master Ben come from Tennessee when he was still a young man, and he bring a whole passel of slaves and my mammy say they all was kin to one another, all the slaves I mean. He was a white man that married a Cherokee woman, and he was a devil on this earth. I don't want to talk about him none.

White folks was mean to us like the devil, and so I jest let them pass. When I say my brothers and sisters I mean my half brothers and sisters, you know, but maybe some of them was my whole kin anyways, I don't know. They was Lottie that was sold off to a Starr because she wouldn't have a baby, and Ed, Dave, Ben, Jim and Ned.

My name is Sarah now but it was Annie until I was eight years old. My old Mistress' name was Annie and she name me that, and Mammy was afraid to change it until old Mistress died, then she change it. She hate old Mistress and that name too.

Lottie's name was Annie, too, but Mammy changed it in her own mind but she was afraid to say it out loud, a-feared she would get a whipping. When sister was sold off Mammy tell her to call herself Annie when she was leaving but call herself Lottie when she git over to the Starrs. And she done it too. I seen her after that and she was called Lottie all right.

The Negroes lived all huddled up in a bunch in little

one-room log cabins with stick and mud chimneys. We lived in one, and it had beds for us children like shelves in the wall. Mammy need to help us up into them.

Grandmammy was mighty old and Mistress was old too. Grandmammy set on the Master's porch and minded the baby mostly. I think it was Young Master's. He was married to a Cherokee girl. They was several of the boys but only one girl, Nicie. The old Master's boys were Aaron, John, Ned, Cy and Nathan. They lived in a double log house made out of square hewed logs, and with a double fireplace out of rock where they warmed theirselves on one side and cooked on the other. They had a long front porch where they set most of the time in the summer, and slept on it too.

There was over a hundred acres in the Master's farm, and it was all bottom land too, and maybe you think he let them slaves off easy! Work from daylight to dark! They all hated him and the overseer too, and before slavery ended my grandmammy was dead and old Mistress was dead and old Master was mighty feeble and Uncle Nick had run away to the North soldiers and they never got him back. He run away once before, about ten years before I was born, Mammy say, but the Cherokees went over in the Creek Nation and got him back that time.

The way he made the Negroes work so hard, old Master must have been trying to get rich. When they wouldn't stand for a whipping he would sell them.

I saw him sell a old woman and her son. Must have been my aunt. She was always pestering around trying to get something for herself, and one day she was cleaning the yard he seen her pick up something and put it inside her apron. He flew at her and cussed her, and started like he was going to hit her but she just stood right up to him and never budged, and when he come close she just screamed out loud and ran at him with her fingers stuck out straight and jabbed him in the belly. He had a big soft belly, too, and it hurt him. He seen she wasn't going to be afraid, and he set out to sell her. He went off on his horse to get some men to come and bid on her and her boy, and all us children was mighty scared about it.

They would have hangings at Fort Smith courthouse, and old Master would take a slave there sometimes to see the hanging, and that slave would come back and tell us all scary stories about the hanging.

One time he whipped a whole bunch of the men on account of a fight in the quarters, and then he took them all to Fort Smith to see a hanging. He tied them all in the wagon, and when they had seen the hanging he asked them if they was scared of them dead men hanging up there. They all said yes, of course, but my old uncle Nick was a bad Negro and he said, "No, I aint a-feared of them nor nothing else in this world", and old Master jumped on him while he was tied and beat him with a rope, and then when they got home he tied old Nick to a tree and took his shirt off and poured the cat-o-nine-tails to him until he fainted away and fell over like he was dead.

I never forget seeing all that blood all over my uncle, and if I could hate that old Indian any more I guess I would, but I hated him all I could already I reckon.

Old Master wasn't the only hellion neither. Old Mistress just as bad, and she took most of her wrath out hitting us children all the time. She was afraid of the grown

Negroes. Afraid of what they might do while old Master was away, but she beat us children all the time.

She would call me, "Come here Annie!" and I wouldn't know what to do. If I went when she called "Annie" my mammy would beat me for answering to that name, and if I didn't go old Mistress would beat me for that. That made me hate both of them, and I got the devil in me and I wouldn't come to either one. My grandmammy minded the Master's yard, and she set on the front porch all the time, and when I was called I would run to her and she wouldn't let anybody touch me.

When I was eight years old old Mistress died, and Grandmammy told me why old Mistress picked on me so. She told me about me being half Mister Ned's blood. Then I knowed why Mister Ned would say, "Let her along, she got big big blood in her", and then laugh.

Young Mister Ned was a devil, too. When his mammy died he went out and "blanket married." I mean he brung in a half white and half Indian woman and just lived with her.

The slaves would get rations every Monday morning to do them all week. The Overseer would weigh and measure according to how many in the family, and if you run out you just starve till you get some more. We all know the overseer steal some of it for his own self but we can't do anything, so we get it from the old Master some other way.

One day I was carrying water from the spring and I run up on Grandmammy and Uncle Nick skinning a cow. "What you-all doing?", I say, and they say keep my mouth shut or they kill me. They was stealing from the Master to piece out down at the quarters with. Old Master had so many cows he never did count the difference.

I guess I wasn't any worse than any the rest of the Negroes, but I was bad to tell little lies. I carry scars on my legs to this day where Old Master whip me for lying, with a rawhide quirt he carry all the time for his horse. When I lie to him he just jump down off'n his horse and whip me good right there.

In slavery days we all ate sweet potatoes all the time. When they didn't measure out enough of the tame kind we would go out in the woods and get the wild kind. They growed along the river sand betaween where we lived and Wilson's Rock, out west of our place.

Then we had boiled sheep and goat, mostly goat, and milk and wild greens and corn pone. I think the goat meat was the best, but I aint had no teeth for forty years now, and a chunk of meat hurts my stomach. So I just eats grits mostly. Besides hoeing in the field, chopping sprouts, shearing sheep, carrying water, cutting firewood, picking cotton and sewing I was the one they picked to work Mistress' little garden where she raised things from seed they got in Fort Smith. Green peas and beans and radishes and things like that. If we raised a good garden she give me a little of it, and if we had a poor one I got a little anyhow even when she didn't give it.

For clothes we had homespun cotton all the year round, but in winter we had a sheep skin jacket with the wool left on the inside. Sometimes sheep skin shoes with the wool on the inside and sometimes real cow leather shoes with wood peggings for winter, but always barefooted in summer, all the men and women too.

Lord, I never earned a dime of money in slave days for myself but plenty for the old Master. He would send us out to work the neighbors field and he got paid for it, but we never did see any money.

I remember the first money I ever did see. It was a little while after we was free, and I found a greenback in the road at Fort Gibson and I didn't know what it was. Mammy said it was money and grabbed for it, but I was still a hell cat and I run with it. I went to the little sutler store and laid it down and pointed to a pitcher I been wanting. The man took the money and give me the pitcher, but I don't know to this day how much money it was and how much was the pitcher, but I still got that pitcher put away. It's all blue and white stripedy.

Most of the work I done off the plantation was sewing. I learned from my Granny and I loved to sew. That was about the only thing I was industrious in. When I was just a little bitsy girl I found a steel needle in the yard that belong to old Mistress. My mammy took it and I cried. She put it in her dress and started for the field. I cried so old Mistress found out why and made Mammy give me the needle for my own.

We had some neighbor Indians named Starr, and Mrs. Starr used me sometimes to sew. She had nine boys and one girl, and she would sew up all they clothes at once to do for a year. She would cut out the cloth for about a week, and then send the word around to all the neighbors, and old Mistress would send me because she couldn't see good to sew. They would have stacks of drawers, shirts, pants and some dresses all cut out to sew up.

I was the only Negro that would set there and sew in that bunch of women, and they always talked to me nice and when they eat I get part of it too, out in the kitchen.

One Negro girl, Eula Davis, had a mistress sent her too, one time, but she wouldn't sew. She didn't like me because she said I was too white and she played off to spite the white people. She got sent home, too.

When old Mistress die I done all the sewing for the family almost. I could sew good enough to go out before I was eight years old, and when I got to be about ten I was better than any other girl on the place for sewing.

I can still quilt without my glasses, and I have sewed all night long many a time while I was watching Young Master's baby after old Mistress died.

They was over a hundred acres in the plantation, and I don't know how many slaves, but before the War ended lots of the men had run away. Uncle Nick went to the North and never come home, and Grandmammy died about that time.

We was way down across the Red river in Texas at that time, close to Shawneetown of the Choctaw Nation but just across the river on the other side in Texas bottoms. Old Master took us there in covered wagons when the Yankee soldiers got too close by in the first part of the War. He hired the slaves out to Texas people because he didn't make any crops down there, and we all lived in kind of camps. That's how some of the men and my uncle Nick got to slip off to the north that way.

Old Master just rant and rave all the time we was in Texas. That's the first time I ever saw a doctor. Before that when a slave sick the old women give them herbs, but down there one day old Master whip a Negro girl and she fall in the fire, and he had a doctor come out to fix her up where she was burnt. I remember Granny giving me clabber milk when I was sick, and when I was grown I found out it had had medicine in it.

Before freedom we didn't have no church, but slipped around to the other cabins and had a little singing sometimes. Couldn't have anybody show us the letters either, and you better not let them catch you pick up a book even to look at the pictures, for it was against a Cherokee law to have a Negro read and write or to teach a Negro.

Some Negroes believed in buckeyes and charms but I never did. Old Master had some good boys, named Aaron, John, Ned, Cy and Nat and they told me the charms was no good. Their sister Nicie told me too, and said when I was sick just come and tell her.

They didn't tell us anything about Christmas and New Year though, and all we done was work.

When the War was ended we was still in Texas, and when old Master got a letter from Fort Smith telling him the slaves was free he couldn't read, and Young Miss read it to him. He went wild and jumped on her and beat the devil out of her. Said she was lying to him. It near about killed him to let us loose, but he cooled down after awhile and said he would help us all get back home if we wanted to come.

Mammy told him she could bear her own expenses.

I remember I didn't know what "expenses" was, and I thought it was something I was going to have to help carry all the way back.

It was a long time after he knew we was free before he told us. He tried to keep us, I reckon, but had to let us go. He died pretty soon after he told us, and some said his heart just broke and some said some Negroes poisoned him. I didn't know which.

Anyways we had to straggle back the best way we could, and me and mammy just got along one way and another till we got to a ferry over the Red River and into Arkansas. Then we got some rides and walked some until we got to Fort Smith. They was a lot of Negro camps there and we stayed awhile and then started out to Fort Gibson because we heard they was giving rations out there. Mammy knew we was Cherokee anyway, I guess.

That trip was hell on earth. Nobody let us ride and it took us nearly two weeks to walk all that ways, and we nearly starved all the time. We was skin and bones and feet all bloody when we got to the Fort.

We come here to Four Mile Branch to where the Negroes was all setting down, and pretty soon Mammy died.

I married Oliver Wilson on January second, 1878. He used to belong to Mr. DeWitt Wilson of Tahlequah, and I think the old people used to live down at Wilson Rock because my husband used to know all about that place and the place where I was borned. Old Mister DeWitt Wilson give me a pear tree the next year after I was married, and it is still out in my yard and bears every year.

I was married in a white and black checkedy calico

apron that I washed for Mr. Tim Walker's mother Lizzie all day for, over close to Ft. Gibson, and I was sure a happy woman when I married that day. Him and me both got our land on our Cherokee freedman blood and I have lived to bury my husband and see two great grandchildren so far.

I bless God about Abraham Lincoln. I remember when my mammy sold pictures of him in Fort Smith for a Jew. If he give me my freedom I know he is in Heaven now.

I heard a lot about Jefferson Davis in my life. During the War we hear the Negroes singing the soldier song about hand Jeff Davis to a apple tree, and old Master tell about the time we know Jeff Davis. Old Master say Jeff Davis was just a dragoon soldier out of Fort Gibson when he bring his family out here from Tennessee, and while they was on the road from Fort Smith to where they settled young Jeff Davis and some more dragoon soldiers rid up and talked to him a long time. He say my grandmammy had a bundle on her head, and Jeff Davis say, "Where you going Aunty?" and she was tired and mad and she said, "I don't know, to Hell I reckon", and all the white soldiers laughed at her and made her that much madder.

I joined the Four Mile Branch church in 1879 and Sam Solomon was a Creek negro and the first preacher I ever heard preach. Everybody ought to be in the church and ready for that better home on the other side.

All the old slaves I know are dead excepting two, and I will be going pretty soon I reckon, but I'm glad I lived to see the day the Negroes get the right treatment if they work good and behave themselves right. They don't have to have no pass to walk abroad no more, and they can all read and write now, but it's a tarnation shame some of them go and read the wrong kind of things anyways.

Oklahoma Writers' Project
Ex-Slaves
10-19-38
1,534 words

TOM W. WOODS
Age 83.
Alderson, Okla.

Lady, if de nigger hadn't been set free dis country wouldn't ever been what it is now! Poor white folks wouldn't never had a chance. De slave holders had most of de money and de land and dey wouldn't let de poor white folks have a chance to own any land or anything else to speak of. Dese white folks wasn't much better off den we was. Dey had to work hard and dey had to worry 'bout food, clothes and shelter and we didn't. Lots of slave owners wouldn't allow dem on deir farms among deir slaves without orders from de overseer. I don't know why, unless he was afraid dey would stir up discontent among de niggers. Dere was lots of "underground railroading" and I rekon dat was what Old Master and others was afraid of.

Us darkies was taught dat poor white folks didn't amount to much. Course we knowed dey was white and we was black and dey was to be respected for dat, but dat was about all.

White folks as well as niggers profited by emancipation. Lincoln was a friend to all poor white folks as well as black ones and if he could a' lived things would a' been different for ever'body.

Dis has been a good old world to live in. I always been able to make a purty good living and de only trouble I ever had has been sickness and death. I've had a sight of dat kind of trouble. I've outlived two wives and eight children. I had 13 brothers and sisters and I was de oldest, and I'm de only one left.

I sits here at night by myself and gits to wondering what de good Lord is sparing me for. I reckon it's for some good reason, and I'd like to live to be a hundred if He wants me to. I'm not tired of living yet!

I was born in Florence, Alabama. My father's name was Thomas Woods and my mammy was Frances Foster. Mammy belonged to Wash Foster and father was owned by Moses Woods, who lived on an adjoining plantation. He worked for his Master ever' day but spent each night wid us. He walked 'bout a mile to his work ever' day.

Master Wash was a poor man when he married Miss Sarah Watkins of Richmond, Virginia. Her father was as rich as cream, he owned 7 plantations and 200 slaves to each plantation. When Master Wash and Miss Sarah got married her father give her 50 slaves. Ever'body said Miss Mary jest married Master Wash because he was a purty boy, and he sure was a fine looking man.

He was good and kind to all his slaves when he was sober, but he was awful crabbed and cross when he was drunk, and he was drunk most of de time. He was hard to please and sometimes he would whip de slaves. I remember seeing Master Wash whup two men once. He give 'em 200 lashes.

Miss Sarah was de best woman in de world. It takes a good woman to live wid a drunkard.

Two of the men ran away one time and was gone till dey got tired of staying away. Master Wash wouldn't let anyone hunt 'em. When dey finally come home he had dem strapped in stocks and den deir bodies bared to de waist and he sure did ply de lash. I guess he whupped 'em harder dan he would if he hadn't been so full of whisky.

He never did sell any of his slaves. He kept the 50 dat Miss Sarah's father give 'em and deir increase. He bought some ever' time dey had a sale. He owned two plantations and dey was about a hundred slaves on each one. Him and his family lived in town.

Me and a boy named John was sized and put to work when we was about nine or ten years old. We was so bad dey had to put us to work as dey couldn't do any thing else with us. We'd chase de pigs and ride de calves and to punish us dey made us tote water to de hands. Dey was so many hands to water dat it kept us busy running back and forth with de water. De next year dey put me to plowing and him to hoeing. We made regular hands from den on.

If we had behaved ourselves we wouldn't a'had to go to work till we was fourteen or fifteen anyway. Slave owners was awful good to deir nigger chaps for dey wanted 'em to grow up to be strong men and women.

Dey was about thirty children on our plantation. Two women looked after us and took care of us till our parents come in from de field. Dey cooked for us and always gave us our supper and sent us home to our parents for de night.

Our food was placed on a long table in a trough. Each child had a spoon and four of us eat out of one trough. Our food at night was mostly milk and bread. At noon we had vegetables, bread, meat and milk. He gave us more and better food than he did his field hands. He said he didn't want none of us to be stunted in our growing.

He bought our shoes for us but cloth for our clothes was spun and wove right there on de farm. In summer us boys wore long tailed shirts and no pants. I've plowed dat way a many a day. We was glad to see it git warm in de spring so we could go barefooted and go wid out our pants.

Our overseers lived near de quarters and every morning about four o' clock dey'd blow a horn [HW: to] wake us up. We knowed it meant to git up and start de day. We was in de field by de time we could see. We always fed our teams at night. We'd give 'em enough to keep 'em eating all night so we wouldn't have to feed 'em in de morning.

Master Wash Foster and his family lived in de finest house in Florence, Ala. It was a fine, large two-story house, painted white as nearly all de houses was in dem days. Dere was big gallery in front and back and a fine lawn wid big cedar and chestnut trees all 'round de house.

He had a fine carriage and a pair of spanking bays dat cost him $500 apiece. Old Monroe was his coachman and dey made a grand sight. Monroe kept de nickel plated harness and carriage trimmings shining and de team was brushed slick and clean and dey sure stepped out.

We lived on de plantation about eight miles from town and we liked for de family to come out to de farm. Dey was four children, Wash, Jack, Sarah and Sally and dey always played with us. When dey come we always had a regular feast as dey children would eat wid us children. Dey had dishes though to eat out of. After dinner we would run and play Peep Squirrel. I think dey call it hide-and-seek now.

My mother was a regular field hand till Miss Sarah decided to take her into town to take care of her children. Dey all called her Frank instead of Frances. I used to get to go to town to visit my mother and we'd have glorious times I tell you.

We'd go out and gather hickory nuts, hazel nuts, pig nuts, and walnuts. We'd all set around de fire and eat nuts and tell ghost tales ever' night. Master Wash raised lots of apples too, and we had all that we wanted of dem to eat.

I saw lots of Yankee soldiers. Sherman and Grant's armies marched by our house and camped at DeCatur, Ala. It took dem three days to pass. We wasn't afraid of dem.

In the second year of de war some Yankee soldiers come through and gathered up all de slaves and took us to Athens, Ala., and put us on a Government farm. We stayed dere till de end of de War. My father died jest before dey took us away.

My mother and us children were on de farm together and dey treated us all mighty good. We had plenty of good food and clothes.

Master Wash came to see us while we was on de Government farm. He was left in a bad shape and we was all sorry for him. A lot of his hands went back to him after de Surrender but we never did. Mother married another man named Goodloe and we all went to Arkansas, near Little Rock. Dis was his former home. I was about nineteen or twenty years old at this time.

I never sent to school. My wife taught me how to read de Bible but I never learned to write. I have good eyesight. I guess dat is cause I never put dem out reading and going to moving picture shows.

When any of my family was sick I always sent for de doctor. We had a few of our own home remedies dat we used also. We boiled poke root and bathed in it for a cure for rheumatism.

A tea made from May apples was used for a physic.

Oklahoma Writers' Project
Ex-Slaves

ANNIE YOUNG
Age 86
Oklahoma City, Okla.

I was born in 1851, makes me 86 years old. I was born in Middle Tennessee, Summers County. My mother was put on a block and sold from me when I was a child. I don't remember my father real good. Sister Martha, Sister Sallie, nor Sister Jane wasn't sold. But my brother John was. My mother's name is Rachel Donnahue. We lived in a log hut. The white folks lived in a frame white building sitting in a big grove yard. Old master owned a big farm.

We ate molasses, bread and butter and milk in wooden bowls and crumbled our bread up in it. Old master had big smokehouses of meat. Dey ate chickens, possums and coons, and my old auntie would barbecue rabbits for de white folks. We ate ash cakes too.

I washed dishes, swept de yard, and kept de yard clean wid weed brush brooms. I never earned no money. All de slaves had gardens, and chickens too. My auntie, dey let her have chickens of her own and she raised chickens, and had a chicken house and garden down in de woods.

I remember in time of de War dey'd send me down in de woods to pick up chips and git wood. All de men had gone to de army. One morning and t'was cold dey sent me down in de woods and my hands got frostbitten. All de skin come off and dey had to tie my hands up in roasted turnips. Sallie she had gloves, and didn't get frostbitten. After my old master died, Master Donnahue was his name, his old son-in-law come to take over de plantation. He was mean, but my sister whipped him.

We had no nigger driver or overseer. We raised wheat, corn and vegetables, not much cotton, jest enough to spun de clothes out of.

At night when we'd go to our cabins we'd pick cotton from de seeds to make our clothes. Boys and girls alike wore dem long shirts slit up de side nearly to your necks. They'd have cornshuckings sometimes all night long. You see I didn't have no mother, no father, nobody to lead me, teach me or tell me, and so jest lived with anybody was good enough to let me stay and done what they did. They'd have log rollings, with all de whiskey dey could drink.

I remember going to church, de Methodist Church dey call it. We used to sing dis song and I sho did like it too:

> "I went down in de valley to pray,
>
> Studying dat good old way."

I been a Christian long before most of dese young niggers was born. My other favorites are:

> "Must Jesus bear This Cross Alone."

and

"The Consecrated Cross I'll Bear 'til
Death Shall Set Me Free,
Yea, There's a Crown for Everyone,
And There's a Crown for Me."

Yes Lawd, there sho is.

One day a nigger killed one of his master's shoats and he catch him and when he'd ask him, "What's that you got there?" The nigger said, "a possum." De master said, "Let me see." He looked and seen it was a shoat. De nigger said, "Master it may be a shoat now, but it sho was a possum while ago when I put 'im in dis sack."

Dey didn't whip our folks much, but one day I saw a overseer on another place. He staked a man down with two forked sticks 'cross his wrist nailed in de ground and beat him half to death with a hand saw 'til it drawed blisters. Den he mopped his back wid vinegar, salt and pepper. Sometimes dey'd drop dat hot rosin from pine knots on dose blisters.

When de Yanks come, business took place. I remember white folks was running and hiding, gitting everything dey could from de Yanks. Dey hid dey jewelry and fine dishes and such. Dose Yanks had on big boots. Dey'd drive up, feed dey hosses from old Master's corn, catch dey chickens, and tell old Master's cook to cook 'em, and they'd shoot down old Master's hogs and skin 'em.

De Yanks used to make my nephew drunk, and have him sing (dis is kind of bad):

"I'll be God O'Mighty
God Dammed if I don't
Kill a nigger,
Oh Whooey boys! Oh Whooey!
Oh Whooey boys! Oh Whooey!"

I don't remember never seeing no funerals. Jest took 'em off and buried 'em. I remember dat old Master's son-in-law dat my sister whipped, he called hisself a doctor and he killed Aunt Clo. Give her some medicine but he didn't know what he was doing and killed her.

I married William Young and we had a pretty good wedding. Married in Crittington County Arkansas. When I left Tennessee and went to Arkansas I followed some hands. You know after de War dey immigrated niggers from one place to another. I owned a good farm in Arkansas. I came out here some 42 years ago.

I have three daughters. Mattie Brockins runs a rooming house in Kansas City. Jessie Cotton, lives right up de street here. Osie Olla Anderson is working out in North town.

Well I think Abraham Lincoln is more than a type a man than Moses. I believe he is a square man, believe in union that every man has a right to be a free man regardless to color. He was a republican man. Don't know much 'bout Jeff Davis but I think Booker T. Washington was a pretty good man. He's a right good man I guess, but he is dead ain't he?

I can remember once my auntie's old Master tried to

have her and she run off out in de woods, and when he put those blood hounds or nigger hounds on her trail he catched her and hit her in de head wid something like de stick de police carry, and he knocked a hole in her head and she bled like a hog, and he made her have him. She told her mistress, and mistress told her to go ahead and be wid him 'cause he's gonna kill you. And he had dem two women and she had some chillun nearly white, and master and dey all worked in de fields side by side.

www.ingramcontent.com/pod-product-compliance
Lightning Source LLC
Chambersburg PA
CBHW070159240426
43671CB00007B/491